THE COMPLETE GUIDE TO WRITING FANTASY™
VOLUME THREE:

The Author's Grimoire

EDITED BY

VALERIE GRISWOLD-FORD

&

LAI ZHAO

D1600428

Dragon
Moon

WWW.DRAGONMOONPRESS.COM

THE COMPLETE GUIDE™ TO WRITING FANTASY
VOLUME 3~THE AUTHOR'S GRIMOIRE

Copyright © 2007 Valerie Griswold-Ford & Lai Zhao
Cover Art © 2007 Dragon Art by Andy Jones
Cover Art © 2007 Business Bot by Janice Blaine
Interior Art © 2007 by Anne Moya www.angelstudios.com

ISBN 10 1-896944-35-3 Print Edition
ISBN 13 978-1-896944-35-7

ISBN 10 1-896944-51-5 Electronic Edition
ISBN 13 978-1-896944-51-7

CIP Data on file with the National Library of Canada

Dragon Moon Press is an Imprint of Hades Publications Inc.
P.O. Box 1714, Calgary, Alberta, T2P 2L7, Canada

Dragon Moon Press and Hades Publications, Inc. acknowledges the ongoing support of the Canada Council for the Arts and the Alberta Foundation for the Arts for our publishing programme.

The Alberta Foundation for the Arts
COMMITTED TO THE DEVELOPMENT OF CULTURE AND THE ARTS

Alberta COMMUNITY DEVELOPMENT

Canada Council for the Arts   Conseil des Art du Canada

Printed and bound in the United States

www.dragonmoonpress.com
www.completeguidetowriting.com
Interior design by Imagine That! Studios www.imaginethatstudios.com

Dedication

Joe Murphy

July 10, 1972 - April 1, 2007

The wonderful guy behind the chapter,
"Birth of a Book Reviewer."
He made us laugh through his podcasts,
his emails and his reviews.
We'll miss him.

Thanks for the laughs, Joe.

THE COMPLETE GUIDE TO WRITING FANTASY™
VOLUME THREE:

The Author's Grimoire

EDITED BY

VALERIE GRISWOLD-FORD

&

LAI ZHAO

WWW.DRAGONMOONPRESS.COM

Foreword

BY C.E. MURPHY

I have noticed something about writers.

Writers—those who wish to be published, which, I presume, make up the majority of people holding this book in their hands—have a very focused end-game in mind: *getting published.* Getting that first contract, getting the promise that their names are going to be on the shelves, surrounded by their contemporaries and their inspirations.

Surprisingly few writers seem to have any clear idea on how you actually get to that stage.

There's the obvious: first, you must write. Obvious, yes, but still surprisingly difficult to impress upon people. Not only must you write, but you must *finish* projects. Thousands upon thousands of words, chapter after chapter, plot point after plot point, even when you hate the story and fear you'll never write anything worth reading.

Let us assume you have made it that far.

What now?

People will tell you that you need an agent. Why do you need one? (Because a good one will tell you how to improve your book as well as get you more money, for starters.) How do you find one? (Network, network, network!) How do you know who to trust, if you do find one? (Network, network, network!) You'll hear that you can't get an agent without a book contract, and that you can't get a book contract without an agent. How do you find the fine line between those two things? (Network, network, network!)

You'll hear endlessly that you need to make your manuscript stand out. What you'll learn here is that this doesn't mean *submit it on pink scented paper with glitter dusted between the pages.* It means turn in a very clean, professional manuscript in standard format. Make it stand out by writing the very best story that you can. That's what editors are looking for, not boxes of chocolate accompanying the manuscript.

You'll read (just as you already have in this foreword) that networking is important. Why? How do you do it? What does it achieve? (An example: networking is attending conferences. At conferences, you meet editors and agents. You can usually arrange to pitch your novel to these people. This may result in a request for your manuscript.

Voila: you've made a personal connection and circumvented the *no unsolicited manuscripts* wall that so many publishers have in place!)

They (the proverbial They) say success is all about marketing yourself, an alarming prospect for many shy writers. How on earth do you put yourself out there, when yourself would rather be at home typing away on the computer? What exactly constitutes marketing, anyway? (Have a website professionally built! Do booksigning! Carry business cards! Memorize an elevator speech for your latest book!)

Make no mistake. These are things that a writer just starting out needs to consider. You have the heart, the ambition, and the drive; this book will help you with the focus of nitty-gritty details that we, as writers, often don't even know we should be thinking about. It can seem overwhelming and frightening. But the wonderful thing is, it can be done. You can learn the things you need to know, and, better-armed, go forth and achieve your goals. It's possible.

I know.

I did it.

Good luck to all of you.

Table of Contents

Yet Another Sequel

THE INTRODUCTION TO
THE COMPLETE GUIDE TO WRITING FANTASY:
THE AUTHOR'S GRIMOIRE
BY VALERIE GRISWOLD-FORD

"There is no royal path to good writing; and such paths as exist do not lead through neat critical gardens, various as they are, but through the jungles of self, the world, and of craft."
— Jessamyn West

When I tell people (or more often, when my mother tells people) that I'm a published author, I get several questions right off the bat. Besides the ever-present "Where do you get your ideas?" (you don't want to know, most times) and "What do you write?" (dark fantasy and paranormal romance), the biggest question is "How did you get your novel published?"

That, my friends, is a tale worth telling, so put up your feet, pour yourself a drink and listen.

Long ago and far away...

Oops, sorry, wrong story.

Seriously, my publishing story goes back to the first book in this series, *The Complete Guide to Writing Fantasy*. I wrote a chapter in that, and when Dragon Moon Press picked the book up, decided I was going to do my part in promoting it. So I called around, got some signing dates arranged, and put out a call to my fellow authors to come up to beautiful New Hampshire and tour.

One author answered: Tee Morris, who in addition to promoting the *Guide* also had a fiction book out from Dragon Moon Press, entitled *MOREVI: The Chronicles of Rafe and Askana*. The two of us set out to conquer eight signings in three states in four days.

Luckily for us, some miscommunication happened, and we ended up with the better part of a Saturday afternoon with nothing to do but write. Since we both had our laptops (a good idea for *any* author who's touring—bring the laptop! You never know when an opportunity like this will fall into your lap!), we commandeered a table in the Student Union at UNH and went to work. Tee started working on the edits for his next book. I stared at a blank screen and wondered what I should write.

There'd been this idea that had been wandering in my head for a while. A novel idea, but I was a bit afraid to start it. It had been about four years at that point since I'd done any fiction writing, and I was really rusty.

However, nothing ventured, nothing gained. I started to type. No outline, no nothing. And I got two chapters of a novel started.

Tee read them and said, "Hey, this is really cool! Tell me more!"

I told him more. He then said, "You realize I'm going to push you to finish this, right?"

I laughed, figuring "push me to finish this" meant he would email me from time to time. You see, at that point, I didn't know Tee as well as I do now.

The tour was in early November. I packed Tee back on the plane to Virginia and proceeded to play (sort of) with the book, which now had the title *Not Your Father's Horseman*.

Fast-forward to early December. December 8, to be precise. I was home from work that day, because there was a wicked ice storm. At approximately 2 pm, (and yes, the details are pretty well burned into my brain at this point) I got a phone call from Tee.

> Tee: *"Hi Val, how's the book going?"*
> Me: *"Okay."* (translation: *"I'm not really working on it at the moment."*)
> Tee: *"Do you have a chapter outline?"*
> Me: *"Sort of."* (translation: *"Not really, but I know approximately what's going to happen."*)
> Tee: *"How long would it take you to get one done?"*
> Me: *"Um, I don't know. A couple of hours?"*
> Tee: *"Good, because Gwen wants it on her desk at 8 am tomorrow morning."*

"Gwen" being Gwen Gades, the publisher of Dragon Moon Press. This was Tee's idea of pushing me to finish it: he'd emailed Gwen and told her I had a book worth her time that I was working on. I spent the next few hours typing furiously, pulling an outline from I don't know where. *Not* what you should do as an author. And then I sent it off to her.

I got an email a day or so later from her, letting me know that she thought I had a very interesting concept, and when would the first draft be ready? I bluffed and said January 1st. She called my bluff and asked to see it.

So I spent December writing. My husband, luckily, is a very supportive spouse and didn't mind (too much) that I was spending every minute I wasn't working on the computer. I pulled 45k together into some semblance of a story and sent it off around January 4th or so.

No, 45k is not long enough for a novel. I didn't even know that. I just breathed a sigh of relief that it was done and waited to hear from her.

And hear I did. Gwen came back and said she liked it, but it was too short. And the descriptions were a little…lacking. (I write very lean first drafts. I've learned that since then.) But she told me to rework it a bit and send it back.

What I didn't know at that point is that Gwen had already decided to offer me the contract. She'd even told Tee that. Tee thought she was kidding, so he didn't tell me. She thought he'd told me, so she didn't tell me either.

Well, at that point, Tee and I were also working on *The Fantasy Writer's Companion*, the second book in this series. Gwen, Tee and I were talking on email one day that winter, and Gwen mentioned how Westercon 58 would be in her hometown of Calgary in July 2005. She said it would be a good time to premiere Dragon Moon's next three books: *Legacy of Morevi* (Tee's sequel), *The Fantasy Writer's Companion* and *Not Your Father's Horseman*.

My heart stopped when I saw that email. I was at work, so I couldn't do anything out loud. However, to make sure I'd read it right, I sent a private email to Gwen, asking her if she'd meant she was offering me a contract.

The email that came back was slightly puzzled in tone. "I told Tee in December I was offering you a contract. Didn't he tell you?"

No, he didn't. In fact, he was as stunned as I was.

That's how I became a published author. The normal route, it was not.

I wrote no cover letter, no synopsis. I didn't do any market research. In short, the opportunity just fell into my lap.

Could this happen to you as well? Sure. Anything's possible. Will I give you Tee's address, so you can get him to introduce your book? No. Sorry.

"Well, then," you say, puzzled, "How can I get my book published, if I don't have Tee's address?"

Welcome to the third installment of the Fantasy Writer's series. *The Complete Guide to Writing Fantasy: The Author's Grimoire* focuses not on how to write the book, but what happens after you've written it and polished it to a shine. How do you go about getting an agent? Do you need one? Should you submit it to a small press, an epublishing company, self-publish? Or maybe just throw caution to the wind and send it off to the biggest company you can find? How about marketing, once you have the contract? How do you write a press release?

Sheesh, where's a writer to start? These are the questions that this book can help you answer.

We've gone to the other side of the publishing business this time for the answers to those questions. Lazette Gifford offers a look at the different paths of publication an author can take, as well as some ideas on project management. Michael Pederson talks about submitting to magazines, another avenue for publication. Jennifer Hagan takes from her years as a reporter to demystify press releases, and Summer Brooks offers a look at another medium of marketing in radio, especially Internet radio and podcasts. Margaret Fisk examines the role of rejections, and Joe Murphy talks about reviews. Tee chimes in with a great chapter on self-promotions, and Jana G. Oliver follows with the whys and wherefores of giving a writing workshop. Danielle Ackley-McPhail explores writer's groups, and Helen Finch gives some sage advice from the editor's perspective. And Lai Zhao looks at networking—always a big plus for a writer.

This book is for everyone out there who has their novel written, and now has no idea how to bring it to publication. Good luck, and remember to follow your own path. There is no right way—only the way you make yourself.

I leave you with a quote from Lewis Carroll, one that makes me smile. Enjoy.

> *"I don't want to take up literature in a money-making spirit, or be very anxious about making large profits, but selling it at a loss is another thing altogether, and an amusement I cannot well afford."*

A long the way, you'll notice extra notes being pointed out to you by our helpful sidekick, Scribble. He had a lot of things to say, but his chapter wasn't up to snuff. So he's been assigned this job instead: pointing out helpful hints that further illustrate the chapters. Keep an eye out for him. He's got some good information.

Five Paths to Publication
BY LAZETTE GIFFORD

Many of you have invested years of your life in writing your novel. Now, with the work written, rewritten, and edited, you are faced with the daunting task of sending your manuscript to a publisher. *Where should it go? Where does it have the best chance of finding publication? What if the editor who reads it thinks it's horrible and sends back a rejection saying I should give up writing?*

Submissions are scary. They may get easier as you do more of them, but this doesn't erase the worry that you are not going to make the sale. Putting those stories in the mail is an act filled with hope, and at the same time, one shadowed with the knowledge that even good books get turned down.

The most important lesson a writer needs to learn is that rejection is just a part of the job description of being a published author. A rejection of your beloved novel is nothing personal, and quite often it isn't even a condemnation of the novel. The rejection only means the book was not right for the place to which you sent it. It might mean the editor doesn't like unicorns, or he just accepted a book with unicorns. In other worlds, it can be totally based on a personal feeling toward the book, or it may have to do with recent purchases and the direction the company intends to take. Always remember that an editor is only another reader, and you cannot please everyone. If your book is rejected, then you need to find the editor who likes the book. It is not a condemnation of your ability to write. Everyone gets rejected at some point in their career.

If an editor sends you back comments on why your story didn't work—which is rare—look them over and decide if you can incorporate the suggestions in a rewrite. If the editor says he would be glad to look over the novel again after these changes are made, then by all means do it if you want the sale. Sometimes, however, you can't make those changes without changing the novel in ways you don't want. Other times you may find that the suggestions open up an entire new aspect of the book you didn't see before.

However, any suggestions are just that—and if the suggestions don't fit what you believe is best for your story, then don't make the changes.

Remember—editors are readers, and they have their own views of how books should work. The next editor might not agree with those suggestions at all. You have to trust your vision of the story and do what is best for it.

Only an unprofessional editor would make more than a comment on the novel itself, so you need not worry about getting rejections which question your entire future as an author.

But to whom should you send your story? There are many choices in the types of places, let alone individual publishers, and it can paralyze a writer before a submission ever goes into an envelope. Understanding the different types of markets can help you in your quest for the right publisher.

PATH ONE: AGENT OR NOT

Too many new writers believe that once they get an agent all they need do is write what they want and turn it over to that person to sell. Unfortunately, it doesn't work this way.

An agent's job is to make certain you are writing material which can be sold to a publishing company.

To that end, the agent will often state the type of material you need to be writing and will edit and require changes in your work long before it goes to a publisher. You will send your agent a synopsis of what you *intend* to write, and the agent will either reject or accept and critique the synopsis until the agent believes it is something a publisher might want. Then the proposal goes to the publisher and goes through another round of acceptance or rejection.

An agent does not make writing easier. He does, however, make it more likely that you will write something that sells, though there is no guarantee even with all the hard work of trying to get it right from the start. An agent will get you through more of the publishers' doors, including those ones that are no longer open to un-agented writers. The agents have become first-level slush readers for those companies, as well as copyeditors. For doing this work, they get a percentage of the sale of any book they find and bring to the publisher. This money (the common amount is 15% these days) comes out of your advance.

Is it worth it? Yes, in most cases, it is. The agent will not only get you through those doors, but he will also negotiate your contract and make certain you are not hit with any strange clauses. And because their cut comes out of the advance, it is in their best interests that you get a good amount of money.

Agents are important for those people who are working toward a career with the big name publishing companies. If you are taking one of the other paths, an agent generally is not important.

There used to be a saying that you couldn't get an agent without a contract in hand, and you couldn't get a contract without an agent. Obviously neither side is completely true. However, it can be easier to get an agent's interest if you have already gotten an offer on a book from a big name company and want them to go over the contract for you and handle future sales.

Agents are an important step for many pro-level writers. However, for those selling to small press and eBook publishers, there is going to be little or no interest on the part of an agent. There is not enough money in either of those areas to warrant an agent taking on the work.

PATH TWO: THE BIG NAME PUBLISHERS

There is hardly a writer out there who doesn't dream of landing a contract with one of the big name publishers like DAW, Warner, Baen or one of the other companies whose books line the shelves of stores. Books from these publishers are the ones most of us have grown up reading, and we have tied our dreams of success to their logos. Most writers will aim for these markets, and with good reason which goes beyond imagining their books stamped with a certain emblem.

There are definite reasons to start at the top in your quest for a novel publisher. First, of course, is that these publishers have the money to pay a good advance. Getting a contract with a New York publisher can mean the first step in giving up the day job and becoming a full-time author.

There is also the prestige which goes along with such a sale. Being able to announce that Baen just bought your latest novel is not just an ego boost – it's also vindication for every writing choice you made along the way. Bad critiques, disapproving relatives and uncaring companions suddenly mean far less than they did when you only had a stack of papers to show them, and for which they were not very impressed.

After the sale it's going to take some time, but eventually there will also be the moment when you walk into a bookstore, go to the fantasy and science fiction section—and there it is! Your book with your name will be right there on the shelf where you had imagined it would be for the last few months. You may even have a pile of books at the front of the store under the 'local author' sign.

You will also have book signings, readings, interviews, though you are likely going to have to arrange for those promotions yourself. You will also have at least one more book on the way because publishers rarely make contracts for just one novel. You are going to have readers! Real people who are total strangers will buy your book because it looks interesting. It's likely you'll even have fan mail from these people.

Yes, there are very many good, strong reasons to try for the contract with the big publisher. The problem is that because it's the top rung, it's the hardest step to achieve. There are roadblocks in the way. As mentioned in the previous section, one of those roadblocks is that many publishing companies now require you to have an agent before your manuscript ever gets through the door. Finding a good agent is going to add considerable time to your quest for publication, but an agent has become a necessity when dealing with the New York Publishing Houses.

Making the sale to a big name publishing company can make your career—but getting one of those coveted few open spots is extremely difficult, even with an agent. Only a limited number of new authors slip into the line up because the publishers, rightly, want to fill the shelves with books they know are going to sell, and those spots usually go to the authors who have already proven themselves.

It's also true that sometimes even excellent books don't make the cut because they are not something the publishing company's marketing department can work into their plans. Having something too unusual might disqualify you, and having something too similar to other work can do the same. It's a hard line to define and one you will not know until you reach it.

Because of the limited number of big publishers, you have very few chances to sell your novel to one of them. Once you have tried a novel, unless a publisher has specifically asked to look at a rewrite, you aren't going to be able to send the novel to that publication again.

A sale to one of these companies has something of a mirror problem when it comes to sales. First, because you have made a sale to the big leagues, you have the best chance at making truly high book selling numbers. However, at the same time, you *must* make exceptional sales in order to keep your numbers high so the company will continue to buy your manuscripts. This is a business, and unfortunately because of the logistics, you cannot be everywhere to personally push those books and get people to buy them. The vagaries of customer buying are beyond your control. You do not even get a say on the cover art, though you can mostly trust the people to do their best in this respect. They want something which will sell the book, after all. And honestly, it's unlikely they'd ever be able to match what you imagine for the cover anyway.

There is a high turn over for books on the shelves at stores. Once the book ships to those destinations, at best you are going to have about a month in which to make good sales and create your niche. It can be done, and is done every month—but it's not an easy path to follow, and it's never one on which you can rest for long.

Some people will tell you this is the only path to take for publication. It has all the hallmarks to make your name famous, and it can offer you a real career and income which might make quitting the day job a reality.

However, there are other paths to publication.

PATH THREE: SMALL PRESS COMPANIES

Small press companies have certain excellent points for choosing them over the big companies. One of them, however, is *not* that they're easier to sell to. In fact, because some are truly niche markets, they're far more limited in what they accept than many of the big name publishers.

However, many small press markets are apt to consider things which might be a little bit more over the boundaries than the larger publishers want to publish. The big name publishers are looking for books which will sell to the greatest number of people, so those books must have a wide appeal. Some small press niche markets are looking at a smaller but devoted group of select readers. Occasionally this might include books which are considered old-fashioned and no longer viable in the current market. While the big market is pursuing the 'gosh-wow' new material that draws the most readers, a small press company might still be filling the needs of those who love, for instance, an old fashioned epic fantasy tale.

Some do, however, also go the other way and pick up material which is extremely unusual. If you have written a story so far out of the norm that the big name publishers will not consider it, you might have a chance with the right small press company.

Small press companies almost always have a far closer relationship with their authors. They have fewer employees and the author is more directly involved in the process of getting the book to print.

Locating such a company which suits your work can be a problem because it's harder to find books by these publishers and therefore harder to gauge what they want. Guidelines, of course, help—but they are not always as detailed as you need. Check websites for titles and then see if your library has—or can get—some of the books which appear interesting to you. Do your best to find out what the publisher offers to see if you like the end product, and if you think you would fit into their lineup. If after you've done your best to find out, you are still not sure—then give them a try anyway. You can't know until you try.

Always approach a small press company with the same professionalism you would use with a larger company. Just because they don't employ as many people or make as large of print runs doesn't mean they take their work any less seriously or that they won't work as hard to make your book a success.

The steps you pass through in dealing with a small press company are essentially the same as a larger company. As with every other place where you send a submission, read their guidelines and follow them as closely as you can. Also note that some small press companies are open to submissions only at certain times of the year. They only publish half a dozen books a year (as opposed to a larger company which publishes that many in a month) so their needs might be quickly filled. If you want a chance, be prepared and get your novel in at the right time. Sending it sooner will only annoy them and make them think you are not paying attention to the guidelines.

If you are accepted by such a company, the next steps will be providing any changes which have been agreed upon between you and the publisher. Afterwards, the book will go to a copyeditor and usually back to you for a final edit. This, again, is little different than what you would expect from a larger company.

For many authors, small press companies are the first choice. They prefer the closer and friendly atmosphere that comes from a small business rather than impersonal feel of a large one. Marketing will be more of your job than it is even in the larger companies.

Some small press publishers do make it to the bookshelves of stores like Barnes and Noble, and others are strictly for sale from the publisher or at conventions and small, independent bookstores. Many are hardcover-only books, though some may do trade (oversized) paperback. Very few do mass market paperback printings because the cost is not equal to the returns.

Some small press companies have long-standing reputations for the excellence in their publications and others are starting to build their way to such a standing. There are a few, of course, who will never make it. However, small press companies are a legitimate and respected form of publication.

PATH FOUR: ELECTRONIC AND POD PUBLICATION

Electronic Publication is a new medium and undergoing change almost from one day to the next. People are still experimenting with everything from marketing presentation to multiple formats which may include audio and even a POD print version of the book. Electronic publishing does not always mean just an eBook these days.

First let's look at the traditional eBook market. This means a book which comes out only in electronic format. There is no print copy. There are many variations to the format to be used with various programs which can be based either on your computer or your PDA. There are also a few hand-held dedicated eBook readers out there, including a new version from Sony.

The number of eBook sales is climbing every year and there are many electronic publishers desperately looking for good authors. However, there are a lot of obstacles to overcome in eBook publication.

The first is that most readers want to hold an actual book, not read lines on a computer or a PDA. Some of this attitude is changing as more people grow up with computers as a natural part of their world. They're used to reading words on computer screens, and while the preference may still be for the actual book, it is not as strong a bias.

A second problem is that when eBook publication first started, many people jumped into the business without a clue of how to edit and present a book. People who read early eBooks were often (rightfully) appalled by the writing quality and swore never to try one again. This is changing as good publishers get a foothold in the market and start making names for themselves so that new readers have a better chance of finding them. There are, however, still a number of electronic publishers who are not well-versed in the actual art of creating books, so both authors and readers have to be careful of what publishers they try.

When should you look at eBook publication as a viable choice?

If you have tried the big name publications and not found your spot, you are left with three choices: trunk the story (put it away and forget it exists), try small press companies, or tempt fate and leap into the eBook world.

The word to remember when you think about eBooks is "potential." There is rarely any advance paid in eBook publication. However, you are given a much larger cut of each book's sale—from 35% to 60%, depending on the publisher. And don't jump at the 60% as a better deal. In my own experience, I've made far more from the publisher offering me 35% because this particular publisher uses company income to actually market their books.

There are expenses which come out of the cost before you get your cut. While there may be no physical book, there are still all the other steps which go before publication plus the work of marketing, keeping up a website, and paying vendors who carry the books. At the time I am writing this, Fictionwise, which is the top vendor of electronic stories and books, requires a per-book set up and takes 50% of the sale price before it ever gets back to the publisher.

So don't be fooled by the numbers. EBooks have potential for making you a lot of money, but you have to work hard for it. Self-marketing is even more important for an eBook published author than it is for one who finds a spot in the print companies. Remember that you have to overcome the 'but it's not a real book' problem just to draw readers.

Finding a good eBook publisher is also a problem. Look for a site which has a good presence—lots of books by many authors, perhaps a few 'these books won awards' links (though, to be honest, there are so few eBook awards available that it's not a fair way to judge). Especially look for three things:

1. Check their submission page. If they say anything akin to "send us your manuscript and we'll publisher you!" run away. You're dealing with people on the fanzine level, and

this means no quality control. Your book may shine like a supernova compared to the rest of the work, but it doesn't matter. Very few people are ever going to see it because they'll see the poor quality of the other work and never come back again.

2. The site should have a book preview for each novel which allows you to read a few pages. Check some of them and see if you like what you read and think you might fit in well with the mix.

3. Check with sites like Editors and Preditors to see if there are any problems. You might even email an author or two from the site and ask about the process, if they have any problems, etc. Some of them are going to find this odd and probably be wary of answering. EBook authors are so used to coming under attack by people who have never even read their books that they can get a little gun shy.

Do not go into eBook publishing blind. Unless you can really push your work and make the kind of breakthrough that few eBook authors have achieved, you'll make far more money with a big name publisher. What you do have with eBooks is more time. One of the good points to eBook publication is that your books 'stay on the shelf' for years and you have time to drive readers to your work.

Electronic publications have several on-line stores, like Fictionwise. com, where you can browse through many books by different publishers. This makes them easier to market, though it will still take a lot of work on your part to get people to try your book. It's not easy, but if the publisher has a good reputation for turning out well-written and edited books, you will find you have a good starting point.

Don't think of epublishing as 'not real' publishing. Someone once told me that epublishing was good practice for the real stuff. No. *This is not practice.* You are going to be read by real people who will be the start of your fan base, whether for more eBooks or to follow you into traditional print. The more seriously you take this process and your readers, the better you will do.

Business travelers are taking an interest in eBooks, having found they can fit a dozen eBooks on their PDA and not have to worry about long flights, boring nights in hotels...or boring meetings. Many people have found it convenient to read an eBook in bed because it's quiet (you won't disturb your spouse as you change pages) and already lit so the room can stay dark. The ability to change the font size, as well as the relative lightness of PDAs, make them great for anyone with eye problems who like to read at night before sleep.

Also remember that several school systems are trading text books for eBooks and laptops. This means another generation growing up with the idea that reading off the screen is natural.

I am not one of those eBook authors or publishers who believe that eBooks are going to put an end to print book publication—nor would I want to see it happen. I love books and eBooks, and they all have their places. I do believe electronic publications will become just another acceptable option for readers and take its place in the line up: hardbound, trade paperback, mass paperback, eBook, audio. And just as some books are published in mass paperback but not hardbound, I believe it will become common for some books to be published in eBook format and not paper.

EBook publication can be fun. You may not have a lot of readers, but they're generally pretty upbeat and loyal. There have been a few eBooks which have been bought up by big name publishers, but it does not happen often enough to be considered a real possibility. Some people have made a big name in the eBook world, and are making good money at it.

Many electronic publishers are experimenting with POD (Print on Demand) hard copies of the books. Print on Demand is a type of technology (like off-set type) and does not refer to a type of payment or a certain style of manuscript. Many self-publication companies use POD as well, and that has given the public an overall bad impression of the term—but the technology can be used by a regular publisher as well as a self-publishing company. Some small press publishers have even gone to POD publishing as a viable way to stay in business when they can no longer afford the costs of off-set print runs.

POD books are most often trade paperback size—that is the larger, oversized paperback books. They can be quite expensive, which is the downside to this technology. However, they can provide a physical copy for those who really want it, and since the book is printed one at a time from electronic files rather than typeset machines, there is less trouble with print runs.

Electronic publication has many downsides, but it has potential.

Path Five: Self-publication
and vanity publishers

If you are looking for a career in writing, then this is not the path you want to consider. The number of people who have made money, rather than spending far too much, in the self-publishing world is negligible. If you want a career, throwing away your book on a self-publication or vanity publisher is a waste of all your hard work.

The two terms can often be synonymous, though in vanity publishing you are apt to pay more money to get the books printed. Self-publishing might be a case where you go to a do-it-yourself epublishing site on the Internet and may not involve any money at all. Either way may look appealing, but they are not an easy answer to fame and fortune. Of course, there are no easy answers along any path to publishing, but this one can actually lead to a downhill slide.

Once the book has been printed, you can no longer sell the first publication rights—and those are the ones that make you any money. Those rights are the ones most major publication companies are interested in, though some may be willing to overlook a self-published history. (As an aside, most eBook publishers ask only for electronic rights, so that you might still have the ability to sell the print rights elsewhere, if you can.)

Some people mistake copyright for first print rights. It doesn't matter if a publisher (or a website where you post something) says you still retain copyright. In fact, under most circumstances, you will *always* retain copyright unless you purposely sign it away. You do not sell copyright when your book is published—you give a publisher *print rights* of various types for a stated amount of time, but you still own the copyright.

So self-publishing a book either in print or electronic format uses those first print rights. This also happens if you put your book up on your own web site. It doesn't matter how many people have seen it. Nor has it anything to do with whether you were paid or not. If your book has been published in any format for the public to see, then you have used your first print rights.

Self-publication is the easy answer to getting your book in print, and —like many things which are easy—it's not the best answer. Many people turn to it because they can't stand the thought of rejection. If you are looking for a real career—if you want a chance to quit your day job and write novels for a living—then you have to get over that fear. This is not a way around the problem. Nearly ever author who has a book on the shelves has survived it. You can too, as long as you remember that rejection is not an attack against you. It's part of business.

If you go to a self-publishing or vanity press, you will have to 'hand sell' virtually every copy of your book. Except for possibly a small local store where they know you, there will be no stores which will take your self-published book and put it up for sale with the others. There are few web sites which will include self-published work, so you will be mostly left to market your book to sites that cater to self-publishing (and where most readers will not go) and to your own website. This means the majority of the sales will have be made by you pushing your books to total strangers and overcoming some incredible odds to get them to buy. If you went to self-publishing because you couldn't face the thought of rejection, how are you going to deal with asking people to buy your book and having them say no?

Are you good at marketing? Are you really good at self-promotion and overcoming obstacles? Is this something you would like to be doing *rather than writing your next book*? If you want to be a success, marketing isn't something which can be done haphazardly. All types of publication take some degree of marketing on your part; however with self-publishing, there will be no other help.

If you are good at this sort of thing, you might have a chance of selling some copies. However, you will do it against huge odds. Self-publishing and vanity publishing have both gotten very bad press, and there's a legitimate reason for it: most self-published books are put out by people who have no idea how to write a grammatically correct sentence, who often misspell words and who don't even understand the fundamentals of writing (like point of view). Those are the things most people will believe about your work when they see that your book is self-published.

Your book could be perfect, but the majority of people will not take your work seriously and will never give it a chance. Is that fair? Probably not—but you can't win by saying it's not fair. It's fact, and there's nothing which can overcome this first major obstacle and suddenly win your book into acceptance just on its own.

Most magazine and newspaper reviewers will not look at self-published books. It's almost always a waste of their time because the books are so poorly written that the reviewers will no longer even bother with one. They have plenty of other books to review, and not enough time as it is. They want books they know have at least seen a copyeditor.

Combined with all the other downsides of not finding many readers, not getting reviews, and not getting your books on the shelves of bookstores, there is also rarely any money to be made in self-publishing. In almost all cases, you will pay for the printing, and you will never make enough to cover the publisher's other expenses, which will be paid to them before you get any of the profits.

Take your work seriously, and give yourself a real chance at having people share and enjoy your story, and stay clear of this type of publication.

A CLOSING WORD ABOUT THE DIFFERENT PATHS

You need not follow only one path in publication. Just because you have published eBooks doesn't mean you can't make a sale of another book to one of those big New York publishers. Some people aim only at the one path, and that's the way they want their careers to go. It's good to have this kind of focus, but it also doesn't hurt to cast your net a little wider. If you are serious about your career, then start at the top and do your best to sell to New York before you move to small press or eBook publishers. If you are not comfortable with eBooks then don't consider them at all. This still leaves you a wide variety of print possibilities.

You can find a publisher if you are willing to work hard, learn your craft, and step outside the bounds of traditional publication if those don't work for you. Whatever you do, give it your best try, take the submissions seriously, and don't give up. You can make it.

Writing for Magazines
By Michael D. Pederson

Congratulations. After lots of hard work, you've finally finished your short story (or novella/novelette). You're happy with it, your significant other likes it and your mom thinks it's the best thing ever written.

Now what?

Well, I hate to break it to you but the hard work isn't over yet. Submitting your manuscript can be a very time-consuming process that requires quite a bit of careful thought. Most people have a first choice for where they would like to be published, maybe even a second choice. But what if your first two choices reject you? Do you have third, fourth and fifth choices lined up? Is your manuscript formatted properly? Should you send a hard copy or a digital copy?

There are a surprisingly large number of things to be taken into consideration before sending your stories to editors. Hopefully we'll be able to clear up a few of your questions here.

What Do You Mean by "Writing for Magazines"?

Specifically, we're talking about how to get short fiction published by periodicals. This can cover a wide range of both fiction and media.

When I say "magazines," that can mean a monthly digest-sized magazine, a bi-monthly glossy periodical, an online publication or a Xeroxed fanzine. *Playboy*, *The Magazine of Fantasy & Science Fiction*, *The Nth Degree* and *SciFiction* all publish short fiction but no two of these publications will ever be confused with each other.

Writing for magazines can also encompass reviews, essays and journalism as well, but none of these (except maybe journalism) constitute fantasy writing. Instead we'll deal with how to get your short fiction noticed by professional editors.

Why Am I Submitting?

This seems like a pretty stupid question on the surface but it's an essential starting point in deciding where you want to send your manuscript.

What do you want to accomplish?

Do you think that you have what it takes to be the next "Big Thing" in fantasy literature or do you just want to see your name in print? Maybe you only have this one story in you but think it's good enough to be published. Maybe you have a couple of dozen stories set in a world of your own devising.

These are the kind of factors that will affect your decision on where to submit. Or even if you should submit. Perhaps you could accomplish your goals by simply posting your story online. Quite often, a popular blog will be read by more people than many of the smaller magazines. Maybe you're more like me though and prefer the tactile sensation of holding a good quality magazine in your hands and saying, "Look what I did!"

It's very important to be honest with yourself at this stage. Just because you've finished a story doesn't necessarily mean that it should be sent to professional editors. Sometimes the process of writing the story serves best as a learning tool.

Maybe the journey is the destination, not publication.

Often it's hard to distance yourself from your work and give yourself an objective opinion. For this reason, every writer needs to find someone that they trust to read for them, someone who is not afraid to tell them that they have written a big stinkin' piece of garbage. If you don't have a realistic opinion of your own work then it's going to be difficult to find the right magazine to send it to.

If you're still cranking out work that looks amateurish, not only will it hurt your chances of being accepted now but it will hurt your chances in the future when your writing has improved. Editors have good memories. I know that if I've read half a dozen bad stories by Author X, I tend to skim over any new stories that I receive from them, not giving them the full reading that they may deserve. Sure, it sounds bad but professional editors receive A LOT of unsolicited submissions (slush) and have a finite amount of time to go through it.

A similar problem: What if your sub-par submission gets accepted? "How can an acceptance be bad?" I hear you asking. There are some publishers that will accept just about anything (no, I won't give you their addresses). It's not an unheard of problem and I've heard of several authors having to publish under pseudonyms because their real name had been linked to some rubbish that was published in their early days.

Remember, this is the Information Age. Once it's out there, it's never going away. Make sure that you're ready for the big bad world of publishing before sending anything out.

WHERE SHOULD I SUBMIT?

This is where the hard work starts again. You're going to have to do some research here. I constantly receive submissions that are totally inappropriate for my magazine. I glare at them and burn the author's name into my memory, asking myself, "What were they thinking?!" If you want to be accepted, you have to find the right magazine for your style of writing.

Good news though. Researching magazines is easier than ever these days. Which is a good thing because (counting online publications) there are more avenues to explore than ever.

This is possibly the most important part in the submission process. Face it, *Analog* isn't going to be interested in a story about fairy circles in your back yard. Save yourself the time and expense of submitting to publications that don't print the type of fiction that you write.

Properly matching your submission to a suitable magazine will increase your chances to be published.

The easiest way to find which magazine is right for you is to search the Internet. Two online resources that I've found to be invaluable to genre writers are Spicy Green Iguana (www.spicygreeniguana.com) and Preditors & Editors (www.anotherealm.com/prededitors/). Spicy Green Iguana is especially useful—boasting to have "genre mags out the wazoo"—with listings for mainstream magazines, fanzines, webzines and book publishers. Each listing generally tells you what genre the magazine publishes, contact information and submission guidelines. Preditors & Editors doesn't have as thorough a database as Spicy Green Iguana but they also have helpful information on agents, industry awards, game publishers and warnings on how to spot scam publishers.

Once you've narrowed your list of potential targets down, it's time to start researching them to see what kind of fiction they print. By this point, you've probably made a list of every magazine that claims to print "Fantasy" but that covers a lot of ground. If you write dark, Gothic romance/fantasy then you need to find a magazine that specializes in dark, Gothic romance/fantasy, and that's not always the kind of information that you're going to find in a generic online listing. You need to sample each magazine's wares. As a publisher, I encourage you to buy yourself a subscription to the magazines that you're interested in. As an editor though, I realize that this can be a pricey venture and offer the following alternatives.

First, see if they post stories online. Many magazines will at least post excerpts from the current issue, and some even run entire stories. Second, most magazines offer a trial issue—sometimes for free, often at a special introductory cost.

If this is starting to sound complicated, then good. There's a reason. Once upon a time, it took considerable effort to submit a manuscript to an editor—you had to type the story by hand and make carbon copies and, of course, you could only make so many carbon copies at a time. So sending out multiple submissions would often require the slow tedious re-typing of your story each time. Only the really serious-minded writer would go to these lengths (in theory, at least).

Today, since anyone can print endless copies from their home computer, we have to find other ways to sort out the frivolous submissions. An inappropriate submission (i.e., a cyberpunk story sent to a vampire magazine) sends up a big flag to the editor. If you really are serious about writing then you want to do everything you can to impress the anonymous editors that are taking the time to read your manuscript.

Which is where your answer for "What do I want to accomplish?" comes in.

If you're looking to start a career as a professional author then you need to start at the top. Find the biggest, best known magazines and start there. For science fiction and fantasy, I refer, of course, to *Analog, Asimov's, The Magazine of Fantasy & Science Fiction* and *Realms of Fantasy*. There are also excellent online publications like *SciFiction* and *Strange Horizons*. Chances are you won't be accepted by the top tier on your first attempt; don't be discouraged, that's just the way these things work. And if you're not accepted right away by the major markets then you simply keep moving down the list until you find someone that likes your story.

If you don't get accepted by the major publishers then set your sights on finding a good small press magazine. There are plenty of semi-prozines and small press magazines that you can try sending to. DNA Publications has a line of science fiction and horror magazines that (although considered small press) publishes a wide range of fiction from both big names and newcomers.

If you're still striking out then look at the fanzine market. Many of the biggest names in science fiction and fantasy got their start writing for fanzines. My own magazine, *Nth Degree*, is a semiprofessional fanzine that was created specifically to help aspiring new artists and writers get their foot in the door. There's no shame in starting small; just take the time to look at the publication and make sure that it's something that you wouldn't be embarrassed to be in.

Of course, if you're just writing as a hobby then maybe it's smartest to start out with the mid-level publishers and fanzines. Sending out manuscripts (though easier than ever before) does still cost time and money, so simply find the magazine that best matches your style and goals and start with them.

How Do I Submit?

Down to the nuts and bolts. This is where people generally make the greatest number of mistakes in their professional submissions.

Most of what you need to know here will be found in your research on where to submit. All magazines have submission guidelines. Some prefer e-mail submissions, some require hard copies with self addressed stamped envelopes. Should you double-space? Are single-sided or double-sided pages preferred?

Always, always, always read the submission guidelines carefully. Remember what I said earlier about editors wanting to make things difficult? This is where it comes into play the most. If you can't follow a simple set of guidelines then you've already lost the respect of the one person that you're trying to impress.

In many ways, submitting to a magazine is no different from submitting to a book publisher or agent.

You will need a cover letter. The cover letter should include all of your current contact information: mailing address, phone number and email address. If you have a website that showcases your work, include that as well. You should also include a word count and a brief summary of your story. Your summary should explain the basic plot, characters and setting. And don't be afraid to give away the ending in your summary; the editor is looking to see if you know how to tie a story together, they don't care if you have a shocking "twist" ending. If you have been published before or have sold stories for upcoming publication, you need to include that information here as well. In fact, any relevant information should be put in the cover letter. Let me emphasize the word relevant. We don't need to know that your mom likes the story or that you have a good contact with your local bookstore. If you teach a class in Celtic history at your local college and you've written a Celtic fantasy, then that would be something the editor would like to know. It's also nice to mention where you came across the magazine that you're submitting to—you've subscribed for years, you found them online, they were listed in Writer's Digest, etc.

Unlike submitting a novel, however, you probably won't need to write a query letter. Again, though, this is something that you need to check your submission guidelines for.

The other major difference between submitting a short story and submitting a novel is dealing with agents. Most major book publishers won't look at a novel without an agent acting on your behalf (this, once again, goes back to the whole trying-to-make-the-process-complicated bit). With magazine publishers, though, you will usually be representing yourself.

The actual formatting for the submission itself will be based on each individual magazine's requirements. A typical submission guideline is: "All submissions must be typed, double-spaced, and accompanied by a self-addressed stamped envelope large enough to hold your manuscript." That's pretty common. However, you will find some variance out there so it's necessary to check with each publication before you send anything. Some will take digital submissions. Some will specify a certain type size. Some will prefer a disposable manuscript. Again, it's very important that you read and follow these instructions to the letter.

One thing that is not usually mentioned in submission guidelines is headers and footers. Use them. Your name and the story's name should be included at the top of every page. A page number should also be included on every page; it's even more helpful if they read " 1 of 16," "2 of 16," etc.

Keep in mind when you are preparing your submission that this is the author's equivalent of a resume. Don't try to get cute or fancy with it. Don't send chocolates. Don't print your cover letter on unicorn stationery.

Simple and professional is the best way to go.

A note on e-mail addresses: Don't get cute. Remember that this is a professional submission; an e-mail from jsmith@sample.com will carry more weight than one from luvbunny21. It's not difficult to set yourself up with a second e-mail address to use for submissions. Think of it as your digital post office box.

COMMON SENSE

Make sure that your submission is grammatically correct. Everything should be spelled properly. Your verb tenses should be consistent. Characters shouldn't change their names in the middle of the narrative.

Again, this sounds like I'm stating the obvious, but you would be surprised at how many writers send out uncorrected drafts. Nothing will get your story thrown out quicker than a misspelling in the first sentence.

If you want to be a professional writer then spelling, vocabulary, punctuation and grammar are the tools of your trade. I wouldn't hire a carpenter that didn't know the difference between a hammer and a screwdriver. Why would I want a writer that doesn't know the difference between first and third person point-of-view?

FOLLOWING UP

Yes, it's perfectly acceptable to check back in on your submission. But use good judgment. Most publications will state in their submission guidelines how long it takes for them to reply to your submission. If they go past their stated deadline, then yes, it's perfectly acceptable to follow up. Just don't turn into Crazy Stalker Guy.

One suggestion that will help put your mind at ease is to include a self-addressed stamped postcard with your submission that reads "Received Submission On _____." Then the editor can simply fill in the date and drop it in the mail and you'll rest comfortably knowing that the submission that you have spent so much time on has made it safely through the mail and rests comfortably on the editor's desk.

REJECTIONS

You will receive lots and lots of rejections. Get used to it. Even the best writers have horror stories about their worst rejections.

These days, many editors don't have the time to give you comments on your story. Don't take it personally when you receive a form letter. If you do get feedback though, remember where it came from. That's probably an editor that will remember you in the future.

What if they ask for changes? Well, there are two schools of thought on that. One: Just because one person thinks your story should be changed doesn't mean they're right. Maybe a different editor will accept your story without any changes. Two: Being published is good and you should do whatever it takes. If Joe Editor thinks that your main character should be a female instead of a male, then make the change.

I can't advocate one outlook over the other. You just have to go with what works for you.

WHAT DO EDITORS REALLY WANT?

One of the questions that I get asked most frequently is, "What makes a good story?"

There is no secret formula for a good story but there are elements that I look for. I generally know on my first reading whether or not a story is appropriate for my magazine. So what do I look for?

Everyone will tell you that a good hook is essential. Well, sure, it is nice, but I'm more concerned with a good ending. I've read too many stories that started out with a great hook but went nowhere. And the ending is very important. Too often writers will cram a resolution in because the story is already as long as they want it. This is a matter of pacing as well as plotting—both of which are essential to a good story.

Originality is something else that I look for. It's hard to come up with a truly original idea but maybe you can find your own interpretation of an old idea. It doesn't even have to be the main concept of the story, just as long as there is something in there that makes me go, "Hey, cool! Wish I had thought of that."

Characters. That's the big one. Nothing irritates me more than writers that insert characters for no reason other than to advance the plot. Once the character exits the scene the reader should be able to fill in the blanks of where they go and what they do. They need to be imbued with a life beyond the page. They don't have to be larger-than-life but they do need to be believable.

Conventions: Fantasy writers are very, very lucky. On any given weekend there is a science fiction and fantasy convention going on somewhere in the country. Not only can you participate in writing seminars at these cons (taught by professional writers and editors) but you can go to panels given by major genre editors where they will tell you exactly what they are looking for. If you are fortunate, you may have the opportunity to talk with these editors and maybe even discuss your fiction. Just remember that cons are for their enjoyment too. This is not the office and they will not take kindly to having you thrust your works upon them. However, if they ask for one you want to make sure to have a clean, bound copy on you.

CONCLUSION: WHY BOTHER WITH MAGAZINES?

It's not uncommon to hear people say that "print is dead." Magazine circulations have been dropping for years and it is no longer possible to make a living writing strictly short fiction. Back in the Golden Age of the pulps it wasn't just common for writers to live off short story sales, but it was practically the only way to earn a living as a genre writer. Mass market paperbacks didn't exist yet and the per word pay rate more evenly matched the cost of living than it does today.

Today, the cost of living has increased exponentially, while the word rate has barely grown or, in some cases, is still the same. So why bother?

Because it's good for you, that's why. Short fiction is a much less forgiving form than the novel. It is the best practice that you can give yourself as a writer. "A job done well is its own reward" may sound like a cliché, but it's true. As a writer you are creating art—it's not necessarily "fine art" but it is art—and as an artist your natural goals are to improve your craft. Short fiction is one of the best ways to do this.

Also, since short stories are (by definition) much shorter than novels it's possible to generate more in a short period of time. If you're good at it then you will eventually start to earn some name recognition.

All of that practice and recognition will pave your way to writing the next great fantasy novel.

Good luck.

EDITOR'S DESK

Submissions
from the Editor's point of view
BY HELEN FRENCH

If you want to know how to structure plots, or what editors think makes a good story, there are a million and one how-to writing books that cover the same ground over and over. In contrast, this chapter aims to look at the business behavior of writers, and how editors view this. For example, an unprofessional query or phone call can persuade an editor that they don't want to deal with that writer again. Any such behavior can reflect badly on a writer and damage or hinder their career.

"When a writer is unprofessional, I am less inclined to want to work with him/her—and less inclined to want to give my time to the manuscript," said Anna Genoese, an editor at Tor.

A fantastic manuscript—from novel length right down to short stories—can overcome many problems. Nevertheless, you don't want to put off an editor or agent before they've had a chance to read it—or even after they've read it, when they might be undecided about whether to see more. And when you manage to snare the editor of your dreams, you want to maintain a good relationship. You can do this and avoid many problems by being professional and businesslike whenever possible.

While writing is an art, publishing is (whether you think it fortunate or not) a business. Ultimately, that's why it pays to be businesslike, as well as artistic—especially when it comes to interacting with your editor (and the same applies to working with an agent, too). Your story speaks loudest, but your professionalism can improve relationships, while being unprofessional can drag them down. As Mary Theresa Hussey, executive editor of LUNA (Harlequin's fantasy imprint) said, "For the initial buy, it's generally all about the story. Although I have to admit that hand-written, hard to read submissions and frequent reminder calls don't make an editor give the author the benefit of the doubt."

I was an editorial assistant for Harlequin—for LUNA and other imprints—for two years, reading thousands of submissions and finding four new authors whose books were bought in that time period. I was keen to forge ahead, find a brilliant new author among the slush, to make my reputation. Even so, the actions of an unprofessional author could put me off their work before I'd even turned the first page.

I then worked as a freelance editor for two years—editing, reading and critiquing books from a variety of genres—and I continued to run into writers who delivered sloppy manuscripts, were rude in communication and refused revision. Whatever their behaviour, I kept an eye out for good writing, of course. Nevertheless, you should want editors to cast their first glance at your story with a favorable eye—try to be professional in your interactions with them from the very beginning.

THE SUBMISSION

Query Letters

Your query letter or covering letter is likely to be the first thing that an editor will look at upon opening your submission package. Some do jump straight to the fiction (if any is included), preferring not to be influenced beforehand, but the majority will use your letter as a starting point. It's an important first impression, which you don't want to mess up by appearing unprofessional.

The most obvious pitfall is writing a shoddy covering letter, which hasn't been properly proofed or structured—or that gets the editor's name wrong. If you treat submitting your fiction as a business, writing a clean and accurate query letter should be a priority. Then, of course, you want to wow the editor with the content of the letter.

Some writers—likely not you, if you're taking the time to read this book—come across very badly, probably without realising it. Telling an editor that they'd be a fool not to request your manuscript, for example, is not a great idea, no matter how good or salable you think your book is. Similarly, saying that a friend or relative loved the book, and therefore everyone else will, is not going to impress. Instead, you'll come across as naïve, and unaware of the nuances of the publishing industry. For example, a friend or relative may worry more about offending you than saying what they truly feel about the book. Alternatively, they may feel so amazed that someone they know could ever finish a book that they may not critically assess the material at all. Besides, as it's such a subjective industry, only the editor's opinion really matters at this point (until you send it to another editor, and so on). They're the best qualified to give an opinion.

There are many other potential pitfalls to avoid. One seen too often is the sob story—the "so many bad things have happened to me that I deserve publication" story. The truth is that nobody deserves publication—only a great story does—and thinking you do is likely to lead to some level of arrogance or delusion. Writing that you do in a covering letter is not going to persuade the editor reading it to come around to your opinion—only your story can do that.

Writers often veer between thinking what they've written is awful and awesome. It is best to have some confidence in your work before sending it out, after all. But there is a difference between confidence and assuming your book definitely will and should be published by the first company you send it to—overconfidence can only end in heartbreak, the majority of the time. Understand that your job was to do the writing, and now the editor's job is to decide how much they like it.

As it's common knowledge that most publishing houses are deluged by submissions, some writers try to stand out above the crowd—but do it the wrong way. Don't, for example, send out query letters or chapters on strange-colored paper, pages of author photographs, resumes that don't have any relevance to your book or its subject matter, and so on.

Lazette Gifford, associate publisher of Double Dragon's eBook fantasy imprint has some good advice as well. "Don't tell me that the book has been rejected by other places," she said. "I don't care where it's been and who didn't want it." The best way to stand out is by stating clearly and concisely what you are offering. The writing will stand for itself.

Know Your Genre

Before you even start writing, it's important to understand the genre that you'll be writing in—in this case, fantasy. While there probably are successful authors who didn't know anything about their genre while writing and submitting their books, their numbers won't be large. It doesn't hurt you to be knowledgeable, while it could hurt you if you're not. Fantasy can be a tricky genre to navigate. It may be impossible (or near it) to read its entire backlist, but if you read broadly across the genre you can pick up a lot of information that may prove invaluable when it comes to submitting your work to an editor. It's only by in-depth reading that you can learn to recognise the most commonly-used clichés, crutches and ill-used techniques.

Fantasy editors see an awful lot of submissions, and become tired of the same material cropping up again and again. You may have written a fantastic piece of fiction, but if it's got elves, dwarves, menacing mountains, prophecies and any other number of oft-used fantasy crutches, there's a danger you could run into an editor who hates all of those. Not that you should necessarily avoid those things, but you should be aware that the more you use, the more you may face prejudice. Writing is a subjective business, and while editors may say they'll buy a great book even if it's not to their personal taste, it'll be much harder to get them to notice that it's a great story in the first place.

World-building is always a challenge (and frequently a very enjoyable one), and you may be tempted to use what some people call "fantasy filler" to save you work and fill in the gaps. This happens more often than you may think—how many fantasy worlds, after all, have a vaguely medieval setting, with little to tell them apart? Not that there's anything wrong with a world that has only a medieval level of technology, but rather that stronger world-building can sometimes make a world stand out. Slavishly following those who have gone before you will win no fans, whether readers or editors. Stronger world-building can make you appear more professional, too—more willing to go the extra mile, more likely to have a long future with a wide variety of books written and published.

Know Your Publisher
Try to learn as much as possible about the publisher of your choice. If you're writing fantasy, you want to be sure that the publishers you target actually publish in that genre. Surprisingly, it's not something all writers do—some submit to every one listed in writing guides. The best way to find a suitable publisher is to go to a bookstore, or look at your own bookshelves, and see which publishers, and imprints of those publishers, put out the fantasy books there.

Once you've done that, go a little further if you can. John Joseph Adams, assistant editor at *Fantasy & Science Fiction Magazine*, advised that "authors should remember to do their research before submitting. With the Internet and the wealth of writing books out there, there's no excuse to be uninformed." That's good advice. Look up the publisher's website, or ring up the company, to check guidelines, names to address letters to and to ensure that they're still there. Businesses chop, change, merge and close down all the time.

Read the Guidelines
Reading the guidelines of the publisher or magazine you're sending fiction to should be mandatory, but it's something that a lot of writers neglect, perhaps thinking that it's time-consuming and unnecessary. Much of the advice in this chapter has focused on how not to be unprofessional. The easiest way to stay on the good side of editors is to do one thing only: follow the guidelines. As Genoese pointed out, why should editors invest time in a submission when the author hasn't bothered? "If a writer doesn't have the time to read and follow my

guidelines, why should I find the time to read the writer's manuscript?" she said.

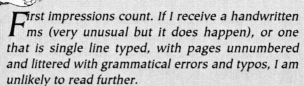

Reading the guidelines will get you farther than just about anything.
— Lazette Gifford, Double Dragon Publishing

Guidelines normally specify a number of things to keep in mind: formatting, genre, word counts and so on. Whether you follow these instructions can by key to acting professionally. Don't submit a manuscript in your favourite font because you feel it suits your characters, for example. Submitting a manuscript in a smaller font because it can save you paper can cost you dear. Nor should you submit multiple stories to one place unless they specify that you can. And finally, don't send the same story to several places at once (simultaneous submissions) unless guidelines state that you can. Even if you think you're saving time, you're likely to be making a bad business move, for these tactics often waste an editor's time.

First impressions count. If I receive a handwritten ms (very unusual but it does happen), or one that is single line typed, with pages unnumbered and littered with grammatical errors and typos, I am unlikely to read further.
— Julia Moffatt

YOUR MANUSCRIPT

Give It Your Best

Don't be fooled into thinking that being businesslike only extends to everything outside of your novel or story. Sloppy fiction writing can also let you down. Some people simply aren't good writers, and may never be. However, when a writer is lazy and doesn't bother to hone their skills, polish the first draft, or even proofread it, that's just bad manners. Editors are very busy and people who submit rough first drafts are wasting time—the editors', and their own.

While a few small mistakes may be overlooked, then fixed by copy editors and proofreaders, editors know that a manuscript littered with errors is going to be hard work. You have to overcome that prejudice with a fantastic story if you want to get anywhere. But it's easier to submit a clean manuscript in the first place.

It's not the editor's job to transform a first draft into a published piece. "I came across one person who said that he wouldn't edit his work at all until he had an editor's interest in it. He seemed to think that was the editor's work. Some people are ignorant of how the business works. And some of them just don't want to learn, either, because it would mean they'd have to work harder," said Gifford. So don't assume cleaning up your manuscript is down to the editor—they'll only reject it. Send out only your best work. Second-best will be rejected in an instant.

I recall reading a romantic suspense which had an interesting plot, but fell apart in the execution—the formatting, grammar, spelling and punctuation were all a mess. The author received a rejection letter and an invite to submit again (with a new manuscript), but perhaps if they'd made more effort in the first place, the outcome would have been different.

> *The bottom line is that if the author hasn't created a compelling opening, dynamic characters and a strong conflict and motivation to move the plot, the author has not done her job.*
> — *Mary Theresa Hussey, LUNA*

It's Not Your Baby

Writing and finishing a book (or a short story, novella and so on) is a massive accomplishment. Most people who declare that they "want to be authors" never get so far. And even the fastest of writers pour hours into their work, as well as their hearts and minds. After all this time and energy has been sunk in, especially as your hopes and aspirations may be resting on it, it's easy to feel very close to your novel—thinking of it as "your baby" is how some people put it. This is where some unprofessional behavior can begin. If you place too much on the outcome of submitting your novel, it can be very distressing to receive rejections and revision comments. It may be difficult to detach yourself enough to read and analyze any communication properly. Similarly, it can make the waiting process unbearable.

> *The reality is that publishing is a business, and only a very small percentage of books can be published and make money.*
>
> — Anna Genoese, Tor

While editors are constantly on the look out for new and exciting fiction, and it's tempting to think that they eagerly tear open the parcels of unsolicited submissions that arrive each morning, the truth is that they have many other things to do first. Aside from looking for new fiction, editors usually have a raft of already-published authors to look after, agents to deal with, scheduled manuscripts to edit, meetings to attend and so on. They might be looking for new talent, but that doesn't stop editors sighing from time to time when a new pile of manuscripts appears. I was always eager to look at a newly-delivered pile of slush, but when deadlines were approaching, contracted manuscripts had to be read first.

Whether or not this particular submission feels like "your baby," there will be many more books to come if you have a successful career in writing. What does it matter if the one you're working with at the moment receives a few rejections? You can write another, and each new book you write will likely be better than the last.

Following Up

Just as authors should be professional while making their initial submission, it helps if their after-submission behavior is also businesslike. There are worse ways to offend or appear unprofessional than through a manuscript or query letter. At least those are recognized and traditional ways to contact editors in the period before you're published. Some editors may invite phone calls, emails and follow-up letters, but the majority do not. If you're going to contact an editor in this way, be sure that you have to, and that you have a query that cannot be answered in any other way.

Email

It's often possible to guess editors' email addresses, especially if a publishing company follows the same pattern for every address. So it can be tempting to send off a quick email, hoping for a speedy answer in return. However, whether it's a query about submission status, or a question about revisions, it's best not to do this unless it's a publisher who took submissions via email in the first place (and is happy to receive follow-up emails)—or a publisher who invites questions in that way.

Being bombarded by email is never fun, particularly when it's from demanding authors who aren't yet being published. Furthermore, using email probably increases the chance that you'll look unprofessional— it's all too easy to fire off an email without spell-checking it first, or to send one when you're angry, without giving yourself the chance to cool down first.

Phone Calls

Phone calls put editors on the spot, which can make them uncomfortable—although they'll certainly do their best to be professional—and which can make them think badly of the calling writer. For instance, many publishers send promising (or otherwise) submissions to freelancers, who in turn compile reports and recommendations for action.

Imagine the editor who rejects a manuscript on that basis, then has to face a phone call from the rejected author. Even if the editor did personally work on or read your manuscript, there's every chance that he or she will have read so many that they can't recall some details from the text. Having to admit that they don't remember what happened in your book can put editors in an awkward situation, and it doesn't endear them to you, either.

If you have revision suggestions that you're unsure about, a phone call may be advisable—the editor obviously thinks it is worth investing some time in you and your work—but if you simply want to complain or ask about a rejection, please rethink it. You'd be better off thinking calmly about whatever comments (or not) that they've made, and wondering how you can (if you agree with them) apply this feedback to future works.

Some writers telephone editors to establish what they think is a personal relationship, and expect personal correspondence in regards to their submission. But telling an editor how great your story is over the phone is not going to win them over. Rather it's the printed words that will do that—they can speak for themselves. In addition, editors have to take many phone calls from their own, published authors. Phoning too often before you're at that stage can create a bad impression. Julia Moffatt, a commissioning editor for Scholastic in the 1990s, said, "Publishers can be notoriously slow in dealing with your material, which can be very frustrating. But they will not be inclined to take yours seriously if they are being badgered every five minutes. In fact I can't think of a faster way to ensure your work will end up on the reject pile than being an author who constantly calls."

Letters

As most communications with publishing houses are done by snail mail, this may seem like the best option when you want to get in touch. Indeed, if you truly feel you have a valid reason for complaint, it probably is. Nevertheless, there are still ways you can appear foolish or needlessly angry, and this can put an editor off from dealing with you again.

If your cover letter says things like "I've never read an eBook" or "I'm practicing for submissions to real publishers" (yes, really, I've seen stuff like that), it's not going to help. I "try" not to see these things and try to judge the book on its own merits, but it's best not to annoy the editor from the start.
— Lazette Gifford, Double Dragon Publishing

Rejection and Revision

Rejection stings, and it's where some writers cross over the line from good to bad behavior. Personal letters show that an editor found something worthwhile in your work (unless they say never to submit again). In such instances, take any comments on board, remembering that you don't have to follow every one, but don't send back a letter complaining that you shouldn't have been rejected, that the editors were mistaken, that one day they'll regret not taking you on. Perhaps the editor will regret that decision, but they'll find that out in their own time.

I sent one author a detailed rejection letter, only to have it returned to me shortly afterwards. She'd written on the top of it "I give up," underlining it several times. I thought she was a promising author until that point, and hoped that a personal letter might help her avoid some pitfalls. But she never submitted anything to me again and furthermore, I'd have been wary of dealing with her after that point because of her unprofessional behavior.

Badmouthing a publisher or an editor or an agent can lead to that writer being handled with caution during the submission process.
— *Mary Theresa Hussey, LUNA*

The majority of rejections are form ones—that is, impersonal, and with no details about why the story was turned down. These can be hard to take—why, writers might ask, won't they tell me what I did wrong? But with so many submissions every day, editors don't always have the time to go into detail.

Sometimes editors are wary of encouraging people—writers might "fix" the reasons for rejection and demand a reread. Many stories are rejected for not standing out—they might be competent works, but not particularly exciting, and so the editor might not have much to say. In any case, editors don't owe anyone a reply, however hard that is to swallow. After all, "[i]t isn't an editor's job to teach an author how to write a better story and make it publishable," Hussey said.

While it's easy to understand why writers might behave unprofessionally about being rejected, it's sometimes harder to understand why they do the same upon receiving revision suggestions.

Yet it happens. The mistake comes in thinking that revisions suggestions are a bad thing—a horrible criticism of a writer's work. Really, revision suggestions are a compliment—an editor thinks that work has potential, and can be improved even further.

The businesslike way to deal with revisions is to complete them to the best of your abilities. That's if you accept them of course—you'd be wise to think about it, at least, but don't go ahead if you think they'd truly change the book for the worse. If you feel that the editor hasn't been clear, they probably won't mind a few questions for clarification. Don't expect them to remember everything about your manuscript, however, particularly if you phone the editor in question—though most editors do have a very good memory.

If you don't want to do revisions, don't do them; it's as simple as that. But don't argue against the revisions, or suggest that your book is perfect as it is. Not doing anything at all will demonstrate that perfectly well, but without offending anyone. Some editors have long memories, and you don't want them to dread your next submission. Moffatt suggested that you "[t]ry and bear in mind when you are being asked to make changes that the editor is not doing it for fun, but because she or he really wants to make the best book they can. And remember, your editor is your best friend in this business. Don't fall out with her!"

Gifts

Some authors, rather than going out of their way to annoy editors, like to try and please them. Not only by writing a great story, but by sending gifts, for example. Yet this won't necessarily win editors over either. In fact, doing so can make them feel discomfited—it can be seen as a way to try and win editorial favor, and there's a very good chance that it will only work in the opposite direction.

It's down to personal preference, of course. There may well be many editors who love thoughtful gifts from as-yet-unpublished writers. But it may be a risk to guess which camp your editor falls into, so it may be wiser simply to restrain yourself. I received everything from tea towels to necklaces, badges and books during my work as an editorial assistant and though I knew it was mostly due to friendliness, some authors seemed to be begging for a personal response to their submissions. It didn't work.

Thank you letters (after a detailed rejection letter, for instance) are often welcomed, but many editors have received unprofessional ones. If you want to send one, do, but don't expect a reply. Think of them only as a way to thank the editor for their time—don't expect that it'll turn into regular correspondence.

One-on-One
In Person

There are occasions when you can talk to editors on a more one-on-one basis. Conventions are one example. You may have an allotted time to talk to them, perhaps in a pitch session. Even here, though, it's writer beware if you want to ensure that you're businesslike and professional. Talk to editors at appropriate moments—not when they're visiting the bathroom or chatting with friends. You want to be remembered, but not for the wrong reasons.

"I do find it rude to be interrupted with a book pitch when in conversation or while eating or while heading down the hotel hallway," Hussey said. "The rules of politeness should always be in effect. Certainly I've looked at material more closely after speaking to someone who has impressed me. But the key will always be in the writing. If the story draws me, I can forget about and forgive a lot of things!" In the end, nothing matters more than the quality of your story, but bad behavior can prejudice the editor who's about to read it, and it's that you want to avoid.

Online

A fairly recent phenomenon involves talking to editors via the Internet—and not just through email. Some publishers have public web sites, where editors may frequently log in to answer queries or to chat. Here, though, they are still working. Don't become too familiar, or write sloppy questions—in a public, yet professional forum such as this, it's not only the editors who must act professionally. Editors don't have time for overfriendly authors, or writers who complain bitterly about rejections on the publisher's turf. And if you don't bother to be polite or use correct grammar, they may assume (whether rightly or not), that the same is true of your novel.

Gifford agreed, saying, "I think it looks very bad for people who are writers not to present themselves in the best way possible where written language is concerned." In fact, this is good advice to bear in mind wherever you surf on the Net. If you're a writer, you should be a master of words—whatever and wherever you're writing. Use Google, or another search engine, to see what someone could find out about you. Something you post in anger one day may still be online several years later. If you must have a moan, try to do it in a "private" area of the Net—such as locked journal entries, or invite-only forums. Moffatt warned of the dangers of being a little too free with your thoughts on the Net, and offered some useful advice: "I would be incredibly wary of publishing an adverse opinion of a publisher online. For a start, if it is too scurrilous, there could be a libel issue, and secondly mud sticks."

Some editors and agents have web logs, online journals, or post on writing web sites under their real identity. As with company web sites, the danger here is that you might feel that you really get to know the editor—be friends with them, even. And so you might expect more from them when you next send a submission than you would've done if circumstances were different. As Genoese, who has a LiveJournal, said, "they [web logs] create a false sense of intimacy."

> *If I were submitting stories, I don't know that I'd gripe about them publicly. I personally don't care about that sort of thing, but other people might.*
> — *John Joseph Adams, Fantasy & Science Fiction*

Adams has a blog that puts him firmly in the public—and writer's—eye. "I think my Internet presence does change the way writers behave toward me. Reading someone's blog or someone's posts on a message board can make you feel like you know him or her… There's nothing wrong with that so long as one keeps in mind that the act of submitting a story is a professional transaction and needs to be treated as such." This is good advice that's worth keeping in mind.

For some reason, fantasy readers, writers and editors seem to have a larger presence online than counterparts who specialise in other genres. It's relatively easy to build up a wide network of friends and contacts that can help you find publishers, critique your work and one day, buy your books. As long as you don't step over the line, and take any frustrations out on the editorial professionals around you, you can maintain a businesslike approach to your writing quite easily.

Do remember that whatever you read may not be true. Hussey said, "I think one of the most important things these days is also trying to winnow the gossip from the facts. Be aware that things you hear online or on loops may be said with an agenda that doesn't match yours or from experiences you haven't shared." Whatever you read about an editor, agent, or publisher, may or may not be true. Facts can be embellished upon and rejections can be exaggerated. While you may aim to be businesslike and professional online, others may not do the same.

Published Writers

So far, this chapter has focused on the unprofessional behavior from writers who are not yet published, and how this can affect the way editors view them. However, having a contract in hand is no excuse or reason to suddenly forget about being businesslike. Published authors have a lot to gain if they act professionally, and a lot to lose if they don't—perhaps more so than unpublished writers.

Holding a contract, or selling one book (or even several), doesn't necessarily mean that you'll have a long and healthy writing career. A lot depends on the quality of your writing and storytelling, but much depends on the relationship writers have with their editors, too. Difficult authors acquire a reputation for their behavior, which can make editors reluctant to deal with them at all. Imagine an editor with two great books, but only one slot available in the publishing schedule. The authors' writing and storytelling abilities are on a pretty much equal level, but their attitudes are not. One author always delivers manuscripts late; one is always on time. One demands the title, cover artwork and copy editing are done exactly as they ask; the other author makes reasonable requests, and is willing to make compromises in some areas. Which author is more likely to get the contract? If the editor is equally passionate about both novels, it'll be the author who's more amenable to work with that gets to continue their career.

Hussey said, "Personal quirks can be accepted, enjoyed and dealt with. But in the long run, editors will only continue working with authors whose benefit to the company outweighs the drawbacks."

Adams shared that opinion, saying, "[e]veryone has his or her limits, and editors are no different. I have heard of book deals being cancelled because the author was a thorn in the side of the publisher, so it's always best to act like a professional, and to treat editors how you yourself would hope to be treated."

That's not to say that you shouldn't raise legitimate complaints once you're published. A good editor should be happy to hear and appease your concerns. But there is a difference between looking out to protect your interests, and simply being difficult because you think you're important. A publishing house will have a number of authors, and aside from a few exceptions, its fortune won't rest upon any one—particularly when it comes to midlist authors. Fantasy fiction is doing reasonably well at the moment, thanks in part to the media behemoths known as *Harry Potter* and *The Lord of the Rings*. But genres fall in and out of public favor, and it may not be so popular forever. Imprints may be cropped, and authors culled, and you'll want to do what you can to remain a published writer. This means continuing to write great books, of course, but being known as an affable author won't hurt, either.

A writer who is unprofessional pre-contract is always unprofessional and difficult to work with post-contract—and smart editors don't try to make their own lives harder.

— Anna Genoese, Tor

Summary

Editors are constantly seeking new and exciting talent. Publishing houses and magazines need new authors. All you have to do to break in is write a great novel—or short story if that's the market you're aiming for—and get it in the right hands. But actually, nothing is that simple. It's true that a fantastic story will get you further than anything else, but understanding that publishing is a business, and accordingly, acting professionally, can help you enormously along the way.

Be clear and concise in query letters, without ordering editors to request your manuscript. Polish the manuscript itself until it shines, and be polite in any follow-up correspondence, or in communications online or in person. That's all there is to it, really. Much of this may seem obvious—it all boils down in the end to "play nice."

While you're writing, treat writing as an art if that's how you work. Once it's done, and you start sending out submissions—hoping to land one at the desk of the editor who's right for you—treat writing and publishing as a business. Be businesslike as well as telling a good story, and you'll soon escape from that slush pile. And if you're already published, being better friends with your editor is hardly likely to be bad for business.

The Mighty Pen
PRESS RELEASES
AND COMMUNICATING WITH PRINT MEDIA
BY JENNIFER HAGAN

So you thought all the work was done. The book is written. You've been through rough drafts, edits, frustration, blood, sweat and tears. Finally you receive the first shiny copy of your masterpiece. And then one, tiny flaw creeps into your almost perfect plan: what if no one reads it?

It would be wonderful if we could all get published by colossal publishing houses who can supply a public relations guy to answer your every beck and call. At least, that's my fantasy. But it doesn't always happen that way. So now you're faced with being the writer *and* the promoter, and most of the writers I've met feel sorely inept when trying to toot their own horns in a public setting.

Don't worry, there are solutions to this dilemma, and one of those is reaching out to your local newspapers. It just so happens that there is a newspaper or three in almost every town in America and like ravening beasts, they are always hungry for news. The key is to dangle a tasty morsel.

That is where the mighty and sometimes misunderstood press release comes in. A press release is like a herald trumpeting your grand entrance, announcing who you are, what you did and why they should pay attention. It can also be an irritating document to write unless you know what some of the conventions are, which is why your humble servant wrote this chapter.

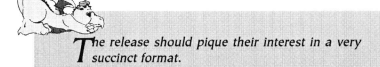

The release should pique their interest in a very succinct format.

But then let's say your press release was successful and reporters are knocking down your door to interview you. How do you talk to them? What are they looking for? Well, after you're done reading this chapter, the whole process will be a little less mystifying.

GUIDING ADVICE

If there is one thing you take away from reading this chapter, let it be this: whenever you issue a release, and I mean every time, it needs to be linked to an event. Yes, the release of a new novel is an event.

However, if the novel was released in February and you want press in June, you're going to have to think of something a little more compelling. Reporters call this the hook. The reason is that the majority of newspaper stories have some immediacy to it because their readers are looking for what's happening now or in the near future or past. So-and-so was arrested last night; Congress is expected to pass such-and-such a bill tomorrow. Even art and entertainment stories are about exhibitions and events. You will occasionally see a profile, or a story about a person or organization without a specific event attached to it, but the expiration date on it is long and god knows when the story will come out. If this is the second time you are seeking press from the same newspaper, it is even more important to link your release to an event. Anything less and it will seem to them like they are repeating what they've already done. Why you ask? Readers aren't looking for what happened last month or a year ago; they want to know what's happening now. So if you want to turn a reporter's head, the best way is to show them why they need to write a story right now.

So let's go back to the previous example: What if your book has been out for months and you need some press to boost flagging sales?

Answer: Arrange a book signing or reading and write the press release to announce it. This really is a lot easier than it sounds. Book stores and coffee houses are usually pretty open to the idea of readings because it charms their customers, and they are especially interested if you tell them that a reporter is planning to attend. A little good press certainly doesn't hurt a business and in this instance you are doing them a good turn in addition to getting yourself some attention too. A little plus here is that if things go well, you have the potential to develop a long standing relationship with the owner of the store and doing readings could become a regular thing. Making connections really is how the world goes round.

Consider Your Audience

One of the first rules of writing a novel is to consider who you're writing for. The same goes with writing a press release. You want it to be read and saved, not tossed into the garbage, so let's consider your audience.

A reporter is typically always running on deadline, even when it's hours or days away. They want their information in bite-sized morsels: quick and tasty. They want a subject that people want to read about, not a story they have to justify to their editors after the fact. They want it to be topical, interesting and, if possible, glib. And most of all, they want a story that they'll enjoy writing. After all, that's why they became professional writers.

An important thing to remember about reporters is that they are not always looking for controversy. Undeniably, some reporters are bloodsuckers some of the time; they have to be sometimes simply to tell the truth. But put your defensiveness away, because if you get a call back about being interviewed, chances are very good that controversy is not what they are looking for. What they are looking for is a good story about an interesting person.

So to sum up, your audience is probably not looking for a press release that is three pages long and includes a complete history of your life, including how devastated you were when your cat died, and which predicts the release of your first book three years from now. No! Bad author!

So try this basic format on for size. Your press release should be about a page, maybe two, although the shorter the better. When writing it, think of your release like you would a resume: it should sum up all of the important information but if your reader has to read too much to get to the point then you've probably lost the job. All of the really pertinent information should be right up front. If you're having a book signing, the time, date and location should be in the first paragraph after your lede. Why make them work for it?

Contact Information

Your contact information is probably the most crucial bit of information in your press release, so separate it out and put it front and center. This information should include your name, phone number, and even times that are best for you to be gotten a hold of if you have an erratic schedule. I suggest putting all of this information up top, just like you would in an English paper, but I've also seen it placed at the bottom. The important thing is to make sure your personal information is in a place of prominence.

Additionally, date the release exactly like you would a letter and number each page. By dating it, the reporter or editor will know approximately when they should get back to you and, of course, numbering the pages helps them organize and keep track of your whole release.

It may seem obvious, but you should put the words "Press Release" or "For Immediate Release" at the top of the front page. So much paper goes into and out of a newspaper office, this tagline will help who ever mans the mail or the fax machine separate what's important from what's not.

Writing the Release

Now that you know what the basic format of a press release is, you're probably staring at the computer screen overcome with the

Fear of the Blank Page. The only thought going through your head is, "Oh, my god, what do I say to these people?" Well, to put it bluntly, you're going to feel like you're trying to pour a gallon of words into a shot glass. Sounds impossible but it can be done.

Starting from the beginning, a release can be broken down into a few basic components: the headline, the lede, the body and the conclusion. The headline is your first punch, where the reader finds out the heart of the story. The lede encapsulates the entire story in one sentence, so all of your most import information should be in this one sentence. The body is where all the other pertinent questions are answered. And the conclusion just draws everything to an end. Easy, huh?

Before you do that, let's talk a little about writing style. Many of the rules and advice that applies to writing a newspaper story also applies to writing a press release, and one of these conventions is style. Although it might seem strange, you should write your press release in the third person. The reason you should refer to yourself as "he" or "she" is because it projects a more professional and objective tone. I know you might want to leap into the air and cheer, but that you can save for the interview. Additionally, your release should be void of colloquialisms, slang or any other casual speech. Your press release is an introduction, so strike a professional tone. This is not to say you shouldn't put your own twist on it. By all means get creative, but remember that you never get a second chance to make a first impression.

When you write a press release, you are trying to convince a reporter or editor that your story should be covered. Using some techniques that journalists use can be very helpful in achieving this goal. One of those techniques is the headline. A headline is a quick way of summing up your entire release in a few words. However, although the headline will be the first thing the reporter or editor sees, it will probably be the last thing you write.

So how do you write one? The key word here is punchy. If your book is just coming out, a typical headline could read "Local author announces release of first novel." If you want to get creative, you could write something like, "Achieving a dream: novelist celebrates release of first novel." If you are announcing an event, then that should get top billing in a headline that could read this way: "Local author plans reading at bookstore" or "Fantasy comes to life at book reading by local author." Stretch yourself and write a headline that is really attention-getting. After all, remember that when you read a newspaper, what is it that inspires you to read a story? That's right, the headline.

Keep it short, omit unnecessary words and use action verbs.

Following the headline is the lede and the body of the release. The suggested format of a newspaper story is a lede sentence followed by the body, which is written in the pyramid format. In other words, the most important details should be in the first paragraph, followed by the next most important, and so on and so forth. The lede should be a brief and poignant statement summarizing the entire release. Ledes are sharp and direct, clever if possible. It's a sort of expanded second headline that acts as an introduction to the rest of your press release.

Referring to our earlier example of a release announcing the publishing of a new book, your lede could look something like this: "Author John Doe is over the moon that his new book about man's first journey to Mars will be published later this month" or "We all have at least one novel inside us, but according to author John Doe, whose first book will be released later this month, one is only the beginning."

Once the lede is written, the remainder of the release is the meat of your announcement. The body should hang off of the lede as a shirt on a hanger, giving your story form in the direction indicated in the lede. Although this may sound cliché, you can determine what the most important details that should be included in the body by asking yourself the essential questions: who, what, when, where, why, and how. The first four should be addressed in the first paragraph after the lede, but why and how usually take a little longer to answer and should be addressed a little later. So to follow our example of a new novel release, your first paragraph could look something like this:

Doe, a Springfield native, has made his living as a cable repair man, but always harbored a secret desire to publish. His dream was realized recently when he received notification from Dragon Moon Press that his novel, A Dream of Mars, would be on the book shelves by the end of the month. The novel is a science fiction story about man's first trip to Mars and the wonders of the universe inspiring a broken-hearted hero to penetrate the mysteries of the heavens.

In one paragraph, the reader gets that the release is about a new novel, written by a local, and also gets the name of the press, the title of the book and an overview of what the book is about. From there the only questions left to answer are why and how. That is where the convincing comes in. These are the paragraphs that will prove to the reporter that your story is an interesting one, so feel free to include a few quick details. For our fictional author John Doe, his press release could read this way:

Doe said it has been his longtime dream to publish a book about Mars. "Ever since I was a small child, I have had dreams of setting foot on the red planet, just like my main character. My imagination would take me on nightly trips to the planet until I finally decided I needed to write all of this down or I would never be able to dream about anything else!"

And so, Doe has worked days and raised his family, while at night he wrote. Doe said he worked on his manuscript for three years before sending it to Dragon Moon Press.

"It was really hard!" Doe said. "Writing is like pulling out a sore tooth; it wants to come out and needs to come out, but it's a painful process."

There are a few things of note in these paragraphs. Firstly, throughout this fictional press release, I've tried to keep the sentences short and to use plenty of action verbs or verbs that describe an action such as pulling or penetrating. This is a style common in newspaper writing because it tends to be attention-getting and easier to read. Secondly, avoid using commas to join many different ideas. This tends to make a sentence confusing. When in doubt, divide a sentence into two and make sure the verbs are interesting and active.

I also used quotes within the release, which can add details to make a story more compelling. It also makes reading the release more interesting, just as dialog makes fiction more interesting. So go ahead and quote yourself, but keep it real. Don't worry about sounding "writerly" in your release. The best quotes are insightful but accessible.

Now that you've written the body of the press release, it's time to wrap it up. One of the most common and effective ways to draw it to a conclusion is to give some biographical information. It gives a little context to the person the release is about and if it is not included in the release, the interviewer will likely ask you those questions when you interview. Ultimately, it makes things a little easier for the reporter. Some information you can include is where you grew up, where you went to school or if you're married with children. With the addition of that information, the release should be finished and ready to mail out.

Details, Details, Details

I once worked with an assistant editor who rolled his eyes every time he saw an exclamation point in a press release. He would, on occasion, pick out a particularly inane comment followed by an exclamation point and read it aloud to the newsroom. "There will be games and toys for everyone!" he would recite from the release, his voice climbing in false cheerfulness. There is no way anyone can be so excited about something that exclamation points follow every sentence. He would then take out the dreaded red pen and start hacking bits out of the press release.

The truth is we all should have listened a little more closely to our seventh-grade English teachers. Yes, folks, grammar really does matter. You don't need to have a black belt in grammar and know how to do things like use a semi-colon or correctly identify a dangling participle. But it is important that you use correct spelling, write the correct form of the word "their" or "except" and know where to use an apostrophe. These are basics, but once again, consider your audience. Think of reporters as your colleagues and good grammar as a good career move. At the very least, bad grammar will open you up to a lot of criticism. Also, reiterating that a press release is like a resume, the last thing you want in print on your resume is a grammatical error or misspelling.

The added benefit is that having good grammar reflects back on your creative writing. It's always so much easier to edit content when you don't have to worry about grammar too. Your editor will love it.

I won't go over a lot here since you can buy handy writing references from the book store, such as *REA's Handbook of English Grammar, Writing & Style* by M. Fogiel or *English Grammar for Dummies* by Geraldine Woods. There is more than just grammar in both books, but in the extras are some helpful little tidbits.

So here are a few pet peeves I've heard editors talk about over the years:

The exclamation point—This one is a little subjective, but my suggestion is just don't use it. You use it in fiction writing to show shock, anger, astonishment and the like but usually very sparingly. Well, take a look in a newspaper and you won't see any exclamation points unless someone is screaming. Probably better to avoid it.

It's and Its—This is a VERY common mistake and it's irritating to boot. You can trace it back to the fact that English is just an erratic language with a lot of exceptions to the rules. So the meaning of these two words is probably exactly the opposite of what you would think. "It's" is the contraction for "it is." "Its" is the possessive. See? Tricky, isn't it? Here are two examples:

It's a lovely day for a walk. "It's" is used as the contraction for "it is."

The sun was shining in all its glory. Here "its" is possessive because the glory belongs to the sun.

Affect and Effect—The simple explanation is that, generally, "affect" is a verb, like "I think Joe was adversely affected by…" "Effect" is a noun, like in phrases such as "cause and effect" or "the effect of the shuttle launching."

Joe was affected by the car crash. "Affect" as a verb.

The effect of the car crash was that Joe had post-traumatic stress disorder.

There is one exception to this rule. "Effect" can be used as a verb in a specific circumstance, and that is when you mean to *bring about* or to *cause* something.

Joe effected a change in the laws after his car crash.

So What Do I Do with It Now That It's Done?

Once your press release has been written, the next step is to submit it to the paper or papers of your choice. In other words you should send your release to every newspaper within about a 50-mile radius. Leave no stone unturned and include even the small newsletters if you can. There are several reasons for this, the first being that all press is good press, no matter how small. The second is a slightly lesser-known fact: newspapers subscribe to each other. Editors and reporters are generally aware of what their competitors write so that they can stay on top of the news. There are always those reporters who are better at researching or simply in the right place at the right time, and the newspaper philosophy is that it is better to cover something late than not at all. So you'll see that oftentimes if one newspaper writes an interesting story about a new author, others will follow suit. No one wants to miss out, after all, and ultimately you are the one who will benefit.

When submitting your press release to these newspapers, you'll want to refer it to a specific person or people. Drawing from an example that has been much used and abused already, think of this as if you were applying for a job. It is always more professional to address your resume to a specific person. By addressing your release to a specific editor or reporter, you lessen the chances that it will go astray. Each reporter is assigned to specific topics or beats, so to get covered your release is going to need to find the right reporter. Writers are sometimes assigned a town and they are responsible for reporting all of that town's news. In other, usually larger newspapers, reporters will have more specific beats, like the police beat or the art and entertainment beat. Sometimes even the people working at the newspapers aren't totally aware of what reporter does what. So without a specific addressee, it could go to the wrong person and get lost in the process.

Finding out who you should send it to should be easy, if you know the right questions to ask. At smaller newspapers, call and ask what reporter covers the town that you live in. At the large ones, ask for reporters and editors who cover arts and entertainment or assignment editors. If the receptionist has no idea what you're talking about, just explain that you wish to send in a press release, what it is for and generally they will be able to direct you to the correct person.

So what do you do if you come up with more than one person at a newspaper who might be a candidate for your release? If you have to choose between reporters and editors, I would go with the editor at first. Reporters generally find their own stories, but assignments will come down from above. The thing is that there are ebb times and flow times in news and if your release goes out during a flow time, there is always the possibility that it will get lost on a reporter's desk. Also editors determine what stories should receive coverage and what stories should be buried on the last page, so by sending it to an editor you tend to cut out a little of the uncertainty.

Even with all of this, there is a chance that your masterpiece of a press release will get lost in a stack of paper and won't be found without some major excavation. Don't panic. If you don't hear from the editor or a reporter within about a week, give them a quick phone call. No, you're not pestering them. In fact, you're making a personal connection with someone. If you are too shy to call, try rewriting your press release so it's fresh and send it again. Again, it won't annoy them. There are enough people calling on a daily basis to complain that if they are going to get annoyed about something, it will be that and not that an excited author is really looking for some attention.

THE MOMENT OF TRUTH

Fast forward a little bit. Time passes. They called, you answered and the time for an interview was set. Okay, the day of your interview has arrived, but before the reporter gets there, just slow down and breathe. It's not uncommon to get nervous, knowing that what you say will likely appear in print, but if you know what to expect there really isn't anything to be afraid of. Preparation is key.

Every reporter has their own style of questioning, whether casual or formal, so be prepared for either. Oftentimes interviewers will prepare several questions beforehand but come up with the others on the spot, depending on the conversation and the interviewee's responses. One interviewing style is to engage in conversation, steering the interviewee to specific questions when more information is needed. Other interviewers will be more to the point, asking you questions, writing down notes and then punching out another question. Quick and dirty. The shape of the interview depends on the interviewer, but remember that although you are not in control of the questions, you can control the answers.

Even knowing that, it would probably make you feel better knowing what questions they were going to ask. The easiest questions to predict are those based on straight fact: Who is your publishing company? When will the book be released? Where will the book be available? How much will the book cost? Just be prepared to give the details but don't worry if you don't have answers to some of their questions.

The reporter will let you know if they really need answers to those questions and you can find out from your publisher or editor and get back to them about it.

They will also likely ask you for some biographical information, like where you went to school, where you grew up, or your other writing credits. Some interviewees I've encountered have written short biographies containing all of their vital statistics which were very helpful. If you feel truly ambitious or truly nervous, feel free. Otherwise, just anticipate some of these questions.

Now that we're done talking about the boring questions, it's time to talk about the more substantive ones. These questions are obviously a little harder to predict because each reporter has their own interests and ideas as to what would make a good story. I knew a reporter who would occasionally ask interviewees what their favorite pizza topping was, just to spark conversation. Generally, the questions won't be quite so random, but don't be totally surprised if something seems to come out of left field.

I used to ask writers where they like to write and then would spend time in the story describing the author in their preferred surroundings. Typically, though, you can expect questions about the book and where your inspiration comes from, why you love to write, or what your future plans are.

Preparation for these questions is a little more difficult because you obviously don't know what to expect. Don't worry about sounding witty or wise when being interviewed; just be honest. Honesty makes the most compelling stories. However, if you would like to think things through and have a little groundwork done before you meet the reporter, start by thinking about important moments in your life or your writing. I mean those interesting and off-beat stories about how you came up with your main character or how your dream is to write while watching the Earth rise over the horizon of the moon. Personal details are what makes a news story fun and unique, and is exactly what a reporter is looking for. Break out your journal and start reminiscing.

If all this sounds a little strange, you could think about it like you would a character in your book. When fleshing out a character you usually pick and chose those details and bits of dialog that show the reader who the character truly is. This is exactly what a reporter is trying to do when writing the story about an author: illuminating a character. So when they interview you, they are going to be on the look out for those neat snippets of information. In a weird kind of way, you are the main character and the reporter is the author looking for a way to make you more real to the readers.

As a side note, face-to-face interviews are not always an option. Do not be surprised or totally disappointed if a reporter schedules a phone interview with you. I have done so on several occasions and generally this happens because there is just too much to do and not enough time to do it in. It can also be a signal to you, the interviewee, that the story may be on the shorter side. This is not always the case, but it is a safe assumption. The important thing is to remember that some press is better than no press and try to make the interview as interesting as possible.

Be a Good Sport

So the story comes out in the paper and you have a few problems with it. Your eyes are closed in the photograph or some of the details are just plain wrong. Just remember, you solicited it. That's not to say that if you have a real grievance, like you were misquoted as saying "Jessie Helms is a constant source of inspiration for me" when you actually said "Jessie Jackson is a constant source of inspiration for me," that you shouldn't give the reporter a call. But if it is a relatively minor mistake like your dog's name was misspelled or the poster on your wall is actually *Star Wars* and not *SpaceBalls*, let it go.

Keep in mind you're building capital with each and every newspaper you contact. Reporters won't only publish one story about a talented and interesting individual if they are given the opportunity to write more. Readers get attached and like to follow careers and reporters know that. Reporters also like to see where someone is going and do have the power to give someone extra press if they can justify it. But they also have the ability to ignore what comes across their desk. So maybe you brush off a few small mistakes or take them up with the reporter tactfully and graciously, maybe even asking for a correction if it is a grievous mistake. That attitude is much more likely to get you coverage in the future than pitching a hissy fit would.

On a related but distinctly separate note are reviews. To put it succinctly, you get what you ask for. I know it's heart-breaking to read a bad review of your book. That stupid reviewer didn't understand the significance of the character's relationship to her mother's cousin twice removed and how it is pivotal to her development. Unfortunately, this is part of writing novels these days and if you ask a paper to review your book, you run the risk of them calling it a piece of tripe.

Fortunately, even bad press can be good press, as cold a comfort as that may seem. The only suggestion I can make is to take your lumps, call the reviewer a Philistine who wouldn't know a good novel if F. Scott Fitzgerald beat him about the head with one to your friends, family, pastor or pet canary and move on. Remember, not everyone has taste. Concentrate on the ones who do.

CONCLUSION

There you have it, a crash course in communicating effectively with newspapers. The final piece of advice I can give you is when in doubt, ask questions. If you are wondering when a piece is coming out, ask. If you are wondering what information they will need from you, ask. The key thing here is that you are building relationships with your local newspapers because you never know when you will need to ask them for coverage again. If you have a good relationship, then the second time you contact them for a story will be easier and more positive than the first. If you don't have at least a professional relationship with them, getting coverage will be more difficult.

So chin up, remember that reporters and editors are people too. I used to tell people that every reporter or editor secretly had a novel tucked into the bottom drawer of their desks that they pull out and work on when no one was looking. Whether that is true or not, there is no denying that a special kinship exists between writers. You just have to pay the respect due to a colleague and usually you'll find it returned.

Get to Know Me

THE SCIENCE OF SELF-PROMOTION
BY TEE MORRIS

The genre of Science Fiction and Fantasy is one of the largest in the publishing industry, and the competition between authors is fierce. While established authors may not wish to admit or even acknowledge it publicly, both corporate and independent press authors share in common the need to self-promote their works. I have only been in the business of writing books professionally for five years, but I remain completely stunned at how many authors consider what I'm about to share with you as a waste of time and a distraction from writing.

"Promotion," I have heard them say, "is someone else's job."

Perhaps promotion was someone else's job back in the seventies and eighties, but that was then.

In 2004, according to several news resources including USA Today, over 175,000 books were published in the United States alone. This includes all genres, all presses. So let's say the numbers haven't changed all that much and 175,000 titles have reached the market this year. Out of those 175,000 titles you have to convince the general public that *yours* is the book to buy.

Welcome to the world of the modern writer.

THINKING AHEAD:
DEVISING A PROMOTION STRATEGY

"I've got a plan so cunning, you could put a tail on it and call it a weasel!"
— *Edmund Blackadder*

Before that first box of books arrives on your doorstep, be they your comp copies or "carry stock" (a supply of books you can buy with a discount from the publisher), it wouldn't hurt to come up with a plan on how and where you are going to sell your book.

You may think, "Well, duh, I'm going to sell it in a bookstore. It's a book, after all."

That's a start.

Relying on bookstores to market, promote, and sell your book is much like raising a child in a home full of happiness, privilege, and wealth, relying on staff to clothe, feed, and transport said child from Point A to Point B without any interaction with the child. So if you want to be a Hilton, then by all means, rely on the bookstores to take care of you.

But, as Edmund Blackadder suggests with his words of inspiration, an even better idea is to come up with a plan: a plan of how, where, and when to promote your books and yourself. Step One of your promotional plan is to figure out first where you will be offering books up for sale.

Bookstores

The initial "bookstore instinct" is a great place to start. Find out what bookstores you want to cultivate a relationship with, where they are located and who your contacts will be. Fortunately, bookstores make this very easy, provided they have a web presence established. For the larger bookseller chains, go to their respective websites and perform a search for stores in your area. You should be able to set up search parameters within a certain radius of miles and obtain store locations and phone numbers.

When you call these stores, remind yourself that you are neither Stephen King nor J.K. Rowling. You are also are not a publicist working for a major publishing house. You are an author taking initiative. This means you have to approach these bookstores with courtesy and a sense of professionalism, easily achieved with the following two approaches:

> (To whoever answers the phone) "Hi. Can I speak to the person who organizes your signing events, please?"

> (To the person in charge of signing events) "Hi, my name is Tee Morris and my first book is scheduled to come out in January 2008, and I'd like to find out what you need to organize a signing event?"

Provided the bookstore is interested, you will want to have handy the following information:

- The title of your book, and its ISBN.
- Your publisher and your distributor (e.g., Ingram or Baker & Taylor)
- Whether or not you have a press kit available.

Once you've talked to larger chain stores, go back to your search engine of choice and perform a search for independent bookstores in your area. Independent bookstores tend to carry fewer titles than larger chains, and are usually managed by the owners themselves. Some pros for working with smaller, indie bookstores:

- They appreciate authors who want to come in for a signing.
- They will work with small press houses.
- They host writing and special interest groups. (The big chains do so as well, but you have to ask their reps if their store hosts anything of the sort.)

- Indie bookstores give every signing their 110% and go out of their way to give it a personal touch.
- Indie bookstores will want to know the same thing that the big stores will want to know: book title, ISBN, publisher, availability, etc.

Take a look at your search results, find out which bookstores carry Science Fiction and Fantasy, and (if applicable) pay a visit to their websites. Find out if there is an interest group that meets there and see if they would love to have you as a guest speaker for their monthly meeting.

When you have finished talking with one bookseller, move on to the next one on your list. This sounds like a lot of hard work, doesn't it? Well, it is. The larger NY houses do have full-time publicists whose sole purpose is to organize book signings at stores you want to visit. With the smaller, independent presses, you are on your own in the publicity department unless you hire a publicist. That can be a steep investment. To save cost, you will have to set aside some time, prepare yourself a script for talking with bookstores and make a few calls.

Book Festivals

Book Festivals are everywhere, and a quick Google search for "Book Festivals" will show you exactly how many are in your area, in your state, and across the country. These one to two day events (or in some cases, week-long extravaganzas!) can be a lot of fun for readers as the authors attending cover a wide variety of genres. Mysteries. Horror. Science Fiction. Self-Help. Fantasy. Romance. Every conceivable way of getting published and every genre that could be published are present at book festivals. Many of these events are either non-profit organizations sponsored by universities, or provide much-needed support for a school or library. Some book festivals go as far as to offer an "Author's Alley" where authors sell books they provide. You may sell books hand-over-fist. You may sell none. Regardless, it is face time in your local area or state; and depending on the event, its proceeds go to benefit a good cause.

While charity events might be considered a "loss" for writers, keep in mind that it is a terrific public relations moment you can bring to the attention of the media (i.e., a local author giving back to his or her school/library/community by participating in this book festival) and it is a tax deduction from beginning to end as your books and time are considered as donations.

Participating in book festivals that sponsor a good cause also makes you feel good.

Along with the variety of authors you meet at book festivals, the potential for networking is ripe. On occasion, editors, publishers, and agents will attend book festivals, and give you an inside look at aspects of the business that still remain a question to you. There is also the networking of authors with other authors, providing leads to potential freelance jobs in writing articles for periodicals and other publications. You may also get a few ideas in self-promotion when watching other authors work.

For a lot more on the art of networking, see Lai Zhao's chapter, coming up next!

Book festivals are great places to promote your work, promote yourself and give back to your community. The ones that are receptive to working with you will truly appreciate the time you give in just being there, so be sure to return the same appreciation when your Fantasy novel is spotlighted along with mainstream fiction.

Science Fiction and Fantasy Conventions

When was the last time you attended a FitzgeraldCon? Or paid your pre-registration to attend DevilWearsPradaCon where Jessica Cutler will be this year's Guest of Honor? And while Mystery and Romance conventions are out there, Science Fiction, Fantasy, and Horror authors are extremely lucky in the number of these events happening across the country and around the world. They are the weekends when freaks, geeks, Goths, gamers, scientists, TV stars, movie celebrities, costumers, Cthulhu cultists and everyone in between commandeer a hotel and celebrate their love of the genre. I speak of the Science Fiction convention circuit, simply referred to as the con.

Cons, provided you know what you're getting into, are a lot of fun to attend, a great way to get the word out on the streets about your work and to get your work into readers' hands. Before I even fully understood what a con was, I contacted and contracted with a few because I knew this was where I would find my target audience.

If you've never been to a con, I suggest reading Sharyn McCrumb's Bimbos of the Death Sun, a murder-mystery set at a Science Fiction-Fantasy convention. The book goes into many aspects of the con scene, the fans attending and the guests appearing there. It's not only a terrific read, but a pretty good idea of what to prepare yourself for and what you are about to experience over a period of three days.

There are several kinds of conventions out there and here's a brief run-down of the most common kinds of cons found in web searches.

Literary cons: These are conventions that are dedicated to the printed word and authors. Usually these conventions feature a Guest-of-Honor (GoH), along with an Artist GoH, Fan GoH, and (more recently) a Media GoH. Programming can include media-, art- and fan-related topics, but the concentration of panel topics and activities are focused on Science Fiction, Fantasy and Horror in print. These are the conventions you as a writer should target. Examples of literary cons include Coppercon (in Phoenix, AZ), Balticon (in Baltimore, MD) and RavenCon (in Richmond, VA).

Media cons: Media cons are the cons that are the biggest and most commercial. Instead of GoHs, a cavalcade of television and film stars from shows like *Stargate SG-1, Battlestar Galactica* (both past and present), *Farscape, Firefly* and the *Star Trek* incarnations are showcased. Many of these conventions go by names like Toronto Trek, BuffyCon, or Creation's Official *Farscape* Convention, clearly designating it as a media con. Some of these events are "author-friendly" and have various SF/F authors on the docket, but the majority of attendees attending are there for the TV and movie stars.

A good way to find out if media cons are truly author friendly or not is to check out their respective websites. Look to see if they are featuring authors (not just media tie-in authors) and try to find out what these authors are known for. Toronto Trek (held in Toronto, Ontario, Canada) features SF/F/H authors as well as media tie-in authors. When I attended as an author guest in 2002, the staff could not have been friendlier, more supportive, or hospitable. Other media cons to look into are Archon (St. Louis, MO), Farpoint (Baltimore, MD), and Dragon*Con (Atlanta, GA).

Gaming cons: Sometimes found at both media and gaming conventions are gaming tracks. Attendees meet up and play a variety of games, ranging from role-playing (Vampire the Requiem) to wargame miniatures (Warhammer 40K) to collectable card games (Legend of the Five Rings). Gaming cons are hosts for major tournaments, entertain guests from various game companies, and serve as a great place to pick up new games for your own collection. You can also network with game developers to pitch ideas and write rulebooks for various games, as well as lock horns with games masters from across the country. Gaming cons include GenCon (in Indianapolis, IN) and Origins (in Columbus, OH).

Anime cons: Anime USA (in Washington D.C.), SakuraCon (in Seattle, WA), and Otakon (in Baltimore, MD) are cons dedicated to the East Asian import of anime (Japanese Animation) and manga (mainly Japanese novel-length comics). Much like media cons, the headliner guests are animators, voiceover talent from both Japan and the US, and artists. Other headliners at anime cons include attendees who participate in "cosplay." Cosplay is usually elaborate costumes inspired or recreated from a favorite anime. In the same vein as media cons, authors can occasionally appear in the programming, but the attendees are geared towards anime and manga. Anime USA (Tysons Corner, VA), Anime Mid-Atlantic (Richmond, VA), and Otakon (Baltimore, MD) are just a few of many anime cons happening across the country.

Many, if not all, of these cons will have websites that will tell you something about their programming. You can also perform a search for "Science Fiction and Fantasy conventions" and then narrow your hit list to cons within your travel vicinity. Research the con as much as you can and then fire off a query letter to the contacts listed on the website. Usually, the websites will specify whom to contact if you are interested in being a guest. If not, try to find a contact in Programming. If there is still no one listed, send an e-mail to the "General Information" address and eventually your query will be forwarded to the right person.

A terrific resource to find out where conventions are happening is the Locus Magazine website (HTTP://WWW.LOCUSMAG.COM/CONVENTIONS.HTML) which lists all registered conventions' essential information and websites.

So what should you send to a con in the way of a query? Keep it simple. You only need to send a few items in the initial contact:

- Who you are.
- What you've written.
- What you are willing to do (within reason, of course) at the con.

For the last item on this list, you will want to offer to speak on panels and do a reading. Here's what you should hope to receive in reply:

- An invitation to attend.
- Complimentary membership for the weekend (in other words, they pay your registration fee.)

Do not expect more than this. Yes, it is true: some pros will not consider attending a convention unless conventions cover the room bill, and in some cases, all other bills associated with said room. If the con-chair (the top organizer of the convention calling the shots) is a fan of this author, then there's a good chance that, yes, the room will get comped. If the funds are in the con's budget, it will happen with all the authors. When new cons are starting up or in their second or third year, their funding will cover the GoH's bills, along with the Artist GoH, Media GoH and other assorted GoHs, and that's it. There's no harm in asking about comped rooms, but as you are a new player, there is little chance that your room will be covered. So be prepared to cover your travel and hotel bills.

On receiving the invitation, it is your turn to let the con staff know what you will bring to the programming, and that you are enthusiastic about participating. Go ahead and send back a reply to the invitation with a list of panel topics (and, if you're feeling ambitious, workshop ideas) and brief descriptions of what you would like to cover in said topics. Don't be surprised if panels you suggest are not assigned to you. (In fact, it's okay to take a bit of satisfaction when hearing the established names are sitting on a panel you came up with, especially if the panel is a big hit!)

Then, within a month or two of the convention, you should receive a list of panel topics to choose from. Try to make your decisions within 24 hours as many of these topics are a "first come, first serve" basis, with the GoHs usually getting first pick. Show interest in topics you feel comfortable talking about and let programming know you would like, at a minimum, three topics. Just remember, the more panels you do, the more face time you clock in. The more face time you clock in, the more books you sell.

ATYPICAL SELLING MARKETS

I hate that business cliché, "Right, let's think outside the box!"

It sounds so "Patrick Bateman" to say something like that, no doubt conjuring images of designer suits, pristine business cards kept in high-tech holders and hair gel as far as the eye can see. Then again, I conjure the same images when I'm at that point of complete and utter loss of patience and I ask the person next to me, "Tell me something, do you like Huey Lewis and the News?!"

So instead of saying...you know...how about we say "Let's think outside the book..." for this section of the chapter?

So far, in our promotion plan, we've targeted bookstores, book festivals and SF/F cons, all of which have something in common: book vendors and readers. It is common sense for authors to target these three venues, but these venues are not the only places you can find a market for your book. While I've heard publishers, editors and authors all talk about the bad in the book business, something I've not heard anyone say is how incredible the book business is in one respect: You can sell books practically anywhere, at any time!

It's one advantage books as a product have—wherever you go, there they are. On commuter trains. In supermarkets. Around restaurants. Books can be found just about everywhere and anywhere, because—for the most part—books are built to be portable. Promoting your books and yourself can also happen in venues that you would not normally consider. At many of these atypical locations, supplying books falls to the author. Depending on how your press handles carry stock, these kinds of unique venues can be an investment, but ones that provide windfalls!

Renaissance Festivals

If you have never attended a Renaissance Festival, the only way I can describe it is stepping through the looking glass into Wonderland. And for seven years, that's exactly what I did. In Crownsville, Maryland, under the direction of Carolyn Spedden and in the company of some incredible actors, I played a variety of characters in the streets of The Maryland Renaissance Festival. Along with actors who provide improvisational entertainment around every corner, you can see terrific stand-up comedians that go to extreme by working in sword fighting, sword-eating, fire-eating and even "stupid human tricks" into their routines. You can also watch Human Chess Games, where pieces literally duke it out for a square on a giant chessboard, and jousting tournaments done in full armor and with full pageantry. All this happens in front, behind and all around you as you walk by tents, booths and Tudor-style buildings featuring artisans and crafters who offer up hard-to-find and one-of-a-kind merchandise.

Pick up a copy of *Renaissance Magazine* or *Pirates Magazine* and you'll find a listing of faires and festivals like Maryland across the country. Some concentrate on the arts and crafts aspects while others focus on theater, dance and music of Renaissance England. The monarchies and famous historical figures dramatized can be as modern as King James, or go as far back as Robin Hood, and even a few festivals take "creative license" and pit the two historical icons against one another, strictly for entertainment's sake.

Oh, and along with actors hired or volunteering time to play characters, patrons attending the festival will also get into costume (formally known as garb) and participate a bit in the spirit and fun of a festival. (And yes, even Starfleet personnel, complete with tricorders scanning for temporal anomalies, get in on the action...) They range in size and scope of presentation, but that is what a Renaissance Festival (also known as Ren Faires) is: stepping back in time, for a day, to a time of romance, chivalry and swashbuckling.

Many Ren Faires also have on their sites bookshoppes. (Yeah, that spelling is on purpose!) Arguably, a quick glance at these bookshoppes will reveal their stock to be historical studies of various time periods, patterns for dress or doublet making, recipe books for authentic

Renaissance Cuisine and Celtic Legend anthologies. Fiction titles, particularly Fantasy novels, are not so commonly found.

This doesn't mean your Fantasy couldn't sell there.

Ask the friendly wench or rogue (a term of endearment at a Ren Faire) at the cash register who organizes signings at the bookshoppe. If he or she is there, introduce yourself and give whatever historical angle is behind your Fantasy, provided it is a legitimate connection to Renaissance history. The patrons attending are looking for the unique at a Ren Faire, and an author signing is something unexpected.

When booking a Ren Faire, all promotion will probably fall back to you. With bookstores, you might get a poster with your headshot and book cover, announcing your signing. At a Ren Faire, you will probably go unmentioned in the program and there will be nothing on the grounds telling people you're there. Have promotional postcards printed up at a print shop and work with the bookshoppe owner to find out whether vinyl banners or posters announcing your signing would be allowed. The more you work with the bookshoppe owner and the more willing they are to work with you, the better the book signing will go.

You will be asked to get dressed in costume. Usually, one is provided for you, if you don't have one. Get into the spirit of things and wear garb. It's something different...

...and it's a lot of fun.

Coffee Houses and Cafés

It was at Stellarcon 29 I got stopped in my tracks by a fan named Betsy Perry. Why? Betsy was dressed impeccably as my favorite renegade Peacekeeper, Aeryn Sun from *Farscape*. We posed for pictures and chatted a bit...and I eventually found out that Betsy was the owner of the Junkanoo Coffeehouse in The Outer Banks of North Carolina.

It was while I was looking over her invitation to Farscape Friday, I asked her, "How would you feel about an author coming to your coffee shop for a book signing?"

Betsy blinked her eyes quickly and asked, "Are you serious?"

Within the week, I had a date and time booked for my first book signing in "Pirate Country."

Coffee houses and cafés that cater to lunch and after-school crowds are always looking for some sort of live entertainment, be it a guitar player, folk singers or a poetry slam. If you have a place you regularly visit for coffee, people watching and perhaps a few long afternoons of writing, ask the manager or owner if their establishment would be interested in hosting a signing or even an informal meet-and-greet with an author (often referred to as a kaffeeklatsch at cons). You could hold the event on a Sunday afternoon or perhaps after-work/after-school on a Friday night? It would definitely be a great way to introduce yourself to the community, network (teachers and professors love their coffee), attract local media attention (especially if you use the word "kaffeeklatsch" in your press release) and are just fun, low-stress signings. Coffee shops can also be a place for writing groups to meet, so you may have a guaranteed audience show up in search of advice, regardless if they write in a different genre to yours.

Coffee shops and lunch cafés that would show interest in something like a kaffeeklatsch will be the privately-owned establishments. Larger chains like Starbuck's and Panera's Bread and Bakery should not be ruled out, but check first to see if the local representatives of these larger, corporate entities host events or groups. If they do, there is no harm in asking to speak with a manager.

WHEN GOOD IDEAS GO BAD: RISK MANAGEMENT

The plan is taking shape, and in many cases these signings will provide some incredible memories in an afternoon, or—if particularly successful—an entire day. You catch audiences by surprise with your appearance. Readers you would normally see at a con pay a visit to the bookstore when a signing is scheduled. Other fans are made when they get a chance to meet you and consider your work at a favorite coffee shop or special event.

Keep in mind, though, that booksellers are different from store to store. The most dynamic of promotions can fall on deaf ears and even the best of original ideas can backfire. So let's take a moment to consider the Worst Case Scenarios that you might encounter when scheduling or attending book events.

You're Who Again?

When talking with bookstores, prepare for some blunt replies, especially if your first book is with a small press. (This is a nice way of saying that some bookstores might hang up on you. Don't let that throw you.) Some bookstore representatives choose to deal with authors in the rudest, most inconsiderate ways possible.

Of course, when a bookstore rep hangs up on you, it's okay to ask yourself "Did Terry Brooks ever have days like this?" (The answer is yes.) Then, after a deep breath, make the same call to the next bookstore on your list.

Cold calls are exercises in patience, and there will be those times when you don't really want to be polite. Remember: you're a professional author now. Adopt a polite, professional attitude.

When dealing with independent bookstores, sometimes the blunt approach is the only approach. It can be a hard sell in getting an independent store to carry your book or even hosting a signing. Keep in mind that it's nothing personal. They have to keep the business running. If it comes between promoting and hosting an event for you, and paying the store's electric bill, you're going to lose, unless you can guarantee your event that will pay the electric bill. (Don't make that kind of promise! These owners have a network and they talk to one another.)

You may not be a big name right now in your career, but remember that you are starting from that same somewhere that all the others—Rowling, King, Ringo and Asaro—started from. It keeps things in perspective.

There's An Author Signing Books? Here? Today?

So you have booked a few signing events and are pretty excited about the prospects...until you hear other authors complain that bookstore signings are hardly worth the effort. This always struck me as odd considering how many authors, big and small press, continuously arrange book signings at bookstores everywhere. After talking with bookstore owners about this, I discovered a few reasons as to why appearances were falling short of some authors' expectations:

- The author didn't tell anyone about it.
- The bookstore or the event's sponsor didn't tell anyone about it.
- The author didn't tell enough people about it.
- There is nothing at the event that is communicating to people you're there.
- All of the above.

Failed signings can be traced back to a lack of publicity, but the fault does not reside with your publisher in not providing promotional materials, or with the bookstore refusing to roll out the red carpet for you. When it comes to letting people know a signing is happening, the responsibility falls on you, the author.

There is a lot of power in self-reliance, and it does not have to cost you an arm and a leg. Put together a 4-up design (the same postcard laid out across a letter sized piece of paper four times) of postcards featuring all the info about your signing (date, time, place, etc.). Postcards can be easily created using any layout application, and can either be printed out or burned onto a CD and then produced on cardstock paper. After two cuts horizontally and vertically, two hundred postcards are produced for less than thirty dollars. These cards can be sent off to bookstores (preferably a month before your event) to be used as bagstuffers or handouts at information booths. Both chain and indie bookstores love promotional postcards because it's promotion they don't have to pay for. For the author, it's a tax deduction. It is also a sign of initiative.

Of course, skeptics may make the sardonic comment, "Chances are, Tee, that your postcard winds up in a circular file."

That could be true, but the point is making the effort. Otherwise, you will have a signing where no one will attend other than family, friends, and people who have already bought your book. While out of two hundred postcards, one hundred and fifty wind up in the trash or ignored, you still have fifty out there, floating about, and fifty people potentially coming out to see what your signing is all about.

If you are feeling up for an investment, you can go to a print shop and, for a small investment, have a 3' x 5' vinyl banner created. It can be something as simple as the words "Author Signing Today" and your website. You can also, for usually less than half the cost of a vinyl banner, have created a dry mounted 18" x 27" poster of your book cover with the words "Author Signing Today" across it. Always ask permission before hanging or displaying such banners, but this kind of signage only helps in informing people that you are there.

Well, It Was a Good Idea in Theory...

"That went well."
— Malcolm Reynolds (naked and alone in a desert)

I have a friend and road trip buddy always looking for unique signing venues, and when he told me about this one particular signing he booked for Halloween, I thought this would be a true slam-dunk. You see, he writes horror. And he had booked a series of signings at a charity-sponsored haunted house.

Now how cool is that? A horror novelist, doing a signing at a haunted house? That sounds like a real gas!

Well, when he first arrived, his table's location was located at the haunted house's entrance, putting him in plain sight. Then audience traffic became an issue, so he was moved by the concession stand, far away from the main flow of patrons. While in the end he sold a dozen books, this was a dozen books over five nights.

It's always a good idea when booking an event to know as much as possible before you arrive. "Where will you have me signing books?" is a good first question. Asking other questions of the hosts of an atypical signing will give you an idea of what to expect. What is your organization all about? What numbers are you expecting at this event? Were you planning any promotion announcing the book signing?

If you are thinking of holding a signing at a location that does carry books, ask yourself questions about the book vendor and their clientele. For example, Wal-Mart and Sam's Club are establishing themselves as major carriers of popular titles. While authors should look for bigger, wider markets to tap into, take a closer look at what these mega-stores carry. They will carry Stephen King, J.K. Rowling, Anne Rice, Dan Brown, Michael Crichton, but when was the last time you saw names like David Weber, John Ringo, Catherine Asaro or Julie Czerneda? They may appear on their shelves, but in far fewer numbers than mainstream authors. Look for your peers in the Wal-Mart's and Sam's Clubs across the country and the familiar names in this genre drop even lower.

"But Tee, Wal-Mart and Sam's Club sell books by the truckloads..." you say.

They can and they do, but numbers of books sold aren't the only thing to consider when booking signing at these kinds of stores. Stop for a moment the next time you're in a wholesale warehouse or a mega-store...on second thought, be careful if you stop on entering a mega-store. If you stop in the middle of any aisle, a cart just might run you down like something akin to *The Road Warrior*. The typical mega-store/wholesale warehouse shopper is in a hurry. Whether it is the Soccer Mom with the 2.5 kids in tow or the newly married couple just picking up quick odds and ends for their new house, these kinds of shoppers want to pick up what they need and get home. Quickly. Thus, such shoppers seldom browse the bookshelves.

While there are stories of "...authors who sold 150 copies of his book at a Sam's Club in one day!" floating from discussion board to discussion board, there is something else to take a moment and look at the next time you see books in a wholesale warehouse. How are the featured books organized? Yep, you're right—they're not. Books sold at wholesale warehouses are stacked up in a center section in no particular order, in no particular genre. Finally, your books are sold at wholesale prices. Look up your contract concerning the profits from those sales.

(And I'm curious—if "this one author" is so successful with Sam's Club signings, why can't anyone remember his or her name?)

Even with the asking of questions, promotional postcards and your best show, book signings are like diets: your results may vary. Every signing should be approached as an individual event, never comparing one to another. One month you will pack them in, and the following month you are begging for people to come through the door. Every signing is different, whether it is at Barnes & Noble, Balticon or Birka. Approach each event with open minds, fresh perspectives, and the right questions to ask in order to make the signing a success.

With venues targeted, you're ready to promote yourself and your book. Outside of direct sales from signings, what other options are available? From here we go into ways of letting people know you are entering the market, where your next signing will be, and what you have planned in the future.

Websites

Designing for the Internet has been made into an easy and effortless task, thanks to a variety of web applications available. Creating an effective website—particularly in an age where a company or individual is represented by their web presence—is an entirely different matter. Uploading a website designed with little or no thought or effort behind can reflect poorly on you. For established authors and publishers, a polished website is low on the priority list; but as you are a new name, you do not have this luxury. Now would be a good time to invest in some basics of design and website construction. Usually, this strikes terror into the hearts of new authors because they believe this is an expensive and time-consuming process. This is not true.

Website development goes only as far as you want it to. Of course, if it is a do-it-yourself website, then your investment will be time. Time to learn, design and proof. With the right tutorials, building a webpage is easy but time-consuming, nonetheless.

You can hire a web designer, or offer a high school or college student looking for artistic credit the opportunity to design a web presence for you. When working with designers, be specific on what you want, and understand what is (and isn't) possible in website design. For example, if you want a website with the capabilities of selling books, ask your hired artist for an estimate on such an interface, if it is in their design capabilities, and if your current web host and the package you've purchased has what it needs to accomplish this securely.

There are numerous titles available that can teach you how to design websites, how to work with HTML and CSS, and how to establish yourself on the Internet. But before you run out and start perusing titles or talking to potential designers, take a look at these time-saving, money-saving, frustration-saving steps that will help you design (either with others or on your own) your website more efficiently and help you avoid any trip-ups or delays in launching your corner of the Internet.

Map out a plan for your website.

Before you even begin the first HTML tag, get the site on paper. Organize a strategy in the same way you would put together a proposal for your book. What do you want to say about your book? How much do you want to say about yourself? Who is your target audience— publishers, agents, or fans? Along with story, characters, and yourself, what else would you like to offer to web visitors? Once you have an idea of what you want to say, then you can begin construction.

Invest in your own domain and web host.

Stake a claim for yourself in cyberspace. Free webspace usually pays for itself with annoying pop-up ads and an address that could choke a cave troll. Reserving a domain with services like Network Solutions or GoDaddy.com can be inexpensive and well worth the investment. Secure your name (either with a .com, .net or whatever works best for you) or pen name, and then begin thinking of where you need to put this domain so people will see it (business cards, tee shirts, book covers, etc.).

When it comes to picking the right domain name for your website, nothing beats your name. You can use your book title for your domain, but what if your next book is a completely different story. How well will that fit under the domain of your debut novel? When thinking about a website for Billibub Baddings, I realized that it wouldn't really "fit" with the mood and natural flow of Morevi's website (www.morevi. com). I also realized the money and time I would invest in securing a domain and creating an entirely new website for Billibub Baddings would drain me dry, and finally anytime I came up with a new idea for a novel, it would mean a new web domain. So, I secured TeeMorris. com, establishing a stronger web presence and a website that would grow with me.

Keep your design and your content simple.
A little bit goes a long, long way and that is so true in website design. Start your website with the basics. Provided you start simply, you can build from the ground up a very clean and easy-to-navigate website. Later, when you get more comfortable with the language and the principles of design, branch out into new concepts and ideas.

When putting together your website, consider the following tips:

- Keep graphics only to the essential.
- Avoid cool or cute graphics unrelated to your work.
- Avoid cool, cute, misspelled or inappropriate content carrying no relevance to your work.

In the end, a website that works is a website that serves its purpose. If your corner of cyberspace keeps readers informed, helps sell your books, promotes your name and meets your expectations, you have a website that works.

CD SAMPLERS

What was once a pricey indulgence in computers—drives capable of burning compact discs—has now become one of the cheapest additions to a computer. Most drives now have ability to burn both DVDs as well as CDs, but for this promotion you need only a CD burner. You will also want to invest in a CD label maker kit (which you should only need to buy once), CD label refills and simple CD envelopes.

A sampler CD of your work, a collection of the sample chapters perhaps featured on your website, is a "test drive" you offer to potential readers. The sample chapters can come in a variety of formats, ranging from PDF to HTML to audio files.

On my own sampler CD, I offer the following:

- A short story of Lisa Lee's (my co-author with *MOREVI*)
- The first two chapters of *Billibub Baddings and The Case of the Singing Sword*
- The first two chapters of *MOREVI*
- My introduction chapter to *The Fantasy Writer's Companion*
- The first two chapters of *Legacy of MOREVI*
- The first four chapters of the *MOREVI* podcast
- A webpage of my current works (with the graphics for the webpage located locally on the CD) and links to where they can be purchased.

The files are saved in the following formats:

- *PDF (Portable Document Format):* PDFs are easy to read on Macs or PC's, laptops and desktops with the Acrobat Reader. They can be created using Adobe InDesign, Adobe Acrobat (Pro, not Reader), and with proper plug-ins, Quark XPress and Microsoft Word. With the right programming, PDFs can be designed with hyperlinks, interactive menus and bookmarking capabilities.
- *HTML (Hypertext Markup Language):* HTML can be read by any web browser, and many eBook readers. Hyperlinks and text anchors allowing for navigation between chapters can easily be implemented.
- *PDB (Palm-powered PDA eBooks):* These files can be read only by Palm OS-driven PDAs or computers loaded with Palm eBook Reader, and easily bookmarked to pick up where you leave off in reading.
- *MP3:* This is an audio compression format, commonly used in podcasting. These files can be played in any computer's MP3 player, played in CD players that read MP3 files, or transferred to portable MP3 players such as iPods, iRivers, or Rios.

When it comes to creating files for CDs, you can use any kind of format. The initial process of creating the files, setting up the directories and creating labels (which should include your name, your website and a note saying this CD is compatible with both Macs and PCs) will take time. The production and printing process goes much faster after setup. I try to burn 100 CDs before every SF/F convention, and set out a few sets of CDs at a time on the Freebie Tables (usually one large table or a series of tables where authors, publishers and other cons leave out bookmarks, flyers, postcards, etc.). A stack of 100 CDs can easily circulate before the end of the weekend.

PODCASTING

It started with two guys—developer Dave Winer and music enthusiast Adam Curry—leading the charge, and has now become the most promising promotional avenue for both new and established authors. However, even with articles from *The Washington Post* and *The New York Times* and many books published on how to do it, the question still remains on many minds: What is podcasting?

Podcasting, in a nutshell, is the process of recording audio, compressing it into the MP3 format, uploading this MP3 to your website with plenty of bandwidth and server space available, and then adding an XML feed file that will tell podcatching clients (like iTunes, iPodder or iPodderX) new MP3 files are available for downloading. You then register your podcast and let people know, "I'm podcasting!" You can listen to them on your computer or any portable MP3 player.

It may sound super-technical, but websites such as LibSyn and Feeburner.com take on the technical work for you (at minimal or no charge), leaving the creative part to you. This is where you have a bit of fun. This kind of promotion can cost under $100—especially if you take advantage of free downloads, providers, and networks— and delivers your name and your work to the world.

People who listen to podcasts come from various walks of life, from various points in the world. My own podcast of *MOREVI* began the week of January 21, 2005, and was soon joined by author Scott Sigler and his novel *EarthCore* and Mark Jeffrey's *The Pocket and the Pendant*. Collected feedback from countries like Canada, Great Britain, Germany and Norway, illustrated the demand for "podcasting novels", eventually leading to the founding of Podiobooks.com. Podcasting can be regarded like placing an ad in a national magazine, and your audience flips through the magazine to specifically find it. With podcasting, listeners never miss your content as they request the download. This is the potential and the power of this exciting new media.

For more on podcasting, check out Summer Brooks' *chapter on radio shows, and the book* Podcasting for Dummies *written by myself and Evo Terra.*

With all these various means to promote your work and your name, and taking caution for when ideas turn sour, you now need creativity and ingenuity on your part to implement these suggestions. Remember one simple rule: Keep things professional. That old saying "There's no such thing as bad publicity..." shouldn't even be a consideration. Perhaps you are looking for ways to improve your business sense; or if you are just starting out, you are trying to plan a positive first impression with booksellers, fans, and event organizers. Regardless of what brought you into this book, your goal should be to create a promotional plan with a professional edge, attitude and approach.

There's a lot to self-promotion and I'm only *scratching the surface with this chapter. If you* *want to hear more, you can subscribe to* The Survival Guide to Writing Fantasy (HTTP://WWW.TEEMORRIS. COM/BLOG/), *a podcast for authors looking to promote their works and themselves.*

TALKING THE TALK, AND WALKING THE WALK: THE PROFESSIONAL'S ATTITUDE

Apart from scheduling appearances, making appearances can be the least favorite part of the modern author's profession. You need to be willing to face this fear of stepping into the spotlight, or your book may move a few copies here and there, but your name will remain under the radar unless you have that breakthrough hit. Until people stampede to their local bookstore for your work, you have to face one of the toughest aspects of being a newly published writer: The general public, including:

- Readers of Science Fiction and Fantasy coming off the street, curious about what is going on in their local Barnes & Noble.
- Hardcore fans that have traveled from all across a con's respective state (and perhaps beyond) to listen to their favorite authors speak, and check out any "new faces" coming up in the business.
- Folks walking from one anchor store of a mall to another, just happening to come across you, your table and your book.

The public comes in all shapes, colors and sizes, and they have an opinion they will gladly share with you—whether you ask for it or not. We can map out strategy upon strategy on where to hold signings, but nothing can really prepare you for actually being there, making eye contact with shoppers, other writers, and a roomful of fans. Every time I attend a con, appear at a signing or take center stage for a speaking event, I am terrified. Public appearances are grueling, exhausting and complete and utter fear in corporeal form.

I love every minute of it.

As you are writing Fantasy, you are lucky to be affiliated with one of the most popular sections of a bookstore. For the avid or casual reader of Science Fiction and Fantasy, meeting an author at a signing is a brush with fame, and that kind of adoration is a little intimidating. Dealing with people can be scary but building a fan base one signing at a time can be made easier when you keep yourself in perspective.

Remember That Fans Are People, Too.

Admittedly, some fans (and let's not forget that the word fan comes from the word fanatic!) are just plain terrifying. I have heard stories about fans requesting writers like Stephen King, Neil Gaiman and Clive Barker sign books with ink coming from self-inflicted wounds, asking media stars why their characters made choices that "just weren't right" (and usually given the unsatisfying, unsatisfactory answer of "Well, it was in the script..."), and making an "unspoken connection" with authors and actors that will lead to "unique" friendships. (These fans are usually two minutes late in catching the non-stop flight on Twilight Zone Air. That's the airline that advertises extra foot room, complimentary drinks, and *something on the wing of the plane*!)

Only steps behind the spooky fans are the abrasive fans. They love to tell you why your book stinks, where it stinks, why you aren't good enough to be published, and all about their work-in-progress that is sitting on several editors' desks. The abrasive fans have one objective: to get a rise out of you. They will go after both big and small presses, and enjoy any victory they can score. These kinds of fan test your patience, can sometimes throw you off-balance emotionally, and ruin a perfectly good afternoon.

These fans also fall into the minority. Never forget that.

The majority of attendees at signings and cons are happy to have you there, and may even follow you from panel to panel and signing to signing, playfully referring to themselves as your "stalkers." These fans are truly appreciative of your work and want to show their support. Authors continue to do signings and even nurture friendships with people they meet at signings and appearances because fans are, on the whole, good people.

All fans share in common an enthusiasm for the Fantasy genre, holding you to their standards because you are coming to their favorite con or bookstore to promote your work. Aggressive or appreciative, they are going to want to know why they should buy your book, and you should be ready to tell them—in a polite manner. Some fans will be smart and supporting, some are tacky and tasteless, but keep it in perspective. They all pay the same price for membership to the convention you're attending, the cup of coffee you got from the bookstore's cafe and for your book.

When Speaking on a Panel, Think Before You Speak.

You're on a panel, in front of people, talking about what you know. At least, that is what your presence on a panel is conveying to an entire roomful of people.

If you want to let an audience know that you're just not thinking, make the following statement when introducing yourself: "I have no idea why I'm on this panel."

Before uttering a sound on a panel, a workshop or a speaking event at a bookstore, seriously think about what you are going to say first. Your comments should not only be educated, they should be positive. Even if the discussion turns to critical, make sure you back up your comments with facts as opposed to opinions. (If, however, you are going for a laugh, make that clear, too!) Panels can quickly turn from lively, constructive discussions to spirited, heated debates. Just remember that what you say is the impression you leave with the audience.

Keep that in mind when you are an author slamming another author. Tread very carefully. You are opening the door for scrutiny. Slamming other authors never makes you look good, especially if you are enjoying successes of your own title. Even if your audience gets you into a one-on-one setting in a bar or over dinner, tread gently. Comments made "in private" can come back to haunt you. Just keep your thoughts positive, encouraging and educated.

Treat Booksellers—Your Business Partners—and Their Patrons with Respect

Take a look at the earlier section about fans being people. Apply it to the staff and booksellers, adding to it a reminder that "Things can go wrong." Shipments can get lost, deliveries can be delayed by weather, and someone can slip up and not place an order for books. When you are heading to a booksigning, prepare for the worst. Have a reserve stock of your titles on hand if, for some reason, the books do not arrive when you do. Call the bookstore hosting your event a week before your signing, just to make sure everything is set. If the staff knows your name, that is a good sign. Be polite and professional, and if a bookstore cops an attitude with you, roll with the punches, smile and stay positive. That is the best defense against the negative attitudes, whether from fans or merchants.

Booksellers are really your business partners from the time they agree to carry your titles. Authors under the mindset of "I'm doing the bookstore a favor by appearing there..." are suffering from delusions of grandeur. The booksellers and you are working together to create a signing that people will talk about. The new author selling 4 - 6 books in a three-hour signing period is considered a success.

For that pocket of time at your favorite bookstore, this signing is all about you. Have a good time! Wave to people. If someone stops, considers your book and then decides not to buy it, smile, say "Thanks for looking..." and mean it.

The same respect you show for the bookstore and their staff should also extend to the folks shopping in the store, browsing across the titles. There is no law saying that you need to make eye contact with patrons, but how approachable you make yourself will affect your sales. I've seen authors create a "zone" (reading a magazine while waiting for someone to stop, work on a personal project, or busying themselves with a coloring book... no kidding, a coloring book...) and no one came near them. On the other extreme, mauling people that are simply trying to get across a crowded mall might guarantee no one stopping by to ask about your work. (And yes, a Barnes & Noble CRM once told me of an author that literally followed customers throughout the store with their book. Needless to say, this author was never invited back.)

So where is the happy medium between unobtrusive and obnoxious? Actually, reading the general public is easier than you think.

- *Pay attention to people that pass by.* It not only gives you a way to read the crowd, it can also provide a lot of inspiration for future characters. Smile and just say "Hi" to people if you make eye contact with them. It will amaze you how far a smile can go!
- *If people stop, pay attention to them and let them guide the conversation.* Let them pick up the book and offer up a polite "If you have any questions about the book, feel free to ask." Then wait for questions.
- *If the interested party looks really engrossed in the back blurb, sum up your work with your quick pitch.* At this point I usually say "I describe *Morevi* in a nutshell as *Crouching Tiger, Hidden Dragon* meets *Pirates of the Caribbean*." This will either start up a conversation (and hopefully lead to a sale) or they will put the book down and walk away.
- *Now here's a really important touch: whatever happens, give them a sincere thank you.* Even for the potential buyers who will stand in front of you, bend back the cover of your book, read it for ten minutes and then put it back on your table and walk away without a word or even a glance to you, say it and mean it.

Predicting signings falls under the same science as hang gliding: depending on the external conditions, you will either fly high or hit the ground hard. Just remember that you and the bookseller are working together. You are a team, set on making this event a memorable one.

Do Unto Readers As You Would Have Them Do Unto You

When you're at a book signing and there's a line of people waiting to pick up your book, take a few moments to talk to the people investing in your work. If you're having a bad day and not feeling all that social, too bad. You're on the clock, so check the nastiness at the door. You need to treat everyone there—especially the people buying your books—with courtesy, respect and a smile. Every sale helps pay off an advance, shows your publisher that you are selling books and continues to cement your future as a writer. The nicer you are to people buying your book, the more memorable you are and the more positive feedback will be generated by writers' groups, other bookstores and online blogs.

What about the people who after chatting with you, looking over your book, maybe even reading a page or two, don't buy it? This isn't your moment to cop an attitude. If you're a new name and have grabbed a moment of attention, be grateful. There are plenty of authors who would graciously accept this moment, and plenty of others unpublished that would gladly trade places with you.

And what about the afore-mentioned abrasive fans in search of that rise? Like it or not, you need to remain gracious and positive. Don't allow yourself to get trapped or baited. At the end of this encounter between you and the abrasive fan, you need to walk away still looking good. You have to accept that people will be rude. In the moment when you are verbally slapped in the face, you have to decide the best way to handle the situation. What works best: allow abrasive fans the opportunity to dig their own grave. Positive responses from the author make great earthmovers.

Making the Difference:
When Self-Promotion Works

When I talk about self-promotion at book signings and with writing groups, I've heard authors-wanting-to-be-published whine and moan, "I don't want to do all that. I just want to write."

Fine. You can go ahead and just write, but don't expect people to know much about your work if you never leave your home, never approach the right people at bookstores and never take a chance.

Self-promotion is now an aspect of both the new and established author. No longer is promotion "someone else's job." While working on your next novel, you should also consider your next appearance, your next con and your next promotion. Some publishers may provide the support you would like, but there are no guarantees when you sign the contract.

What is a guarantee: Face time sells. Self-promotion is not a matter of personality, but matters of professionalism, determination, patience, attitude and initiative. It is up to you to get the word out to every avenue you can and try to keep the publicity up. Publicizing your novel sounds like a full-time job, but it is merely an aspect of your career. It's a challenge to meet, and if you conquer it, opportunities present themselves on account of your efforts.

Make it happen. Good luck, and enjoy the ride.

Communicating with Others:
NETWORKING
BY LAI ZHAO

Everyone here, consciously or unconsciously, networks. Those who are successful at it generate business; those who are not, do not. I am in Hong Kong—a city where who you know, how well you know them and what your relationship with them is counts for much more than straight promotion. (What you know also counts, but what you don't know, you can learn.)

Networking is part of the Far East cultures. It stems from millennia of societal structure and practices. One of the most noticeable examples was the Imperial Chinese court—strife, intrigue, politics, feuds. All to gain favor with the Emperor. Not all that different to the Royal Courts of the Western world. In fact, networking has been a part of human history for a long time.

But what techniques can you use to network successfully? What do you do if you dread the idea of it?

To cover all aspects of networking is beyond the scope of this article. Instead, an overview is provided, with a little extra that I've yet to encounter in such articles written for writers.

INTRODUCTION AND DEFINITIONS OF NETWORKING

Are You Networking?

- Do you talk to your family, relatives and friends, people at conventions, and at exhibitions?
- Do you talk to people in online chatrooms?
- Do you email people, send greeting cards?
- Do you speak to people regarding your research?
- Do you ask for, and give, help?

If you answered 'yes' to any of these questions, you're networking.

Definitions

Networking is:

- (3) a group of system of interconnected people or things—
Concise Oxford Dictionary, Tenth Edition
- Just a fancy word for communication—
students.nebrwesleyan.edu/students/cfox/html/chapter6.html1

So, what is communication?

- (1) share or exchange information or ideas—
Concise Oxford Dictionary, Tenth Edition

Communication is also the verbal and non-verbal exchange of information or ideas: In the physical environment, your tone of voice and gestures speak volumes more about your message than vocabulary used.

---

1   STUDENTS.NEBRWESLEYAN.EDU/STUDENTS/CFOX/HTML/CHAPTER6. HTML— unfortunately this link is no longer active.

THE WRITER'S NETWORKING

I came across an interesting analogy: The article, *Networking Lessons We Can Learn From Cats* by Debbie De Louise (Autumn 1999)2, talks about how cats get the best out of life just by doing what they do naturally.

Expand their world to the human world and networking is no longer 'confined' to the neighborhood or even to the country. It is an international tool, reaching places that other forms of promotion may not.

But where else can you network besides conferences and conventions?

The following lists places or tools that I've used:

> Book signings/launches
> Book-buying events
> Book fairs
> Exhibitions
> On the street
> In a restaurant/queue
> At rest in the park
> At the gym
> Attending a martial arts class
> On holiday
> During festivals
> At concerts (provided you can hear the conversation, that is)
> At parties/movie premieres
> During research/interviews
> Standing still on escalators
> While traveling on a bus
> Sitting on a plane
> Enjoying sea spray on a cruise
> On the phone
> In letters/postcards/greeting cards
> Through celebration wishes
> In chatrooms, discussion forums
> On mailing lists
> In email

---

2   Networking Lessons We Can Learn From Cats, Debbie De Louise, Autumn 1999. (WWW.CATWRITERS.ORG/ARTICLES/NETWORKING.HTM)

Simply: anywhere and any time you communicate with another person.

THE FEAR OF NETWORKING

But the thought of communicating with strangers, or not via the written word, fills you with fear. Introducing yourself to strangers fills your stomach with butterflies, makes your heart go *pitter-patter*, turns your palms damp, and gives you cold sweat-shivers.

While these feelings may be intense for a novice, experienced networkers can feel them. I've been doing this a while now, and still feel nervous when I have to work a room full of people I don't know. Sometimes, it takes everything I have to say, "Hello, I am Lai Zhao, co-editor of *The Author's Grimoire*. I'm wondering if you know about this book, or its publisher, Dragon Moon Press?"

But can't someone else network for you? No.

You wouldn't ask another to come up with your ideas and write your book. Networking is the same way.

Fear is natural, because this is personal; people are accepting or rejecting you. However, this is where authors have an edge over others who need to network: we're used to rejection.

Consider the rejections you have. Look at the number of negative or non-existent remarks about your work. Perhaps your work has been attacked without the attacker perusing the content. Maybe that review was less than favorable. And still you continue your publishing career.

Why? Because you believe in your work, you know it's publishable and there are people who love your work.

THE PACKAGING / SELF-PRESENTATION

It's easy to argue that rejections deal with your work, not you personally. But I've found it's part of the same process.

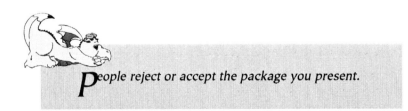

People reject or accept the package you present.

If you want to enter various circles, you need to present the package that will appeal most to those circles. For example, you want to be part of an elite group that frequently visits art galleries. A favorite is Rembrandt. How do you get accepted into that group without pretending to be something you're not? If you're interested in art, you brush up on that interest, particularly Rembrandt.

But what if you're not interested in art? Then you need to have a solid reason to enter that circle. If you don't have one, is it necessary for you to enter it?

Not all efforts need to result in concrete friendships or inclusion in exclusive clubs. Sometimes the best results come from not belonging to any specific club, but instead, belonging on the fringes of lots of clubs with a few solid friendships.

What's the Big Deal about Networking?

Why should so much emphasis be laid upon it? What can you do with it? How does it benefit you? Isn't 'word of mouth' the same thing?

The Emphasis

Networking is one of the best marketing resources for an author—it's free and it uses what you do naturally: communicate.

'Word of mouth' is a very similar tool. But a fine, sometimes indistinguishable line exists between the two: The former is sales, in that other people help promote your book, but you're not one of them. The latter is marketing in that you are communicating to others the worth of your book. In this way, it includes 'word of mouth.' But garnering book sales isn't all. You also build up a group of people around you who will support you and help you promote your book. You're part of this group.

The Usefulness

In business, saying the right thing, presenting the appropriate attitude and cultivating the essential relationship can help you obtain almost all that you want:

Two colleagues work at the junior level of a company. One of them calls it as he sees it, regardless if he offends the employer; he nurtures no relationship with the employer. The other phrases her observations in such a way that it pleases said employer; she ensures she has a good relationship with them. It's time for a salary review. Who gets the raise? She does.

Adapt this to the writer's world:

Two newly published writers. Same scenario, but the employer is now a big-name editor from a big-name publisher. Both writers pitch their second books; they're as good as each other. Who gets the contract?

The Big Deal

Authors need to network because though a writing career can be seen as an Art, to sell your books, you must promote. Hence, professional writing is a profit and loss enterprise—a business.

Many authors work full time (like Stuart MacBride (crime novelist, last noted day job was Project Manager) and Toni Morrison (African-American novelist, professor at Princeton University), and promotions, like national tours and advertisements are usually beyond their means (in terms of time and costs). To promote their work and stay solvent, one of the most effective promotion methods used is networking.

THERE ARE SECRETS TO NETWORKING?!

This question is like asking, "What's the secret to getting published?" If one exists, none of the authors or marketers I've talked to know it. They only practice what knowledge and advice is already available.

A successful author has a good product. Obtaining a good product means writing it. The same principles apply to networking: If you don't do it, you will not improve at it and no one will care.

Who cares most about your book? Who knows how best to represent it? Who can answer all the questions that will crop up about it? You.

Your agent or publicity team (if you're lucky enough to have one) know your book well and can help you promote, but only you know the book's emotions, its background, characters' thoughts you never put into the book but which impacted the story and so on.

It's up to you to convey that knowledge, that passion, to your target audience: Communicate your enthusiasm and belief in your product. (And if you hit it just right, you can create a wonderful, momentous impression that will help carry your product for a long while.)

Benefits of Networking

You invest your time, effort, knowledge, referrals and money. What do you get out of it?

- Encouragement when you're down
- Ideas to beat writer's block
- Critiques aimed at helping you improve
- A way to by-pass the slush pile
- People to give you a leg up when needed
- Care and support where and when you least expect it
- Expansion of your 'social circle'
- An expanse of knowledge for your non-fiction and fiction projects
- Professional advice
- More referrals
- Book sales
- Readership
- Friends

But these benefits don't arrive immediately; they take time. Expecting immediate results is unrealistic. A good, reliable network with people you can depend on takes time to build. About three years is average for a base of solid contacts.

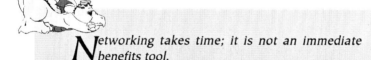

Networking takes time; it is not an immediate benefits tool.

Networking Essentials

But what are the basics, where and how do you start?

The Basics

There are two things that you should note and practice.

Courtesy:

This is important. It's surprising how often the basic 'hi,' 'please,' and 'thank you' are forgotten.

Sometimes, someone has taken an author's or an agent's time, obtained the information they wanted and gone away, all without the basic courtesies. Although that person may be grateful, they neglected to show that appreciation and thus they've unintentionally created the impression of ingratitude. (The writing world is not unique in this aspect; it happens with CEOs and senior management, too.)

If someone is not courteous, you don't have to match them. Obviously, there is a level of rudeness none of us will tolerate, but these encounters are rare. In such situations, though, I've found it best to say, "Thank for your time; I won't disturb you any longer," then walk away. But if that person looks like they're having a bad day, you can let them calm down and approach them again later. Or if they are genuinely unaware of their self-presentation, you can either forgive them for it, or leave them alone.

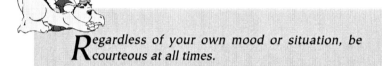

Regardless of your own mood or situation, be courteous at all times.

Listening:

This is a skill that gets overlooked. It is perhaps the best skill in the world to master, and may be one of the most difficult. You hear the other person's words, but do you listen to their meaning? Or are you thinking of your own response?

When you listen, your mind is focused on the meanings and message(s) that person is trying to convey.

An obvious fundamental to remember and practice when pointed out. But how often have you interrupted the speaker to voice your viewpoint without hearing the speaker's remaining explanation?

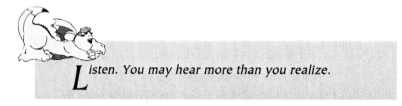

Listen. You may hear more than you realize.

Generally:

Be yourself. If you try to be something you're not, you'll be regarded with disdain when the truth is discovered.

Offer help first. Being 'in it for yourself' limits your success. Help others to help yourself.

Follow up on referrals within 24 hours. Leads grow cold fast, so you need to stay on top of them. Remember to thank the person who passed you the referral.

Respect the other person's time. Monopolizing someone's time is not good for anyone. You risk creating problems for yourself when you next want to contact that person.

Consider if interrupting a conversation is appropriate. Interrupting one that does not invite you paints you as unprofessional, leading to your loss.

Be professional at all times. For whatever reason, if someone overreacts to a situation, or their attitude becomes inappropriate, don't react in a similar way. And if you must be angry, choose your moment.

Deliver on your promises.

How and Where to Start Networking

Online Networking

I keep mentioning my physical location. Depending on your goals and the circle(s) you want to move in, where you are may hinder or help.

Offline, I network in the business world; online, I am in the writing world. Though the focus of each is different, the techniques are the same and the business world offers many tools that writers can use.

In the writing world, I'm mainly in chatrooms and at discussion boards. E-mailing lists, email and online journals are also part of my toolset.

Chatrooms

These are linked with their discussion boards, usually as a bonus. The reverse, however, isn't always true. The most useful chatrooms are those that are bonuses to an active discussion forum.

Chatrooms are prevalent on the Net. Finding one is simple; choosing one is much harder. I use a list of questions to help:

- Is the associated discussion board more active than the chat?
- Is the main focus of the chat writing or everything but?
- How many active chatters are there?
- How are you greeted when you first enter?
- Are the chatters helpful if you have a writing question, regardless of novice or pro level?
- What happens if a flame war starts? How is it handled if a moderator is not present?
- Are you comfortable there? Bear in mind, it takes a while to acclimatize to a chatroom, but if you find you like it and it meets your needs, you can opt to stay.

I also try the chatroom. This means making an effort to fit in. And if you're accustomed to chatrooms you can tell within a week or less if the room is right for you. If you're new to them, you will need more time.

Chatroom networking essentials you need to know and practice include dos and don'ts. Here are some of the basics:

Don't:

Ask A/S/L (age / sex / location) on arrival. A/S/L belongs mainly to chatters on IRC, to those who know no better way to start a conversation, or to those who are after one thing. (IRC is 'Inter-Relay Chat'—a system used before web-based chatrooms became more user-friendly and popular.) If you've found a good writer's chat, the regular chatters there will ask you what you mean, or ignore it, or laugh it off.

Use Netspeak. This is 'how r u,' 'wot u doing,' 'l8r' and other similar phrases. As a writer, you should use the language's proper form. However, popular abbreviations, like LOL (laughing out loud or lots of laughs), BRB (be right back), AFK (away from keyboard), ROFL (rolling on the floor laughing), etc., are acceptable.

Use 1337. In the same vein as the last "don't," do not use 1337 (LEET, short for Elite). It's a language comprising numbers and letters. For example, "disis 1337, d0 j00 pwn @ + 1 h3@D@ch13 j3t?" (This is LEET, do you have a headache reading it?).

Act like a troll. In other words, don't be a trouble-maker. Be aware that while it is not your intention to be a troll, you may have conveyed this through your words. Just as it is important in written business communications to be clear and sincere, so it is true of chatroom communications.

Ask for crits the moment you get in. If you're new to a writer's chat, asking for a crit the moment you enter is a good and fast way of getting yourself onto the regular chatters' annoyance list. Take the time to introduce yourself, return greetings, get to know others and understand the chatroom's traits.

Interrupt a snippet. If you enter and it's clear someone is posting part of their work for other chatters to comment on, don't interrupt. You can say hello afterwards. Or, if you've inadvertently interrupted, wait till the end to apologize.

Do:

Be humble. Nothing annoys regular chatters like an arrogant new chatter who appears to know everything. You can, however, be confident.

Be genuine. It's inadvisable to be someone you're not, regardless of how appealing the idea may be. Chatrooms rely on written words to convey meaning and personality. Falsified information and personas will be met with scorn and loathing. You may also be banned from the chatroom and discussion boards. On the other hand, if you're asked questions you don't want to answer, you don't have to. Just don't lie.

Be patient. A chatroom's character is not always immediately obvious, especially if you've entered during an internal writing event, or a quiet period. Be patient if no one answers at once. The writers aren't being rude, they're busy and may not be monitoring the chatroom. However, if a long while has passed and there's no activity, feel free to say goodbye and move on.

Be polite and respectful. Don't assume every chatter in the chatroom will welcome you. Not everyone has manners. However, that doesn't mean you should emulate them. While first impressions aren't always accurate, they do count in networking.

Act intelligently. That is, if other chatters insist on their viewpoint or belief, they have their reasons. If you ask them to explain and they do, acknowledge their viewpoint as valid, even if you disagree. Don't insist your belief is the correct one; you'll end with more bad feelings toward you than good. On the other hand, if you're proven wrong beyond reasonable doubt, admit it and make an effort to correct your stance. Don't insist on being right when it's clear you're not.

Apologize if you've made a mistake. None of us are perfect. Sometimes our words convey the opposite of our intentions. In this case, apologize and explain. While it's easy to say "it's online, no one knows who you are," there may be editors, publishers and agents present (very rare, but not unknown). Make your first impression a positive one.

Relax and have fun. Be honest that you're searching for a writer's chat. You don't need to admit it when you enter, but if asked, you need not hide the fact. However, "I'm here to network" is not generally a well-received response. While it's an opportunity to do so, you can be informal. But if it's a scheduled Chat event with a special guest, treat it as you would a business meeting. Those of us who frequent writer's chatrooms are mainly there for the company and friendship.

Discussion Boards

Once you've found a discussion board you like, how do you network there?

Generally, familiarize yourself with the board's layout, its forums and threads. Note discussion threads you can contribute to and any questions you have.

Look for an introduction area. Discussion boards for writers normally have a separate forum, or thread, to introduce yourself. Post a short description of yourself. What you write depends on how others have introduced themselves. You can follow their examples, or strike out on your own. Keep it respectful, though.

Contribute to those threads you noted earlier, or ask your questions.

A note on questions: before you ask any, search the boards, or review the FAQ. Your question may have already been asked and answered. If not, feel free to ask.

Overall, the dos and don'ts of a discussion board are close to those for chatrooms. A few extras for discussion boards when posting your comments:

Format your posts so they're easy to read. This includes putting blank lines between paragraphs, spelling and grammar checks, no unnecessary abbreviations and no Netspeak or 1337 (LEET).

Ensure your post is clear. Does it say what you want it to say? Can it be misconstrued? Granted, some of your audience will misunderstand no matter how you word your post, but if you're as clear as possible, you will minimize the misunderstanding.

Post a contribution first if you're new—a.k.a., offer help first. While you're there to learn and network, the "what's in it for me" approach will limit your enjoyment of the board's community. If you've asked for help and received it, thank the people who took time to provide that help. Reciprocate as appropriate. When boards are active, a post sometimes gets overlooked. If you've not received a response after a week, feel free to 'bump' your post by either editing the original, or using the reply function.

If you've made a mistake and someone's pointed it out, remember: they're not attacking you. They've done you a favor. Thank them and correct your mistake.

Use 'please' and 'thank you.' Be respectful.

Networking Correspondence
General:
Other forms of written networking include business stationery, emails, faxes, letters, queries, proposals, synopses, even this chapter and so on.

The main point here is to remember that your written words represent you. If there are mistakes, or your presentation is sub-par, you will give the impression of being sloppy. Whether you are or not, is negligible.

Some of the worst correspondence includes junk mail. Occasionally, one crops up that is purportedly about a charity. Scanning through, however, you know it has to be fake: Grammatical and spelling errors riddle correspondence teh; punctuation has been inserted, in ? any; old! way; and capitalization Is haPhaZard.

How much worse, then, would such errors be if they appeared on your stationery? Particularly if said stationery is part of a query and synopsis package heading for an editor in your network? Or what if it's a mailing list that includes a number of editors and published authors?

Before you hit that send or print button, or seal that envelope, check that your work is perfect. Ensure it's free of errors, unnecessary creases and crumpling. Is it easy to read and to the point? Double-check that your work is professionally presented. When you're certain you have a perfect copy, send.

Mailing Lists and Writing Groups:
E-mailing lists are a great way to meet people who share the same interests. And because it's a mailing list, you can share a lot of information that members have opted to receive. While minor typos are accepted, major errors are frowned upon; they make your contribution hard to read. That is, if it's a true contribution. In business, you don't join a business discussion list to solely promote your company's products. In the same way, you don't join a writing list just to sell your book.

When a mailing list or a writing group welcomes you, there are certain expectations they have: you're there to contribute and learn. They don't expect immediate promotion in your first communication with the list—the fastest way to alienate yourself and obtain a reputation for being disrespectful and self-serving.

Every author promotes, but why set yourself up for disdain? Especially the disdain of your peers?

Treat all networking correspondence as you would job interviews or business correspondence; even one mistake could be costly.

Mailing lists are just one type of a physical networking environment.

Physical Networking Environments
The physical environment affects your attitude, behavior and perception. Being comfortable in my environment greatly contributes to my networking success; the opposite is also true.

There are pros and cons to various environments. I've listed some and the following draws mainly from personal experience:

The Telephone

Telemarketers are irritating, but they're doing their job. I sometimes wonder if their company trains them before they call, though. Case in point from the other day:

At sonic speed, a telemarketer said, "Hello, Miss, our company's recorded sales pitch system called you the other day. I'm following up on that call. Our company is X Research Limited and we'd like to ask you some questions..." At that point, I hung up.

To lose a contact, adopt the clueless telemarketer's approach. But keeping a contact can be surprisingly effortless:

Speak at a pace slower than breakneck speed. Telemarketers tend to race throughtheirwordslikethissoit'salmostimpossibletodetermine whatthey'resayingandtheyrarely... pause... for breath.

Give your name first, then the reason you're calling.

Ask if your contact has time to follow up with you on that enjoyable conversation you had at that conference. If not, schedule a time.

If they have time, detouring and wasting their time is not recommended; not letting them get a word in edgewise is also detrimental to your networking. And by the time you get to the end of your detour, what was your point again? Respect your contact's time and stick to the point.

Treat this as an informal business meeting.

Conferences

Conferences are where much networking takes place. But if you dislike crowds, conferences are not the 'be all, end all' of networking. There are other avenues. However, let's assume you love conferences and want to get the most out of them.

These events yield a lot of contacts, some of which may be essential while others are 'nice to have.' Their downside is cost.

If you live far away, larger conferences are worth the investment, but you have to work at it. Following are some questions you should ask yourself before signing up for any conference.

What are your networking goals? What do you want to specifically achieve? For example, speaking to three agents and three editors in the Fantasy genre in detail, and securing a lasting, positive place in their memories; also obtain their contact information. This is a concrete goal.

Who's attending that you want to connect with? Check out all the attendee lists. Additionally, check the predicted number of attendees. After you know who and how many people you need to face, list those that you must contact and prepare accordingly.

What programs do you want to attend? Check who's taking the programs. If they are someone you'd like to connect with, make a note of it.

Do you know anyone going? Sometimes, it's daunting to think that you're going alone. Going with a writer you know can be a good confidence boost, but don't always hang around them when you get there. Split up so you can cover twice as many programs and communicate with twice as many people. Pool your resources and you'll find you've doubled your network using half the effort.

When you arrive, there a few things you should note:

Freebie tables

You can pick up information on the conference you couldn't get prior to attending. Also, authors may be promoting their latest works and have giveaways, i.e., freebies. Feel free to avail yourself of these.

Registration

Talk to the registration staff. They'll make you feel welcome; they may also be authors, editors or agents volunteering. And if they're not, they're the people who know who's attending and could help get you in touch with your target contact(s).

Con Etiquette

Remember to be courteous. General don'ts:

Accost people aggressively or rudely. Give them space and time. This helps everyone relax and you can steer conversation as you need to.

Interrupt conversations when it's clear an interruption wouldn't be welcome. I was at an exhibition helping at a stand that sold various business products and found myself in a queue, waiting to buy lunch. Two businessmen stood behind me and were interested in why I was in the States. We got into a pleasant conversation. In time, it turned to other matters that didn't include me.

At length, the pair wondered where a particular stand was. I knew because it was diagonally opposite the stand I was helping at. So I interrupted their conversation to give them precise directions. I thought

I was helping. I did. I helped the conversationalists to their destination and helped myself to losing two contacts who may have benefited a project I was working on at the time. Lesson learned? There are times when interruptions are welcome and when they are not.

Monopolize someone's time, regardless of who that person is.

Babbling. This is someone who talks at you non-stop seemingly without breathing or punctuation and they don't let you get a word in edgewise because they have so many interesting topics to offload on you and this is just the start... and you get the picture.

Interrupt an editor conversing with someone else to pitch your own book. If you do, the best-case scenario is that the editor and conversationalist will listen politely, then send you on your way.

Worst-case scenario: editor and conversationalist spread the word that you are unprofessional and rude, and use you as an example of what not to do at a conference.

Chase an editor on a bathroom run because you want to pitch your book. If the editor invites you to do a 20-second pitch on the way, go for it. But if not invited, save it for a more appropriate time. It's inconsiderate and do you really want to be remembered as the author who made the editor uncomfortable? (This goes for publishers, agents, authors, visitors, all attendees, and conference staff, too.)

General dos:

Remember the Golden rule. "Do unto others as you'd have done unto you." Be polite, friendly and helpful. (You'd be surprised at how many visitors and pros are the exact opposite.)

Watch what you say. Everyone says the wrong thing at some point, but a conference is not the ideal place to practice getting that right. Be considerate of others, even if you think that person is not worth your time, or someone has infuriated you. While visitors may outnumber the guests, you are not invisible to the guests and they network, too. In networking, first impressions count.

Listen. Give your full, undivided attention to the speaker. They may not be your ideal contact, but ideal contacts spring from the unlikeliest of places.

Say 'please' and 'thank you.' You don't need to do this after every phrase, but insert them appropriately and remember the final 'thank you.'

There are pros and cons to going to conferences. Some of the major pros:

You can lose yourself in conferences and people might not remember you. This can be used to your advantage, especially if you make a minor social gaffe—a forgettable incident, and lots of people will miss it.

An abundance of networking opportunities allows you to warm up for your major contacts. The problem is choosing the right people to warm up on. Generally, not recommended as it can be detrimental to your networking efforts.

You can meet the right people just by ensuring you're in the right place at the right time. This is not as difficult as it sounds: check for updates made to the program line-up and guests list, then get yourself there. Prior to the conference, if applicable, sign up for one-on-one meetings with your target contact(s) or sign up for panels. There will be plenty of research opportunities for your work, as well as for finding an excellent way of starting a conversation and common ground to break the ice.

It's a conference geared toward writers, publishers, agents, editors, etc. You're part of this world; enjoy it.

However, there are also cons.

You can get lost in conferences, and people won't remember you. A disadvantage when you want your target contact to remember you. To counter, do something different to make yourself stand out when talking to them.

They cost a lot. Especially if you need to include a plane ticket, accommodation and car rental in your budget. Try sharing accommodations with friends and car pool. There's not a lot you can do about the plane ticket.

There can be a bewildering amount of networking opportunities. Where do you start? Start with the Opening Keynotes presentation. That introduces you to people at the conference, to the programs and events you should note. Visit the dealer's room. It contains friendly people who may also be publishers, editors, authors, or people who know them.

Seminars & Workshops

These environments are akin to conferences, albeit, on a much smaller scale. However, the same courtesy and common sense applies.

Some of the pros to seminars are:

A limited number of people attend. At a seminar, you spend at least half a day with the same people, so your meetings are more leisurely and relaxed.

Meeting people who do the same thing you do. When you fit in, seminars and workshops can be thrilling, inspirational and rewarding. In a small event, one person's actions are visible to the whole group. You can learn much through observation.

Exposure. If you volunteer to help out, it's a prime opportunity to show the audience part of your talent. If you are an amateur stand-up comedian whose humor colors your work, or you're a character-actor who can bring your characters into existence, this is a great opportunity for you.

Informality. A workshop can be a great informal setting in which to have writing fun.

However, there are always cons to consider as well.

A limited number of people attend. This is an acting test: you're not pretending to be someone else; your professionalism is being tested. And in a small gathering, everyone sees.

Meeting people who do something similar to you. If you don't fit in, it's painfully obvious from the start. I attended a workshop by Nury Vittachi (author of *The Feng Shui Detective*). I read crime and detective, so it didn't faze me that I attended. But this workshop stood out.

It soon became apparent that besides one other and myself, everyone else wrote solely non-fiction or literary fiction. Normally, I discount this. However, I got the impression that saying I wrote fantasy was not a good thing to say. People were respectful, but at the same time, I felt apart from it all. The result: Except for one or two people, I've lost touch with all participants of that workshop.

Exposure. If you are 'volunteered' to take part in the seminar or workshop's exercise at the front of the room, it can be frightening.

Informality. An informal setting where you can have too much writing fun. Moderation is key.

Presentations

Whether you're the one giving them or watching them, these environments are more of a one-way communications channel than true dialog. However, networking is still possible.

Things to look out for in your presentations:

If you're not presenting but are a natural leader, or like to talk, be careful that you don't dominate the presentation. Should you find you're talking most, finish what you're saying and let others communicate their ideas. Lots of information can be gathered when you listen.

An insatiable curiosity is a good thing, but it needs to be used in moderation. Ask the right questions at appropriate moments and most of your related questions will be answered, too.

On the other hand, if you don't like talking but you have something to contribute, work out the crux of your message, find the appropriate moment and say it. You can't? If it helps, think of the event as a writing discussion—everyone has a valid viewpoint to express and no one's going to laugh at you (if they do, they're being unprofessional, so don't let it upset you).

Pros to presentations:
- You can take notes on how to present yourself, or not.
- An opportunity to study people and their conveyed attitudes.
- A chance to learn how others communicate.
- The subject may be one you do not know in detail—time to learn.

Cons to presentations:
- Presentations can be an unnerving experience, like a panel interview whether you're interviewing or being interviewed.
- If you say nothing at presentations, you can become invisible.
- The subject may be beyond your expected understanding, which may limit your contribution.

Informal Gatherings

A great place to make friends and acquaintances. General chatting is expected and business is not. If it's a party, or barbecue, etc., leave the formal networking at home, but keep some business cards handy. Should someone ask if you have contact information and you think it's acceptable, you can use your business cards. At other times, it's best only to exchange phone numbers or email addresses. You can always follow up after the event.

Other Physical Environments

There are many more physical environments in which to network, including, pubs, SCA events, film premiers, awards, weddings, church gatherings and more.

However, recommended places to not network include the bathroom and changing rooms. While some may accept these places as a chance to do so, you have to pick your time. If you're not sure, leave it out. Of course, if you like what the other person's wearing, or trying on, you can start a conversation. A word of caution though: if your target contact does not appear to invite conversation, don't force it.

A NEGATIVE EXAMPLE
FROM A TV PROGRAM (NO LESS)

What's the good of all positive examples if you don't know what a bad example is?

On *Queer Eye for the Straight Guy*, one episode featured a sports commentator meeting an Internet friend for the first time in their online friendship. This friend's self-presentation was negative; they were unappreciative of efforts made on their behalf.

The commentator countered with positive remarks, not allowing the negative to faze him. However, later that same day he hosted a gathering. He did not introduce his Internet friend; his friend noticed this, too.

So, if you're going to be unceasingly negative and critical, be prepared for this result.

When you network, be positive—no one likes being around a negative person.

A POSITIVE NEGATIVE EXAMPLE

A company once asked me to go to a 'networking beach party.' Knowing I handle beach parties badly, I refused to go: Had I attended, it would have gone south for everyone. I can't say the company gained extra projects because of my absence at that party (that's silly), but I can say, the company would not have gotten those extra projects if I had gone.

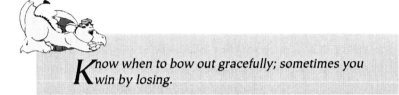

Know when to bow out gracefully; sometimes you win by losing.

And a word about bluntness:

Being blunt is sometimes necessary, but it can be mistaken for rudeness. Consider the following conversation:

"When's your next workshop on Horror?"

"Halloween."

"That says a lot."

"That says a lot" is blunt, but spoken a certain way, it can be sarcastic and rude. Might it have been better to say, "You mean October 31, right?"

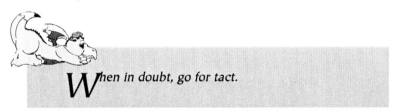

When in doubt, go for tact.

NONVERBAL COMMUNICATION

Tone and unspoken words are part of non-verbal communication.

Statistics say nonverbal cues are responsible for at least 60% of face-to-face communication; others state it's over 90%. However, verifying these statistics is difficult. The conclusion to draw is that nonverbal communication comprises the majority of face-to-face dialog.

Defining Nonverbal Communication

According to Answers.com, nonverbal communication (NVC), is:

> "Communication without the use of spoken language. Nonverbal communication includes gestures, facial expressions, and body positions (known collectively as 'body language'), as well as unspoken understandings and presuppositions, and cultural and environmental conditions that may affect any encounter between people."
> Source: Answers.com[3]

Nonverbal Cues

At its most basic, this is body language.

For example, consider a conversation you chanced upon. Were the participants hostile or friendly towards you? How much was said? How much was not said? In vis-à-vis communications, oral comprises surprisingly little of it. The main conversation takes place using facial features (expressions), body movements (posture, stillness, fidgets, etc.), physical appearance, environment, culture, the relationship between the conversationalists and many other factors.

For instance, at a conference, you encounter two editors who are standing facing each other and side-on to you. This means they do not welcome outside intrusion into their conversation. However, if they were standing at an angle to each other, and were three quarters facing you, you would be able to join their conversation:

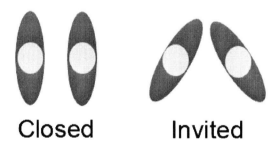

Closed   **Invited**

Body language is also present in someone sitting.

---

3   Answers.com

(HTTP://WWW.ANSWERS.COM/TOPIC/NONVERBAL-COMMUNICATION)

If you're at a table and the other, an agent, faces the door, are they really comfortable sitting like that, or do they want to leave? Are they glancing at their watch, scanning the room, or even drumming their fingers? Or are they making notes? Are their replies genuine?

Superficially, someone so successfully stifles a yawn no one notices it. But you're watching their reactions and listening analytically to yourself. Is your conversation boring them? Do they want to be elsewhere? Ask yourself: have you been dominating the conversation? If so, you need to change track or lose that person's attention. However, if not, they may be genuinely tired; it's a good time for everyone to take a break.

On a deeper level though, consider the following.

Let Me Outta Here

The person sits facing the door, legs crossed and gazes everywhere but at you. At times, they yawn (politely), and they nod to show they can hear you. Clearly this person wants to leave this conversation.

Liar Liar

He's leaning back in his chair, ankles crossed, but arms and hands open; he's right-handed. With his first and second answers to your questions he looks left. Knowing he has lied to you before, you realise he's lied to you just now. However, his third answer causes him to look right, but his fourth response causes him to look left again. He told the truth then reverted to lying.

This is a simplified illustration of detecting truth and lie in a conversation; you must take into account other information and factors before deciding if someone is lying or being truthful. (A full exploration of detecting truth and lie is beyond the scope of this article.)

Keep Your Distance

She's standing with her arms crossed and her feet shoulder-width apart. Her mouth smiles, but her brow frowns and her gaze sweeps the crowd, never resting on one area for long. Just as well she's in slacks, casual shirt and canvas shoes, and you know she's an agent; she'd be forbidding in a security uniform. But if you didn't have to, would you want to approach her, anyway? She doesn't seem to welcome contact with anyone.

Me, Myself and I

He talks. And talks... And talks. He doesn't seem to breathe. He gestures, looks at you but doesn't wait for your response. His jaw muscles are getting a good workout. He leans forward, but occupies over half the table surface, leaving little room for others. There's a lot of air being passed over his larynx resulting in intelligible sounds. But listen closely: is he saying anything of substance?

Refreshingly Genuine

She sits opposite you, leaning back in her chair, relaxed. Her feet are side by side, hands and arms are open. She faces you fully and patiently awaits your next word. Everything around her is ignored as she focuses on you. Occasionally, she repeats a cogent point, or clarifies another, or summarises what you've just said—all to ensure she has understood you correctly.

Observe yourself and others: much information lies in your posture and gestures.

Fun Comparisons

In advertisements, have you noticed the models never look accidentally miserable, even if they aren't smiling? Why? Do you also get the feeling they're inviting you to purchase that brand? Why?

Compare President Bush and President Hu Jintao, or maybe President Thabo Mbeki and President Chen Shui-bian. Who fills you with irritation or doubt? Who fills you with pride or confidence? Why?

Tone & Unspoken Words

Is the tone upbeat? Down? Neutral? Does the tone indicate that the unspoken words could harm you? What remains unsaid can give you a greater insight to the speaker than what is said. However, if you cannot say for certain, do not second guess, but remain professional. You can always investigate later if you feel you must.

On the day after I called in sick, a colleague rang to ask for help on a document. This is not unusual, except it was Saturday morning—a non-work day, unless it's urgent. The next unusual aspect was the question when the answer was already known: did I have Microsoft Word™ at home? No.

The colleague's tone throughout the conversation was friendly. But it was the false caring tone that alerted me to the caller's true intentions. Suspicious, I followed up that Monday.

My colleague insisted they were referring to the work computer. (Microsoft Office™ is standard at work and installed on all computers.) But I remained unconvinced: they would not look at me directly and their tone was too sincere to be genuine.

Under the guise of needing help, my colleague wanted to know if I had truly been ill.

A word of caution regarding sarcasm and inappropriate tones:

Sarcasm has its moments. But not in professional networking! An acquaintance of mine is sarcastic and blunt. He comes across as arrogant, sneering and superior. While a nice person, I've noticed no one is around him for long.

Inappropriate tones may be good for a laugh with close friends, but when networking, remain respectful and, if necessary, conservative. You're meeting strangers or acquaintances, and while some may appreciate the joke, not all are so easy-going.

Should the conversation be going south, remain professional and end it appropriately. Even if your opposite doesn't do so, observers will acknowledge your professionalism.

Networking in person is about conversations and exchanging business cards, and also about nonverbal cues and unspoken thoughts. The impression you give and how well you interpret these communications and cues depends on how observant you are and what you know of body language.

Choosing Your Network

You need to get close to people, to connect with them at some level. But not everyone is suitable: I keep certain colleagues at a distance—they're not the type of people I want too close to me, even for networking. I don't trust them at all.

However, be aware that if you choose to distance yourself from various people, you may inadvertently harm your network.

Do you trust your acquaintance enough not to exploit you or stab you in the back? Granted, there are those who will do that regardless of circumstance, but why invite it when you can prevent it.

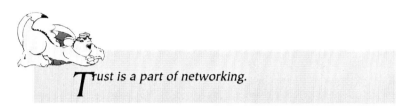

Trust is a part of networking.

Notice the technique of successful, professional networkers: they select people they want in their 'inner networking circle,' but they do not shun those not elected. The latter are kept on the circumference.

Who do you want in your 'inner network?' Who do you want to keep on the fringes? And who do you want to forget completely?

Factors for choosing who should be in your network include that person's industry, what they can offer you and what you can offer in return, your relationship with them, their trustworthiness, and more. Just remember to trust your own judgment and don't shun anyone; ideal contacts sometimes come from the least expected of places.

Contingency Measures

And a word about contingencies: You can't plan for all of them, but you can prevent many by being friendly and professional from the start. However, if you find yourself in a jam, stay calm and find out what's happening; this is about being professional.

CONCLUSION

Networking is not a 'one-off' thing. It is a continuous, sometimes exacting task. It can't be used in isolation of other marketing efforts because it's part of marketing. And to be truly successful, you must implement it.

The quality of your network and how you present yourself can be summed up as "garbage in, garbage out"—you reap what you sow. But you don't need to remember all the networking knowledge you've encountered. Create a summary list of points as a checklist for yourself:

- Participate in networking events—go to conferences, chat online, contribute to mailing lists, give workshops, etc.
- Follow up referrals within a day—a lead can grow cold very fast.
- Practice networking daily—it takes time and effort to build a relationship
- Have specific networking goals—achieving them becomes more feasible and fun
- Say "please" and "thank you"—basic courtesy
- Reciprocate—return favors as you receive them
- Listen—have you heard what the other person is saying?
- Don't ask "What's in it for me?"—help others to help yourself.
- Deliver on your promises.

If you read *The Author's Grimoire* from cover to cover, you'll find that every article contains a little of word-of-mouth or networking. This is because, like marketing, networking is an integral part of business. Talking to people is about communicating and presenting yourself—verbally and nonverbally. Remain professional, friendly, and helpful, and others will soon see you as someone reliable and worth knowing.

The Joy of Writing Workshops
By Jana G. Oliver

You shift uneasily from foot to foot, surveying the landscape. Faces stare back at you. Some are openly eager, others wary. Pens are poised in mid-air and virgin sheets of paper wait to record your every word. Sweat runs down your back and you move your notes around on the podium for the hundredth time.

Why would anyone put themselves in this position?

Though occasionally unnerving, workshops serve many purposes for the audience and the presenter. The obvious goal is to educate, to nurture new writers and bring their talent to fruition. But just as there are layers to onions and ogres, there are other reasons for presenting writing workshops. Besides the satisfaction of imparting knowledge to a group of (hopefully) eager students, one of whom might someday earn a Hugo Award or become a New York Times Bestseller, there is another side of the coin.

The "What's in it for me?" side.

Whoa, that sounded crass, didn't it? Still, it's an honest question. You will spend considerable time creating a course outline, polishing your presentation and collecting your reference materials. Besides the joy of teaching, there should be an upside to all your efforts. In my experience, you should benefit from workshops on at least four levels.

PERK #1: FEED YOUR BRAIN

I'd much rather throw words on a page than read about the mechanics of writing. It's a lot like reading about mountain climbing or sex; while informative, it just doesn't give you the same thrill. Since workshop planning requires a lot of research, I find myself reading about such "riveting" topics as point-of-view, plotting, hooks, trends in genre fiction, the state of publishing, etc. At the same time that I'm gleaning content for the workshop, I'm nourishing my brain. Your little gray cells need constant updating or they get sluggish and inclined to watch late night infomercials because they're "cutting edge." In short, a well-fed brain is a creative brain.

By wending your way through books, articles, author interviews and industry reports, you immerse yourself in the writing craft. Part of that knowledge you will pass on to your students; all of it helps you become a more savvy writer.

PERK #2: YOUR AUDIENCE, JUST LIKE KIDS,
WILL ASK THE DARNDEST QUESTIONS.

What's it like to be an author? Why can't I finish a story? Why can't I spend thirty pages detailing the intricacies of my warriors' armor? Why won't I get a $4 million dollar advance on my first novel?

Students have an uncanny ability to know which questions to ask. It's as if they'd obtained a copy of your workshop outline and spent the night before the class preparing queries for which you have no response. It's your job to find the answers, if nothing more than for the next time someone pops one of those beauties on you. Workshops are a two-way street; you learn from your audience while they learn from you.

Perk #3: Building Street Credibility.

Teaching a workshop "brands" you as an expert. Ever since we sat around campfires and listened to the village elder spin us tales of great battles and mythical beings, we have regarded our teachers with a certain reverence. The ability to teach skills to others is an art. Fortunately, that reverence rubs off even for those of us who teach workshops.

By branding yourself as knowledgeable in your field, your visibility increases and doors open. Conducting a workshop polishes your professional image and puts your name on people's lips. As the adage goes, "It's not who you know, but who knows you." Writers who rise above the pack are more likely to be at the proverbial right place at the right time.

Perk #4: And then, of course, there is the money.

Some venues compensate you in non-monetary ways. Conventions, for example, may supply free admission, while others will pay your food and hotel expenses. Some workshops will be gratis and others will allow you to command a healthy paycheck for a day's work. Where you offer your course (and who hosts it) will affect your potential income. If you teach workshops at a junior college, you're probably going to make more money than if you offer an adult education class at your local parks and recreation department, who often split the take 50-50.

I keep two goals in mind when I teach: impart my hard-won writing knowledge to a new crop of writers and build my reputation. Both of my goals have succeeded admirably, culminating in the penning of this article, an unexpected and rewarding outcome of my workshop experience.

Bore Me at Your Own Peril

Let's climb in a time machine and pop back to your high school or college years. Was there one particular teacher you really liked? One whose class you never missed? Now discarding the lithe-limbed mini-skirted art teacher or the hunk of a gym instructor who had biceps that begged to be squeezed, who most influenced you by the way they taught? What was it about that teacher that captured your interest?

In my case, it would not be the monotone sociology professor who droned on about his work amongst primitive societies at eight in the morning three times a week. There was not enough caffeine on the planet to keep me awake during his lectures. The professor who riveted me was the odd little gnome of a fellow who taught Western Civilization. With a penchant toward suits (when most of us wore love beads) and a mischievous gleam in his eye, he enchanted us with history's tragedies and triumphs, all in vivid and occasionally lurid detail. I'm still mining plot lines from his lectures.

I judge a workshop by how well the teacher inspires me. If he/she is able to convey enthusiasm for the writing craft, you've got my attention. You might be able to explain to me what a gerund is, but I want you to make me fascinated with those little grammatical critters and show why they're important to my writing (or not).

Enthusiasm. If you don't love what you're teaching, don't inflict yourself on the innocent public. If you're doing it solely for the money, the audience will know.

Working Knowledge. At what point in your writing career do you feel you know enough to teach? That's a personal call. I started offering workshops on novel plotting after a year of writer purgatory during which I arm wrestled a particularly recalcitrant plot. When the plot won, I realized what I'd endured was ideal workshop fodder. By struggling through a bad patch during which I sincerely questioned both my sanity and writing ability, I can easily relate to my students as they slog through their own personal writing swamps.

Be Real. When a teacher tries to make me think he or she hasn't screwed up a plot or blithely states they've finished every novel they've started, my skeptical gene kicks in. A teacher, above all, must be honest with their students. If you tell me you've never made a mistake, I'll suggest your name for sainthood but I'm not likely to take your course or believe what you tell me.

"Students, regardless of age, are on the lookout for fake or hypocritical teachers. I've always found it's best to be myself—warts, eccentricities and all. I'm not afraid to tell them what I'm good at and what I'm still learning," said Tyra Mitchell, Professor of Marketing at Coles College of Business, Kennesaw State University. Marketing yourself as a teacher is as important as marketing your course. Being fallible turns what could be an adversarial relationship into one of mentor and student. A shared journey is always more meaningful than the one we make on our own.

Teachers can only open the door; the student must step through by himself.
— *Chinese Proverb*

BUILDING THE PERFECT COURSE

Workshops are a bit like Frankenstein's monster, kludged together from bits and pieces of knowledge accumulated from a variety of sources. The trick is to put the information into a form that makes sense to the audience. Here are a few ways to help you pull off that trick.

Just like in writing, showing is better than telling. If my sociology professor had related scintillating anecdotes about his life amongst the aboriginals, fertility rites and all, we would have listened with rapt attention rather than catching some zzz's. Once you tap into your audience's frame of reference and create a workshop that educates, entertains and energizes, your students will be keen to hear what you have to say. When your students leave your classroom, they should be filled with new ideas, eager to tackle their current writing project. In truth, you are both teacher and cheerleader.

The key to a great workshop is flexibility.

Imagine for a moment you're an actor in an over-the-road theatrical production. One night you're in a grand theater with fabulous acoustics, all the latest hi-tech electronic wizardry and acres of stage space. The next night you're in a small town jumbled up in an old Vaudeville house with a dinky stage, erratic lighting and a sound system that was new when FDR was president. Not only does the venue change but so does the audience's expectations: some will laugh at every nuance, others balance their checkbooks and gaze longingly at the exits. Teaching is like theater: you adapt or fail.

Now for those of you who suddenly perked up and said "Flexible? Hey, does she mean I don't need a course outline?"—just sit down and behave. You need an outline to keep on track, but at the same time you need to be open to those off-ramp opportunities to see the World's Largest Strawberry.

The first trick is to judge your students' skill level. If your course material didn't specify a certain level at the time of registration, then you must be prepared to present a "broad spectrum" workshop. If your audience is confused by the difference between a noun and a verb, you will present an entirely different class than if your students have a few short stories or a novel under their belts. Your content will also change based on the age and frame of reference of your audience. Junior college students are an entirely different breed than retired folks. Different viewpoints, different expectations.

If I find my charges are new to the craft, I focus on the basics. I explain how to get a story off the ground, what elements are necessary for a good read and what happens when you start spinning your wheels halfway through a plot.

If I discover I have a more sophisticated audience, I pull out more esoteric content. I'll focus on the work at scene level, how to wring as much as possible out of the prose and how to use emotional and physical layering to bring the characters to life. Above all, I make sure what I'm teaching has value to their current work-in-progress. I want my students to go home armed with a new set of gadgets in their writing tool box.

But what if the audience is a mixture of newbies and seasoned veterans? Ah, that's where you earn your keep. It's not easy to layer the content so that the fledgling writers aren't overwhelmed and the old salts aren't bored out of their socks, but it can be done. Most writing topics are universal. I touch on the basics while adding a couple techniques that both the new folks and the experienced writers can use at their own levels.

How do you tailor your workshop on the fly? By leaving some "scoot room" as I call it: extra time in the schedule where you can delve deeper into a particular topic. When I first started teaching, I didn't do this; I felt the need to pack every moment of the class full of information. Now I grant my students adequate time to assimilate what I've taught. That assimilation phase allows them to ask in-depth questions, personalizing what they've just heard. The knowledge is of no value if the individual writer can't use it once they get home.

The best way to determine the lay of the land is by introducing yourself and then delivering a brief overview of your accomplishments, stating why you're qualified to teach the class. Then allow the students to introduce themselves, detail their own writing feats and explain (briefly) their current work-in-progress and why they're taking the class. (This, of course, isn't an option in classes larger than about twenty persons). I make notes during those introductions and tailor my presentation based on the 'level' of the audience and their overall goals. This exercise also builds a sense of community.

For larger audiences you have to work without a net, taking your cues from the participants as the workshop unfolds. If your students are sincerely interested in publishing contracts, spend some time on that. If they'd like to know the ins and outs of royalties, delve into advances, returns and sell-through. If they want an in-depth understanding of point-of-view, trot out your lesson on third person omniscient and have at it.

The ability to shade content on the fly is an acquired skill. I couldn't do it during my first workshop or even the second or third. Slowly I learned that there are certain patterns to what my students want to learn. Almost all are interested in the basics of how to get a book published. Most want to know how to obtain an agent and what a contract involves. Some are strictly focused on the craft itself, to their credit.

Your goal is to tap into their brains and present your material with energy and enthusiasm. If you succeed, your students will be clamoring for more.

Written Exercises

— Or —

Where's the Mother Ship

When You Need It?

I admit to a love-hate relationship with in-class exercises. I grit my teeth when an instructor asks me to create a scene using three different shades of the color blue. On the other hand, some of my most informative and craft-changing work has occurred during a workshop exercise.

Donald Maass, premiere NY agent and author, often requires his students to stress their pens during his popular workshops. His exercises aren't just time fillers, but a challenge to examine character and scene in new ways.

An example: Take your character back to a location where a particularly horrific event occurred. If your character survived a grueling car crash that killed his spouse, have him view the mangled vehicle a week or so afterward. What goes through the character's mind? How does he react to the crumpled metal, the blood-spattered seat, the shattered windshield? Do the sounds of the accident reverberate in his ears? Does he remember his wife's last words?

That's heady stuff from a writing exercise. In my case, I chose a scene where my character had no choice but to watch a relative drown while both were chained in the hold of a rusty freighter. Bringing that character back to the ship a week later evoked devastating memories of guilt and anger that raised the bar for my entire story.

I stick to technique-oriented exercises that highlight a particular writing skill, such as changing the point-of-view character or how to layer all five senses in a scene. You'll have to judge what exercises are appropriate for your workshop. By allowing students to play with their words in a non-threatening environment, they have the opportunity to "try on" new methods and internalize new skills that, in turn, lead to more powerful stories.

PAY NO ATTENTION TO THE WIZARD
BEHIND THE CURTAIN!

Though it costs a few trees, I utilize handouts even if I offer a PowerPoint® presentation. Nothing is more aggravating than trying to balance a notebook on your knee while scribbling at warp speed. If I know the information is available in paper form (or on a website for later reference) I can chill and focus on the teacher. Because of this bias, I'm generous with handouts. When using a PowerPoint presentation, I will even duplicate some of the pages in the handouts. I also include a bibliography of 'how-to' books, useful websites, photocopies of writing articles (after obtaining permission from their respective authors) and printouts of web pages that might be of interest. I package all of the handouts in a colorful folder, include my business card, a pen and blank paper for notes. And of course, I include my promotional material.

PowerPoint presentations can be a kick or they can be as tedious as sorting grains of sand under a microscope. Here's where "eye candy" comes into the picture. If you create a "theme" for your workshop, include an identifiable element of that theme on your slides.

An example: A writing seminar entitled *How to Write Urban Raptor Fantasy* might include the image of a velociraptor (think *Jurassic Park*) in chain mail, teetering on stiletto heels while leaning on a broadsword at a bus stop. Chain mail and heels? Outrageous, admittedly, but it catches your interest. In future slides you only need have one portion of that image to carry the theme forward—the heels or the raptor's tail for example. Whatever element you devise can be carried over to your handouts and in your advertising.

Besides using a theme, keep your slides easy to read.

- Use bullet points to break up long blocks of text.
- Use different colors or fonts to highlight important information.
- Use concise language.

And now a word from those of us who view eye charts with suspicion (or not at all). *Use readable type.* Not everyone can spot a fly on the wall at two hundred yards. Tiny type is not your friend, especially if the room you're working is wide and deep. Folks all the way in the back won't see a thing, which inevitably leads to fidgeting and grocery lists. Keep the finer details of the presentation on your notes, not on the slides. You are the teacher, after all, not PowerPoint.

And while we're talking about electronic presentations, please verify your equipment is in working order. If you're using your own computer, is there an electrical plug nearby and an extension cord available to bridge that gap if needed? If you are using a remote, does it need fresh batteries? Do you have all the correct computer cables, electrical adapters and software?

Besides rehearsing your workshop to work out the verbal bugs, run through the technical aspect of the class as well. Faulty equipment or technical ineptitude give the impression you're disorganized and that impression will bleed over into your teaching, no matter how hard you've worked to polish the actual course content. And of course, always have a backup plan in case the technology croaks.

INDULGING YOUR INNER THESPIAN

Today an elf, tomorrow Robin Hood! You, too, can be a walking, talking prop simply by showing up in costume. If presenting a workshop on research, I might wear my 1880's Victorian outfit. If my workshop is on how to write medieval Celtic fantasy, I'd break out my corset, my 'fairy' skirt and my hooded cloak. Wearing unusual garb indicates that this presentation will be different because you're different.

Christopher Paolini, the teenage wunderkind who penned *Eragon*, wasn't afraid to channel his inner thespian while he promoted his self-published book. Wearing medieval garb, he made over one-hundred-thirty personal appearances. His age and his costume immediately resonated with his audience and helped the book find a home with Knopf/Random House, who paid him a handsome half-million-dollar advance for the rights.

On the personal side, some outfits are too uncomfortable to wear for any length of time. Be sure your costume allows you to move with ease. Can you sit, bend over and take a breath? All of those, especially the latter, are important so your presentation doesn't suffer from the effects of your costume. Being different doesn't mean being blue, unless you're dressed as a Smurf.

And now for a wee note of caution. Alas, depending on who is hosting your course, costumes are not always welcome. There are some who find leather, chain mail and sharp pointy objects a bit over the top even if you are slated to teach about how to write fantasy. Often schools have rules about weapons and take violations very seriously. Play it by ear. If all the lights are green, go for it. Nothing captures attention quite like a costume married with a snappy presentation.

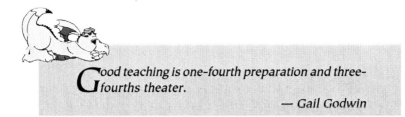

Good teaching is one-fourth preparation and three-fourths theater.

— *Gail Godwin*

And This Workshop is Brought to You By....

What could be better than finding a sea of bright faces ready to hear your words of wisdom? Having someone else pay to get them there. To successfully promote your class, you need to know your potential audience and target that demographic through an appropriate advertising medium while trying to find nifty ways to avoid spending your own hard-earned cash. In other words, do it on the cheap.

In the case of adult education classes, the host (usually the parks and recreation department or the school district) places a free listing in their course catalog. The catalog is then mailed to addresses throughout the metro area. None of that costs you a dime. That's part of the reason they often split the course fee with you. To augment their efforts, I always pick up extra copies and hand them to anyone who sounds remotely interested.

Use your personal website to good advantage by listing future courses. I have a special page for my workshops that includes descriptions, costs, location and how folks can register.

Creating flyers for your course is as easy as using your computer's word processor. You can either print them at home or at your local copy center. Be aware that some venues require approval for any advertising you create so allow yourself enough time to get their okay. Sometimes it's just easier to ask for extra copies of their flyers or catalogs, which most are willing to provide.

If your writing course is aimed at senior citizens, leave those flyers at senior centers, assisted living residences and where local writers congregate. If you're presenting a workshop for a special interest group, ask permission to advertise in their monthly newsletter at no charge. If you're charging for the course, offer to rebate back a certain percentage of the registrations as a donation to the society in return for the gratis publicity.

If your workplace has a community bulletin board, tack up a notice that includes your website address so your fellow employees can find out more about the course without impinging on work time. This will keep the boss a happy camper and still allow you to reach a new pool of potential students.

Conventions and conferences offer free advertising in the form of their flyers, mailers and their website. If pre-convention media interviews can be arranged, be sure to capitalize on the opportunity to swell the ranks of your audience. Also be sure to leave flyers at other conventions you attend.

Place course information in your neighborhood newsletter, at the local library or at your place of worship. But wait a minute, you say, why would the neighbors or the folks three pews away care about my workshop? Because nearly everyone harbors a desire to write a book. A good number of folks have a dust-bunny entombed manuscript under their bed or in a closet stashed behind the bowling trophies. Writing courses have universal appeal. The further you cast your net, the more students you'll catch.

BAITING YOUR HOOK

How you describe your workshop is as important as where you advertise it. Note the difference between the following course descriptions.

Plotting Class—A four-hour course on plotting.
No skill level required. Handouts will be available.
    —Or—
Oh Plot, Where Art Thou?—
Students will learn how to plot their current
work-in-progress. All skill levels accepted.
 Come prepared to work!

The first description lacks punch and includes a negative (no skill level required). It sounds like you're going to give them a handout and send them on their merry way. The next description is closer to the mark. The value of the course (plotting their current work-in-progress) is stated up front. "All skill levels" sounds positive and the "Come prepared to work!" adds a note of enthusiasm and hints the course will not be boring. The title only reinforces that.

Writing catchy course descriptions does not come easily and takes a fair amount of practice. Once you've mastered the technique, you can make any workshop sound like a once-in-a-lifetime event.

A CAVEAT

Who hosts the course is as important in determining your advertising strategy as where it is being held. Mindful of community sensibilities, I would not offer a class entitled "No Virgins Need Apply: How to Write Scorching Sex Scenes" in the adult education venue or at a local church, despite the fact it would probably be standing room only. I would readily offer the same course at a convention or to a local writer's group.

How about a course entitled "Interspecies Sex?" Offered by multiple award-winning fantasy and paranormal author P.C. Cast, the class teaches, "How to make believable intimate scenes between humans and fantasy characters." Cast pulls no punches. "I don't shade my presentations. I let [my audience] know the subject is inappropriate for those under 18 or those who might be offended by a frank discussion of sexuality." Once that warning has been issued, she's free to rock-n-roll. It's no surprise her workshops are always well attended.

It's best to go with your gut as to what is appropriate and what might not pass muster. When in doubt, ask. If you're still concerned, have the hosting organization sign off on the course content. Then you're free to teach as you see fit.

Word O'Mouth

People compare notes; it's part of our nature. If we enjoyed a restaurant or a movie, we talk about the experience. For an author, having a bookstore clerk "hand sell" your book is a dream come true. I found my dentist, chiropractor and massage therapist because of personal referrals. Why should your workshop be any different?

If you've done your job and offered an excellent learning experience, the students will want to talk about it. To facilitate that desire, I do the following at the end of each class:

- Thank them for their participation.
- Tell my students when my next class will be offered and give them a handout with the course particulars.
- Ask them to spread the word.
- Ask them to tell the hosting organization (the adult education department, convention, college, etc.) they enjoyed the course.

I've had students immediately register for another class. I've also acquired new students based on personal recommendation. Word of mouth works. Be sure to add it to your arsenal.

Audience Management 101

Audiences are usually a well-mannered lot: attentive, patient and keen to learn what you have to teach. The trick is to keep them that way. To that end, there is a formula you should memorize:

NUMB BUNS = NUMB BRAINS

The longer your students sit, the less aware they become. We've all hunkered down though long lectures or sermons while our brains idled in screensaver mode.

At least once per hour, have your students stand and move around. They can chat amongst themselves, visit the restroom; it doesn't matter, just as long as they're not sitting. A five-minute break can help recharge their batteries and keep them focused on the workshop, not the clock. If your course extends over a meal, allow for what I call "kindergarten syndrome." After a snack, little people roll out their mats and take a nap. Adults would love to do the same. Try to offer more upbeat material after a meal and schedule frequent breaks to prevent postprandial lethargy.

Does the thought of talking in front of an audience frighten you witless? Consider attending Toastmasters, an international organization dedicated to helping the presentation-challenged. Started in 1924, Toastmasters offers a supportive environment to help you learn how to deliver great presentations, give and receive constructive evaluations, conduct meetings and become a better listener.

HTTP://WWW.TOASTMASTERS.ORG/

CLOWNS TO THE LEFT OF ME,
JOKERS TO THE RIGHT....

Most students are quiet, respectful and see no reason to challenge the teacher's authority. Occasionally you will encounter someone who is disruptive for any number of reasons:

1) The Know-It-All. This person honestly believes they know far more about your topic than you do, but somehow through the whimsy of the gods they're not teaching the class. Still, they feel compelled to hijack the class with their own pearls of wisdom. The key is to integrate the Know-It-All into the group, allowing them to impart their knowledge without ceding control. I've run into such students and it's difficult to rein in their enthusiasm to demonstrate how much they know. Tactfully mention that others need time to express their views. As a last resort, have a private conversation during one of the breaks pointing out that not all of the students are at Know-It-All's level and so could he/she lighten up a little so the others can catch up.

2) The Oh-So Clueless. This person just doesn't get what you're saying and the more information you give them, the more helpless they become. Scolding will only upset these folks, so gently guide them along even if it is evident they're not fully digesting the workshop material. It is vital that you not "dumb down" the course to accommodate one person. If it becomes plain that the student is just not on the same wavelength, allow them the option to take the course at another time after you've supplied them some homework to bring them up to speed.

3) The Chaos Generator. We all have hectic days. Some people have hectic lives and manage to spread that erratic energy around them without realizing it. If you have one student who seems to attract "drama," it is vital not to let them distract the other students. You may try having the class take a few deep breaths, rolling their shoulders, followed by a writing exercise that has them pen a paragraph or two about a quiet, restful location they've visited. Both tasks should help settle the unfocused energy. If your Chaos Generator continues to unnerve the group, insist on keeping the workshop on topic and on schedule. Hopefully, the student will fall under your spell and the disruptions will dissipate.

Not all of us are able to play well with others. If you've tried to negotiate with a problem student and all your efforts have failed, you may need to offer that individual a refund for the course and show them the door. Your first priority is to insure that your students have a good experience. If that means reducing the class by one to achieve that goal, then take that step as diplomatically as possible. Then return to the job at hand as if nothing had happened. Your students will thank you.

Teacher Tips
1) Feed your brain—eat a well balanced meal before your workshop.
2) Keep hydrated to aide your vocal cords.
3) To avoid hypoglycemia, bring "finger foods" that will maintain your blood sugar at a decent level so your brain can think.
4) Don't lock yourself in front of the microphone or sit at a desk for the entire presentation. Use a lavaliere microphone and roam at will.
5) Take breaks at the same time your students do.
6) Remember to have fun!

TAKING THE SHOW ON THE ROAD

—OR—

WHADDYA MEAN I SHARE A ROOM WITH THE FIRE EATERS?

If you are blessed with a guardian angel that looks out for you every time you go "on tour," slip that little cherub a pound of chocolate every now and then. Most of us don't have such luck.

New Location = (Murphy's Law)2

I like checklists. There's something reassuring about them, even as things go off the rails. To keep my head straight, I create a list for each new site. That way I know if I've missed something that will come back to bite me in the workshop down the line. Design your own and check off the tasks as you go.

For example:

Course Location: United Martian University (UMU)
Workshop: Where Spielberg Got it Wrong—How to Write Realistic Battle Scenes
Date/Time: 7/4/2010, 1-5 pm (Room 2354 Bradbury Building)
Liaison's name and contact information: Ms. Eureveni XII

Check off as completed:

__ Date, time, location verified
__ Materials List Sent—LCD projector and screen, dry erase board, markers, lavaliere microphone, thirty foot electrical cord
__ Hotel reservations confirmed (confirmation #_____)
__ Plane tickets ordered __ Tickets received
__ Determine number of registrants & assemble workshop packets
__ Workshop materials shipped to contact (Tracking #_____)
__ Workshop materials received?
__ Follow-up on Materials List request

Arrive at least one hour early to inspect the site. If the contact person is mysteriously absent (it happens), find yourself someone who can act on his/her behalf. All the while, remember the Golden Rule of Workshops: Your Students Come First.

What if the room just isn't suitable? Water dripping out of the ceiling? Bugs crawling around? (Yes, this has happened.) An energetic gospel group in the next room singing praises to the heavens, complete with booming bass guitar? (Ditto.) Or the media star who had his rabid fans shouting and clapping every time he cleared his throat? (Don't remind me.)

Overcoming adversity is a sign of a pro and often that requires the bargaining skills of a Bedouin camel trader. Another class room not available? How about a board room or someone's very roomy office? If the weather's pleasant, take your class outdoors and work off the paper copies of your PowerPoint presentation you placed in each student's packet. Think outside the box and find solutions. Often, it's easier to act and then apologize later.

Let's fast forward—you survived the disaster with aplomb. Once the students have departed, how do you handle your displeasure? Tempting as it is to pummel your location contact senseless with a Thesaurus while shouting like a Vogon, that won't get what you want—an apology and a promise to make it better the next time.

Barring those "Act of Deity" situations which are not really anyone's fault, it is important that your contact understand that they owe you big time. If the contact seems ambivalent, work your way up the food chain. If the indifference is institutional, take that as a hint and find a new place to offer your workshops.

Got Sunscreen, Will Travel

The gentle rolling waves, the sea breezes, the sound of a blender concocting some fruity brew that demands a miniature umbrella. Sound inviting? It does to me. Cruise ships, in particular, offer on-board *edutainment* for their passengers, usually during the days the ship is sailing from one port to another. Cruise lines know that happy passengers are less likely to mutiny and they plan accordingly by offering classes that appeal to a cross section of the cruising population. If you can present a short talk on an interesting aspect of writing (and meet the cruise line's criteria), you can make the sea journey at reduced rates. How reduced? It depends on the cruise line.

There are, of course, a few caveats. PowerPoint presentations are pretty much the norm. Coupled with your nifty slides, you need to provide *edutainment,* that certain panache that beguiles your fellow travelers and makes them pleased they chose XYZ Cruise Line to go to Bora Bora instead of the ZZZ line to Vladivostok.

Depending on the cruise line, most of the presentations are 30 minutes in length with an additional 15 minutes for questions. To earn your keep you will be required to offer three or four of these talks (each unique) during the course of a week-long cruise. Your responsibilities don't end there, however. As you are a "guest" of the cruise line, you need to mingle, answer questions and generally be approachable during the entire voyage. Some cruises require more comprehensive responsibilities: post-lecture sessions to allow passengers to ask detailed questions and hospitality hours that may feature a general topic as their focus.

Cruise lines have specific codes of conduct for their guests and excessive drinking, use of illegal substances and rowdy behavior will have you marooned on an island faster than Captain Jack Sparrow, minus the rum.

The positives definitely outweigh any potential negatives. Though cruise lines do not want you selling your books directly to the passengers, you can make arrangements to have copies placed in the ship's gift shop. Your name is touted on the daily activities sheet and the on-board cable network. For example, when Cindy Daniel, author of the *Death Warmed Over Mystery Series*, served as Special Interest Lecturer on a Celebrity Cruises ship, she was thrilled with the publicity she received. "Having my video on the ship's in-room cable loop was a great form of advertising. I was reaching all 3000 passengers a dozen times a day."

What sorts of topics play well to a general audience? Daniel reported, "Knowing I was part of the entertainment and enrichment series there was a lot more pressure. I didn't want anyone to have a bad experience." She said she purposely chose topics that zeroed in on what everyone wants to know about being an author: *Finding Your Writing Style, How to Get Published* and recounting her own personal journey in *My Road to Publishing*.

THEME CRUISES

On a grander scale, "theme" cruises are tailored to reach a specific "niche" market. Whether the theme is baseball, quilting or writing, specialty cruises are a tremendous draw. If you make the cut as a guest, you could find yourself rubbing elbows with some of the biggest authors in your field. Again, you are a "celebrity" and owe your allegiance to the cruise line and your fellow passengers. If you favor emulating a prima donna, stay home. But if discussing the finer points of Tolkien or debating who your favorite fantasy author is while you glide toward a tropical island paradise appeals to you, consider theme cruising and pack those bags.

Hitch Your Workshop to a Star: Sixth Star Entertainment & Marketing in Ft. Lauderdale serves as an entertainment resource for cruise lines and resorts. To learn more about their requirements and the types of Specialty or Destination speakers they seek, visit www.SIXTHSTAR.COM

THE INTERNET ATE MY HOMEWORK

For those who prefer to remain at home and not schlep their suitcases from city to city, the Internet provides an excellent medium for online education. Online courses offer many benefits, both for the teacher and the student, not the least of which is convenience.

Anyone who has access to a computer and receives e-mail can take your course, whether they're in Belgrade or on a sheep station in Australia. At any hour of the day a student can log on and work through course material. If life intrudes, the student can usually catch up without too much hassle. Daily lessons can be printed and saved for future reference. No more writer's cramp.

Cyber-courses run the gambit in length from a few days to a couple of months, depending on the topic. As an instructor, you can assign homework and then review the lessons in an electronic format. Assignments can easily be posted for class critique, building a sense of community.

On the flipside, online courses present unique challenges. Someone, preferably not the instructor, should be in charge of organizing registration, collecting fees (via the mail or PayPal) and be responsible for any Internet hassles that arise (missing emails, overzealous spam filters, etc.)

There are issues for the instructor, as well. Unlike a class that runs from noon to five on a given day, an online course is virtually 24/7. Students check their e-mail at different intervals so the instructor may be barraged by questions and comments at all hours of the day. And some cyber-classes can field up to 100 students, which can mean a lot of email traffic, even if half of your students lurk in the background. You must be prepared to spend a considerable amount of time reviewing your emails, answering questions, responding to comments and posting new lessons.

Some students are more visually oriented than others and that will require you to occasionally include a diagram to illustrate a particular lesson. Explanations need to be thorough, but not too verbose. Condense your content to help highlight the important points. And have no fear: you can be assured your students will let you know if you're not hitting the mark. The fifty e-mails you will receive will be your first clue.

GEE, LADY, THE CLASS WAS GREAT, BUT....

Everybody is a critic, especially if they paid money for something. Your writing workshop won't be any different. The only way to fine tune your presentation is to solicit honest feedback. The "you were awesome" comments are great for buffing the ego, but not that helpful in structuring future classes. I ask for input, usually in the form of written evaluations. I also allow the students to remain anonymous so that I can be assured of honest feedback.

I review those evaluations before my next class, incorporating suggestions while polishing my delivery. I constantly update my material to keep it current. The publishing industry is always in a state of flux and today's writers need to stay ahead of the curve.

On a personal level, I consider a class successful if each of the students finds at least one useful piece of information that will transform their writing journey. Whether that's coming to grips with point-of-view or how to create a story arc that holds a reader's interest to the last page, my goal is to give my fellow authors workable tools to hone their craft.

A FINAL THOUGHT...

When a student masters a difficult concept, you grow along with them. When you hear they've sold their first short story or novel, that's a feeling that's hard to top. You won't be the sole reason for their success, but your guidance helped them a little further on their journey.

After all, someone taught you along the way. It's time to return the favor.

Shouting From The Mountain:
MAKING THE MOST OUT OF TALK SHOW APPEARANCES
BY SUMMER BROOKS

I love reading. I feel wonder and joy when I discover a story that pulls me in completely, a tale that makes me feel like an observer living in that world. I love the illusion drawn by making me feel as if I'm the protagonist's silent confidant. Best of all, I love flipping through page after page of luxurious, velvety-rich prose that can actually make me forget I'm reading.

Finding a book that can do these things is like finding a treasure; a precious gem I can enjoy again and again. The challenge is in finding the gems that might be overlooked in the flood of new and reprint titles engulfing bookstore shelves every month. Even I need help keeping track of what's coming out next, given the sources I keep in contact with and the outlets I follow. It's easy to imagine how hard a time casual readers might have in finding a wonderful book to read.

So what can you do to help get your book noticed in the crowd?

One suggestion: find a media niche in common with your story, a place that would show an interest in your story if they knew about it. Once you find that place, talk to them about your book. Talk passionately, talk hard, talk soft, talk true. Talk about your book with the same love that drove you to write it. Help them to want to talk it up, too.

You have to be dedicated to spreading the word far and wide, because it isn't enough to get the word about your book out to one or two outlets. Targeted publicity for your book is just as important as finishing and selling it for publication. The new economics of publishing shows that good publicity might be more important than most new authors realize, and not just because of the many books and other diversions competing for any potential readers' attentions.

Published authors already know that if a previous book didn't generate enough bucks or buzz, there's a strong chance the publisher won't be as interested in repeating the process for the next book. In fact, unless the publisher truly believes that your book could be their next smash hit, the chances of it being carefully guided through their publishing mazes and supported by the full might of their marketing machines are slim.

So take some initiative and find out what help you can provide. If you're with a publishing house that has a dedicated publicity team, find out what you can do to work with them. Ask them what you can do to actively help spread the word about your book.

Now, some people might tell you to let the publicists do their job without interfering, but I know from experience that at times, author input is called for. There were publicity departments at several major publishing houses had no idea that *Cover to Cover* existed, much less knew that it was dedicated to promoting new science fiction, fantasy and horror novels, despite the fact that the show had been on the air for 3 years when I came on board. Some small press imprints were just as hard to talk to about the show at first, but with some persistence, it paid off.

If you don't have the luxury of a good publicist, then you have far more work ahead of you. And by work, I mean that you have to do more than just put together a slick website, submit a link and a blurb to a few dozen search engines, then sit back and wait for the eager reading public to come find you. I mean you should plan to pound the proverbial pavement. I mean search for and bring your publicist a handful of marketing leads they may not previously have been aware of. And whatever you do, be diligent about following up on the opportunities they bring you.

Step up and make a positive pest of yourself if you feel the need; remember, it's all for a good cause—you and your book!

Now that I'm done with that little soapbox, let's get to some of the fun stuff. There's a wide variety of marketing strategies any author can pursue—mainstream and alternative, viral and underground—but some of these ideas are covered in other sections of this book. I'm going to focus on two closely related outlets: talk radio shows and podcasts.

Radio-related promotions could be one of the easiest and least expensive ways to get news and information out to a large number of potential readers. The first challenge lies in finding out if your book and the audience of the shows you're considering are a good fit. Since we're focusing on readers and potential readers of fantasy novels, it makes our search for potential outlets simpler. But that doesn't mean that getting to the right station or show contacts will be just as simple.

Finding the Shows that Fit Your Work
Radio Guides
With so many new portable media technologies hitting the market, and so many ways to get connected to the Internet, it's easier to search the richest resources to help you find the best radio programs and podcasts to approach about your book. Sometimes, though, too many choices can make it harder to find the best fits for your needs.

There are web directories that specialize in national and international radio station listings, and most of them maintain links to the websites of the stations they track.

The major radio station guides that are good starts are:

Radio Guide USA	HTTP://WWW.RADIOGUIDE.COM/
Radio Locator	HTTP://WWW.RADIO-LOCATOR.COM/
About.com:	HTTP://RADIO.ABOUT.COM/OD/
	RADIODIRECTORIES/
State History Guide	HTTP://WWW.SHGRESOURCES.COM/
	RESOURCES/RADIO/

It's also just as easy to find a radio guide for the state or province you live in by entering the right combination of keywords.

For example:

New York Radio Guide (NYC radio)

HTTP://WWW.NYRADIOGUIDE.COM/

So pick your geographical area and do a quick search, because you never know when that information can come in handy for a book tour or special promotional trip.

If you plan to travel out of your home area to any conventions or conferences where you'll be a guest or panelist, find out if the organizers have local media contacts, or know of any genre-friendly shows or show hosts in the area. If they don't, try asking your publicist if they know anyone in the area you're traveling to… you never know which people know each other from their college drinking days.

It might take some extra digging to find something relevant, if you find anything at all. Most major metro areas have a book-related show of some type lurking on the dial at odd hours of the weekend, and even a casual mention on local talk shows in two or three cities could be that extra nudge your story needed to get noticed.

You could also look for local Book Festivals. There are city, state and regional Book Festivals all over, and most of them have media sponsors. Those media sponsors are likely to have some involvement with literacy and promoting books, making them the best first place to ask if they'd be interested in hearing about you and your novel.

The one drawback is for shows out of your area. If they don't have streaming audio of their programming available across the Internet, there might not be an easy way for you to listen to the show for yourself and find out if you and your book would be of interest to that show's target audience. Ingenuity and improvisation might be called for in this case, depending on how creative you want to get in spreading the word.

Podcasts

Delving into the world of podcasts might sound just as daunting as going into the world of broadcast radio, but it isn't. Your work might even end up being a little easier. With a podcast, there are usually fewer levels of contacts to make your way through in order to reach the person who can make things happen. In fact, you're more likely to end up talking directly to the fantasy geek whose interest you want to pique on the first email or phone call.

Since that person or group started a podcast to share and spread the love for their interest, you know the geek was strong with them. Listen to a few promos and a few shows, and then decide for yourself if a particular show would be a good place to talk about your book.

If you can't find a podcast that would be a good fit for an interview in their format but does have the right listening audience , consider making a 30-second audio promo for your book and asking the podcaster to play it on their show. Promos and reciprocal links are essential in podcast show notes, so a short mention and a link can be a wonderful placement in a popular show.

For our needs here, the best guides for locating podcasts are:

Podcast Alley	HTTP://WWW.PODCASTALLEY.COM/
Podcast Pickle	HTTP://WWW.PODCASTPICKLE.COM/
Yahoo! Podcasts	HTTP://PODCASTS.YAHOO.COM/
iTunes	HTTP://WWW.ITUNES.COM/

The best part about podcasts is that it's easy for you to listen to a couple of episodes of the shows you're interested in. You can find out in a few hours whether or not a particular show is the one you've been looking for.

PREPPING FOR THE INTERVIEW

In just about every situation, it's a good idea to make sure that the relevant people involved with the show you'll be talking with has copies of your book well in advance of the show. You can send either advance reading copies or review copies of your book a few weeks before your interview. It's important to cover this detail because some outlets provide book reviews along with the author interviews. The show may also be able to put a promotional blurb on their website, or air a 15-second promo spot during earlier episodes of the show for your book, so don't be afraid to ask about the possibilities.

Here's a moderate but not all-inclusive checklist of questions to ask and items to consider prior to your interview. You don't need to follow all of them, but this list can be a good place to start working from. Add in different points that work best for you and subtract any of the ones from this list that don't.

For more on interviews and press releases, see Jennifer Hagan's chapter The Mighty Pen: Press Releases and Communicating with Print Media!

Will the Interview Be Live or Tape-Delayed?

Finding out if the interview will be broadcast live, or if it'll be recorded and edited for later broadcast is a key bit of information to have. Most local radio shows might run a segment like this live, such as during a morning or afternoon drive-time talk show, or they might make a mention of a signing event during a popular drive-time or lunchtime music show. However, most of the specialty and niche shows whose topics would be have a better-fitting target audience for your novels are syndicated, and syndicated shows are more likely to be pre-recorded.

The same scenario could apply for satellite radio shows, and would definitely apply to podcasts. With those shows, your interview would be recorded and produced before being cut together with other segments to create the final product that everyone hears at a later date.

How Long Will the Interview Run?

Find out ahead of time how long the interview will last. Most producers should tell you how much time will be needed when they schedule the interview with you, but in case they don't, be sure to ask.

A typical morning variety radio talk show that airs on the standard AM/FM frequencies might consist of a 5-minute segment, where you'd be able to talk about your local appearance along with a brief mention of who you are, and a quick overview of the book.

However, many of the specialty or niche shows follow different formats. For instance, some shows might plan to run their interviews in 10- or 20-minute segments, and use them as just one element of a longer show. Other types of shows may run longer interviews, like a 40- to 50-minute segment to be used as the primary element of a show. It all depends on what kind of interview you feel can best suit your style and energy levels.

Podcasts can follow a similar breakdown, so ask as many questions as you feel you need to get comfortable with their expectations from you when the time comes.

Will This Be a Canned Interview or a Free Form Interview?

People who are more familiar with a press release and public relations firm-style interview session might want to have such an agency prepare and distribute a list of questions that they'd prefer to have the interviewers strictly follow. This has the advantage of helping the author to stay close to the commercial marketing message the firm wants to send out about the book. While some authors might be more comfortable with that format, it's not something I care for personally. I think it drains the life and spontaneity out of the interview before it's even begun, and that tends to create a less enjoyable interview atmosphere for the audience.

In the pre-arranged interview situation that the "canned questions" structure defines, listeners can often discern the back-and-forth pattern of "Question #1" and "Answer #1" that both the interviewer and the subject get quickly bored with. Some of those listeners and potential readers might also be disappointed by the appearance of keeping to a tightly-controlled session, especially if that's not the typical style found in the show format that they've become used to.

With a free-form interview, the questions come from the interest the interviewers have in the writer and the book, and are more likely to lead to unexpected places. This can include bringing up gold nuggets of history, or of back story, or some other hardly-known fact that will hook a listener and turn them into a new reader. Use the interview process to make your story come to life, and make the listeners eager to dive into the universe you've lovingly created.

But not following a script doesn't mean you can't guide the interview to go to a few places you need it to go. There may be a few key things you want to highlight from your book: key elements from your story, a few items of note about you and your background, or about any special situations regarding you and the marketing of your book, such as a unique promotion or contest. One of the most interesting things I came across in 2005 was a contest put together by Deborah LeBlanc. She ran a contest in conjunction with her book tour that was both promotional for two of her novels, and a promoting literacy campaign sponsored by area libraries in each stop she made during the tour. Her contest offered a top prize of $5000, but you had to have read the current book and the previous one in order to get the information necessary to win the prize.

When you're talking to the producer or the people doing the interview, ask if you can submit a handful of questions ahead of time that you'd like them to use. Try to keep those questions simple, to be used as guides rather than a script for the entire interview.

The well-timed use of a prepared question when the interview seems to have run aground is more organic, and aids the interview process instead of rigidly structuring it. The same result can be obtained when there's a need have the conversation gently guided back on point: just drop one in as necessary. The answers to those few questions might just be the ones to give the listeners a little more insight into the story you're hoping they'll go out and purchase and enjoy, or into you as the writer, which to some readers is the more intriguing aspect.

Will the Interviewers Have Read the Book Beforehand?

If the interview will be focused on your novel rather than any local appearances, try to find out if the interviewer will have had a chance to read your book before the interview. Sometimes it's not necessary, depending on the type of interview the show format allows for. If you're only on for a 15-minute slot, there may not be time to get into great detail about the book, so expecting the interviewer to read an 800-page epic less than a week before the interview can be unrealistic.

Depending on how far in advance the interview is scheduled, you or your publicist may be able to get review copies there in time for someone to read it. It's nice to have someone become familiar with the book and the story beyond the standard promotional sheets. That kind of familiarity can result in a more engaging interview, because the interviewer might be better able to come up with questions about story setting or characters or world characteristics that someone less-acquainted with the story might not think to ask.

If you know whether the interviewer will have read the book or in some other way have familiarized themselves with the book before the interview, try to find out if they will be asking any specific questions about the book that they'd like to have answered on the air. Of course, this brings into consideration whether or not you want to include answers or discussions that would be considered spoilers for the story.

The length of the interview would also be an indicator of whether or not spoilers may become part of the interview. A short, 5-minute interview will not be likely to include any of the deeper, probing questions that would spoil a plot twist or character resolution. But a 35-minute interview could easily go to depths that would cross into spoiler territory.

If you want to talk in detail about the story while still avoiding spoilers, write out some enticing events that would not risk ruining the enjoyment of the story. You could refer to your notes and mention them, and it would still be effective in luring in those potential readers.

WORKING THE INTERVIEW

The act of going through the interview still makes some writers nervous, anxious and sometimes nauseous. If this is the case for you, the first thing to remember is: you don't have anything to worry about! Just breathe and get down to the fun of the interview.

Remember, you're a published writer, and they're talking to you for any number of reasons. It could be because you and your book are starting to generate some word-of-mouth buzz, or it could just be that you were persistent and kept bugging them until they scheduled you on the show. Whatever works!

If your energy is high and you sound like you're having fun, the interviewers will pick that up, and all of you will start to feed off each other's high energy levels. When that happens, everyone sounds like they're having fun, and the interview will be livelier and more interesting to listen to.

That lively intensity is something that audiences will also pick up on, and in turn they'll start to listen more closely to what everyone has to say. Enthusiasm about the book, about the series, or just about what the author has to say will carry over to listeners. By the end of the interview, you want the audience to be saying to themselves, "Hey, I've gotta check this book out!" And since encouraging more people to buy the book is the goal of this game, this is a very good thing.

And who knows? Maybe after they enjoy the book, they might turn around and tell their friends about the book, or even go out of their way to tell casual online acquaintances to go check out the book. I've been on a number of mailing lists where every few months, someone will pipe up and ask for book recommendations, so why shouldn't your book be one that a few people offer up to the group?

Also, expect the unexpected, and take what seem to be setbacks in stride. Technical glitches and human error happen all the time. If the interviewers are calling you for the interview, and the call isn't on time, take a breath. There may have been delays from earlier interviews, or worse. There are also logistical differences between live interviews and pre-recorded ones, and between the ones done in a studio with the interviewers and the ones done over the phone.

Farpoint Media Studio is our home base. We record everything there, from shows to ads to promos for other shows, and that studio's lifeline is a high-speed Internet connection. Once, we had to reschedule an entire day's worth of interviews because a traffic accident took out a junction box in another part of town, taking out our Internet and phone with it. Quick wits and cell phones saved us from having 4 busy authors get testy from waiting around for us to call.

Simple human error also comes into play. We missed an interview with Gene Wolfe because I lost his phone number the day we were supposed to call him, and there was no one at the publisher's offices to contact on a weekend to ask for it. My bonehead, but all was forgiven and life went on.

One other note for the unexpected category: be prepared for a question about your story that might surprise you. Even if you don't have an answer, don't panic and "um-uh" your way through an answer that you think might sound deep or clever. Be honest, and think fast on your feet as you go! Both you and the interviewer might learn something different, and good banter that's organic and heartfelt can also get potential readers interested.

I've seen plenty of emails and comments come in about our interviews saying just that. I've seen messages from listeners thanking us for talking in a direction they didn't expect about a book they were familiar with, and I've seen messages from listeners who couldn't wait to go buy the book because the interview was so engaging. I am always happy to pass on notes and comments like that to the authors.

Closing Info for the Interview

Most good interviewers will repeat the pertinent information: author's name, most recent book that's already out or coming out, and any additional sources such as the author's website, or a website dedicated to the book or series. Just in case, be prepared to mention a website that listeners can refer to, be it your publisher's website or your own, or one specifically designed for your book or series. Podcast show notes are ideal for an abundance of links like this.

Use your appearance on the show to your best promotional advantage. If you're on a local or regional show, or a show with a wide local reach for the area you'll be appearing in, make sure you mention any signings or other appearances in that show's broadcast area that will be coming up in the near future. Ask on-air if anyone who heard the interview plans to stop by your appearance to mention that they heard about it from the radio show. It's a good double plug for the show and for you.

After the Interview

The interviewers might chat with you for a minute or so before going on-air or recording, to let you know what'll be going on during the interview. *Pay attention here* since there may be some key instructions about how they want to close the interview.

It's truly funny to watch Michael and Evo's reactions after someone they've been talking to hangs up right after saying the on-air goodbye, especially when I know how much they wanted to talk more afterwards!

Some show hosts might not have the time to chat afterwards, and some might, but give them the chance to close things out first. Listen for them to say something like "We're clear," and wait for the host or the producer to finish up the call. If you hang up early, you might miss out on a compliment, a request for more information, or even an open invitation to come back on the show!

Depending on time constraints, after the interview would also be the best time to ask more questions, ones that can help you make the best possible use of your time spent with the show. If you're working with a live show, there might not be any time to ask the interviewers anything, but see if you can stay on the line with the show producer or whoever may be running the switchboard and the computers, and ask them.

If that's not possible, you can always send a follow-up email, thanking them for the interview, and ask these questions in that email.

Time constraints aren't likely to be an issue when dealing with podcasters, but it can't hurt to ask before launching into the million-questions phase.

When Will the Interview Be Aired?

Find out when and where the show featuring your interview will be aired or published. Forward any information about the show's airdates as far and as wide as you feel comfortable with. Post updates about it to the message boards where fans of your writing or ones dedicated to topics similar to your story's genre or theme hang out .

If it's on a local show, see if you can provide airdates for any articles that might mention your signing or appearance. Get those times listed in the events calendars in the local papers and magazines.

If it's on a syndicated show, find out which areas will air the show, and how often. While it's not highly likely, see if you can find out if the network or the individual stations are going to run promos mentioning that you'll be on the upcoming shows.

If it's on a podcast, find out when the show will be available online, and for how long. Make sure to check back with their website after the show you're featured on goes live, and get the direct link for it to pass around.

And by all means, tell your publisher or their publicity staff, if they weren't involved in landing the interview. They enjoy hearing about developments like this, and may go so far as to discover if other writers from their imprint are welcome on the show or podcast as well.

Will copies of the interview or the show be provided for me?

If you're working with a broadcast or satellite radio show, ask if they can provide a copy of the show for you, either before or after it's aired. Also ask if the material from the interview is free for you to reuse in any of your marketing materials. Having a good pull quote from a show host or an audio review could make your publicist happy, and putting the recording on your own website for fans that aren't in that show's broadcast area is a step above that people will notice.

In the case of a station or network that provides live streaming of their shows, that gets a little trickier, but still ask. If you're working with a podcast, find out when you'll be able to get a copy of that show online.

No matter which outlet carries your interview, distribute the information about the release date to as many outlets as you can, especially to those you think would be interested in hearing an interview about your newest novel.

How Can I Use That Interview?

Fans become fans by having a cocktail of minute details and a smorgasbord of choices to go where they can indulge in information overload. Help them, if you can! Just try to avoid doing something that results in a bad URL a few months later.

If you simply use a URL to a mention of the interview, or one to an actual audio recording of the interview, find out if that link will actually be there six months later. It might be worth it to save a copy of the show to your own website, but be prepared for any extra bandwidth costs that may ensue.

When more and more people know that you've been interviewed on the radio, it'll be much easier to arrange another one.

There is one bit of caution about distributing promotional information to message boards, though… don't spam the boards.

In case that wasn't clear enough: *Do not spam.*

Before you post any kind of promotional message, take an extra few minutes to read through any posted rules of etiquette. Each online community has varying rules, so repeat as necessary for each site where you'd like to post your interview notice.

Some forums don't allow promotional postings of any nature, but most have one specific topic or other special area dedicated for announcements and self-promotion notices.

Taking those few moments to check could potentially save you from months of aggravation from an online community that views your enthusiastic marketing announcement the same way city officials view graffiti.

Being on the receiving end of their irate reaction is an experience few souls intentionally seek out. It isn't worth the risk of losing your chance to make new fans before they've even read or heard about your work, at least not because your announcement didn't follow the standards of practice for their online home.

Will the Book Be Officially Reviewed as Well?
It can't hurt to ask if your book will be officially reviewed. Having a good review (or a controversial one) read on the show or posted on the show's website would make a good addition to your book's marketing package.

WRAPPING UP
As with most journeys of this type, all good things must come to an end. But that doesn't mean you're done yet!

Follow up is necessary. Find ways to let people know about the interview ahead of time, and find ways to keep people listening to it, even after it's been aired. Send updates of new works coming out as soon as you know about them. If you had fun, tell your other author friends about it, too!

Remember, radio takes you places, be it through music or through talk. Hop on for the ride yourself, and see how far it can take you and your book.

Birth of a Book Reviewer
WRITING AND RECEIVING BOOK REVIEWS
BY JOE MURPHY

Most writers start their first works with a passion, an idea so clear and bright, they feel if they don't get down what they have to say, they will burn alive from the inside out.

Such was my first book review. I was listening to The Dragon Page, an interview show for science fiction and fantasy authors. Evo Terra was singing the praises of Piers Anthony's *On a Pale Horse*. Evo spoke with such passion, promising so much, that I went out and bought the book that night, and finished it the next day.

And as I finished reading the last line of the last page, I decided at that moment to make it my life's ambition that no one else would ever read that atrocity ever again.

And so, on The Dragon Page's forum, my soul erupted onto the keyboard. I tapped into a fury and an eloquence that to this day I believe came from gods of old. One thousand words later, my rebuttal, my critique, my newly discovered life's foundation, uploaded into the Ethernet.

A couple of months later, someone hacked the forum, and it was lost forever. But at that point it didn't matter. The metamorphosis had already happened. I had started the post a simple audiologist, I had ended it a Book Reviewer.

And that's all there is to know about me. I have no degree in English, literature or publishing. An author who disagreed with my review of his book once asked me what qualifications I had to write reviews. I responded by asking him why he wasn't concerned about that before I wrote it. I'm just a guy who enjoys reading and writing about what I've read. I've learned a lot doing just that, and I hope I can pass something of benefit on to you.

Now that you know who I am, I'm going to tell you who you are. I wrote this chapter for the author who is being published for the first time, maybe the second. You want to get reviewed, but you have no idea where to submit your book, or how. I aim to show you what you need to do, whether you're published by a small or large press. I will also tell you what you need to do with your reviews once you get them.

WHY SHOULD YOU GET YOUR BOOK REVIEWED?

I was of two minds about writing this section.

It seems to me that very few new authors need encouragement in sending out their books to get reviewed. After spending months, if not years, researching, writing, rewriting and editing, authors are understandably proud of what they've accomplished. And what's the point of writing a novel if no one's going to read it? However, as thrilling as it can be to see someone else talk about your book, there are also practical reasons and goals to have in mind when soliciting reviews for your work.

Feedback

This is probably the main reason authors want to get reviewed. An author wants to know that someone other than her mother has read her book. There is no easier way to feel like you've hit the big time than to have a complete stranger write an essay about you... I mean, your book.

Of course, there is the possibility that the reviewer won't like it, but I think that is a relatively small fear for most new authors. The rush of creativity and optimism that carried them through the entire writing process seems to carry over after the book has been published. Most novels from first-time authors seem to come prefaced with cover letters and emails explaining how the debut novel by so-and-so is the best thing since Angelina Jolie in a tank top, and I would be a fool to deny myself the pleasure of reading it. The letters have a restrained earnestness that makes me believe they really mean it. If I weren't so jaded, their enthusiasm might be infectious.

If your first reviews are negative, I'll cover what to do a little later. If you're fortunate enough to receive a positive review, or several, of your work, bask in the glow for a bit, download and email the review to everyone you know, and then put that review to work.

Your Website

You have a website for your book, right? If you're a fantasy writer, a large percentage of your future fan base is going to be self-proclaimed geeks, and self-proclaimed geeks who surf the Web. If you don't have a website with a user-friendly domain name related to the title of the book or your name, get one. Then read on.

Dedicate one of the pages of your website to collecting reviews. The positive ones, if you want to make life easy on you, or both the positive and negative, if you wish to make life unnecessarily hard.

If you plan to post the entire review on your site, ask the author of the review first. Reviews, like all forms of writing, are copyrighted, so get the permission of the copyright owner, which will be either the reviewer or the publication. Make it clear that you will link back to their website, in a bit of cross-promotion.

If the review is very long, you may simply want to show the first few paragraphs, ending on a particular juicy sentence, then have a link to the full review, housed either on your site, or the reviewer's.

Whether you post the entire review, or just an excerpt, include the reviewer's rating of your work, the reviewer's name and the publication or website the reviewer works for.

Blurbs

Blurbs are one- or two-sentence quotes about your book.

Blurbs are marvelous little things. In less than a paragraph, they can often accomplish the same purpose as an entire review. They prove to the potential reader that someone other than your girlfriend read and enjoyed your book. If given by a popular author, celebrity, authority or publication, blurbs can add significant weight to your presentations and marketing.

Blurbs are often pulled straight from reviews. When Tee Morris published his second novel *Billibub Baddings and the Case of the Singing Sword*, he sent early copies to The Dragon Page and *Nth Degree* magazine. He took small segments from the reviews and used them as blurbs for his book cover and for his book listing on Amazon.com.

Your small press book is being printed as we speak, but you ain't got no blurbs to put on the cover? If your book is hardcover with a dust jacket, try to get your publisher to order a small run of dust jackets to begin with. Once you collect some reviews and blurbs, reprint the dust jackets with the blurbs on the back.

Blurbs are so effective that some authors blurb hunt. They ask anyone and everyone with the smallest amount of clout for a quote for their manuscript. Open up the books of some established authors, especially nonfiction authors, and the first three or four pages may be nothing but accolades from others in the same field.

Why are blurbs so useful? Versatility. They can be used as part of any form of promotion, including: your webpage, press releases, radio, television or Internet ads.

Using blurbs adds an air of professionalism to your promotion campaign. By professionalism, I'm not referring to a professional attitude to promoting your book, or working with your publisher and editor. That's a given. I'm talking about professionalism in the sense of making your product and presentation look as professional as possible when compared to other presentations.

The big publishing houses use reviews and blurbs in their promotions, so you should to. If you don't bother to do the same, your promotion will not appear as professional. Even if book sellers, interviewers and reviewers don't notice why the promotion is weak (and they most likely will), they'll still sense it.

Even if you're one of that rare breed who couldn't care less what others think and say, to generate any kind of buzz about your work, you will have to put your book in the hands of people who do. Be sure that what you hand them measures up to the other dozen or so packages they receive every week.

In fact, once you have a good blurb, you can use it for pretty much the rest of your career, even using it for other books. For instance, you've just completed book four of the *Tribellian Trifecta*. You've only managed to get one decent quote for the book. You use that at the top of the cover letter to the reviewers. Then, two thirds of the way down, you put: "Praise for the *Tribellian Trifecta*," and proceed to use quotes you've accumulated for Books One, Two and Three.

Recently on The Dragon Page, we interviewed author Cory Doctorow. His new novel *Someone Comes To Town, Someone Leaves Town* had just been released. With the review copy of the novel came a press release from Tor Books and the Sci Fi Channel, who had just teamed up to promote Sci Fi Essential Books.

The press release came with a "Praise For Cory Doctorow" insert of two pages, printed front and back. The insert contained forty-two blurbs about the author. Three of them actually pertained to *Someone Comes To Town, Someone Leaves Town*.

So mine your reviews for catchy and memorable quotes, and use them.

Creating Momentum

Books sell by word of mouth. Wait, I'm sorry, you didn't catch that last sentence? Let me say it again. Books sell by word of mouth! If your book opens to solid reviews from several sources, some of them with significant weight, that won't be enough. If you think the sales will start rolling in and you can retire to the white sand beaches of Mexico, you're kidding yourself.

Good reviews won't add up to a glut of sales, they will add up to some sales. If readers buy your book based on good reviews and like what they read, they will tell their friends, and maybe loan them their books. That's okay, because if the friends like the book, they will pass your name on to others, who will buy the books.

Ripples in a pond, grasshopper. Ripples in a pond.

Then, based on the strength of your reviews, you may land some print or radio interviews. Then some readers will hear your interview on The Dragon Page, or Writer's Roundtable, or Hour 25 Online, or read your review in <u>Nth Degree</u>, and a few more people will buy the book, who will then tell their friends, who will then tell their friends.

See the pattern here?

Reviews, like interviews, signings, touring and all other forms of marketing, are a way to get your name out there, get some people reading your stuff and let the word of mouth spread. And once your name starts getting mentioned, when the next book comes out, and the next favorable review comes out, not only will your past fans rush to get your book, but someone will come across the review, think to himself, "Oh, yeah, that's the author Suzie likes," and decide to finally give your book a try. Then, if he likes it, he'll tell his friends, who will tell his friends. And then you'll rule the world.

When Tor bought *Eye of the World* by Robert Jordan, they knew they had a potential hit on their hands. So they printed up the first two hundred and fifty pages or so and sent it out as a free book to reviewers and bookstore owners to build word of mouth before the book got published. Doubleday flooded the public with free copies of Dan Brown's *The Da Vinci Code*, and that seemed to work out well. *Harry Potter and the Philosopher's Stone* became a best seller in England based on word of mouth alone before coming to the States.

Books are sold by word of mouth, and reviews help generate word of mouth.

WHERE DO I GET MY BOOKS REVIEWED?

There are two types of review sources, Pre-publication review publications, and post-publication review publications.

Submitting to Pre-Publication Reviewers

Most of the big names in the book review field are pre-publication sources. These periodicals generate buzz about books that are soon to be released. They are important because they are read by librarians, book store owners, and other potential buyers.

Pre-publication reviewers generally need copies of the book at least three months before publication to be considered for review. Preferably four or five. They also tend to have policies against reviewing self-published authors, especially self-published fiction authors.

Despite their bias towards large, established presses, if you want to see your books in libraries and book stores, these are where you want to get your books reviewed.

I can already hear you asking, "How am I supposed to send my book in to get reviewed when it hasn't even been produced yet?" In order to submit your work to pre-publication reviewers, you need two things: a galley and a press release.

Galleys

A galley (or "Advance Reader's Copy") is essentially a preview version of your book. They are generally bound paperbacks with little or no cover art. Most of the galleys I see are plain white stock covers with the title of the book and author's name on the front, and some variation of this information on the front or back:

Book's title
Author's name
Category (Fantasy, Mystery, etc.)
Edition (i.e., First, Second, etc.)
The publication date
ISBN
Library of Congress Catalog Card Number
The publisher's name and contact information
The price
Number of pages—approximate if necessary
Number of illustrations
Trim Size (the book's dimensions. 6x9 inches, for example)
Contact name and information for the publicist
"Advance Reader's Copy: Not for sale."[1]

And don't forget to throw on a good blurb or two if you have them!

Many galleys are printed from earlier-than-final drafts of the book, and require a few more eyes to look at it before it is sent off for the first run of printing. These galleys should notify the reviewer of this on the front cover with the phrase: "Uncorrected Proof."

Where do you get your galleys? If you're working with a small press that cannot afford to print galleys, or your big press doesn't want to risk the investment on you, the untested author, there are print-on-demand services that specialize in galleys and "small-run" releases. Take, for example:

Crane Duplicating	WWW.BOUNDGALLEYS.COM
Country Press Inc.	WWW.COUNTRYPRESSINC.COM

You could, of course, shop around to different print-on-demand services to see who can deliver the best price, and ask if they can meet your needs.

Once you start price shopping, it'll be evident rather quickly that printing galleys is not an inexpensive investment. And it equates to something of a gamble, as you can send out the galleys and still not receive a review. And if you do receive a review, it could be negative. You could conceivably spend $500—$700 on bad publicity. What do you do when you can't afford bound galleys but still want to get reviewed? Colleen B. Lindsay from Ballantine Books offers this trick[2]:

Print off several copies of your finished manuscript. Print it in a format that is easy to read. The regular manuscript format is fine; avoid printing your 6x9 formatted book on 8.5x11 paper. On the cover page of each manuscript, have the book title and the author. On the second page, print the other essential information. Take the manuscripts to your local printing store and have them bound in comb bindings with heavy card stock covers. These are your galleys.

Many reviewers will accept these, but they are not necessarily the first choice, so be sure that the copies are easy to read and all the important information is presented clearly. Don't give the reviewer a reason to toss your manuscript aside.

Press Releases

A press release is like a coming-out party announcement for your book. The press release gives all the essential information about your book, and also gives the reviewer a summary of the book. This summary should, of course, not only provide information about the plot, but also entice the reviewer to choose your work over the other dozen he received this week alone. A sample press release follows:

Contact: Gwen Lastname, Dragon Moon Press publicist
520-555-0156 -or- gwen@dmp.com

JOSEPH MURPHY

BONK LOVE
"A novel of the future, of the past, of love, and murder"

Mr. Murphy certainly puts a new spin on the futuristic palentology shtick. Original storylines and a quick, light prose style makes this a great read at the beach.

— *Kansas Examiner*

Well, now i know who to nominate for a Hugo this year.
— *Robert J. Sawyer, author of Hominids and Calculating God*

Not just a "romance with fossils," bonk Love is hard science fiction at its best. Those who bitch about the current state of science fiction, I have just one word: Joseph Murphy

— *hardslghphi@hardassspacegeeks.com*

Joseph Murphy's daring debut novel blends the genres effortlessly in this futuristic, Paleolithic, cross-species, erotic, murder mystery. Bonk Love (Dragon Moon Press, Paperback, August 15, 2007) begins a saga that catapults the reader across the lengths of the galaxy and into the depths of the human heart.

The year is 3098 CCC-A. Adria Vog has made history as the first synthetic person to command a long-term space mission. Adria leads the voyage from nino to Nina, the sister planet that shares her world's orbit around a triad star system.

During the ten year archeological excavation, the team discovers the frozen body of Tagor, the biological predecessor to the Tribellian Race. the team thaws and revives the caveman, against the explicit orders of Space Station One.

Thus begins the dangerous love affair between Adria, the android scientist who faces reprogramming, and Tagor, who has become the target of religious extremists bent on keeping his discovery a secret.

Can love bridge the gaps of language, biology, and civil unrest?

About the Author:
JOE MURPHY spends his nine to five working as a freelance dry cleaner and part-time massage therapist. when he wears his other hat, he reviews books and movies for The Dragon Page radio program. Joe lives so very much alone in Tuscon, AZ with his stuffed animals George and Spike. You can read his reviews at www.dragonpage.com/reviews.html.

Visit Dragon Moon Press at www.dragonmoonpress.com

While there are services available that can write press releases for a fee, I don't see the need. There are plenty of websites available online that provide you all the information you need to write a serviceable press release. By merely entering "write a press release" into Google, I found dozens of sites showing how to write press releases of various kinds. Just keep the following in mind:

You preferably want to print the release on the publisher's letterhead. If that isn't possible, at least have the publisher's logo prominently displayed, and be sure you have permission to use it.

Be sure to have the publisher's contact information on the press release. Review the section on galleys for all the important information that should be found on the press release.

If you want to send out press releases but don't have any blurbs to display, send them without blurbs. As you begin to collect reviews, add quotes of reviews as blurbs to the releases.

Most press releases for books I see use double-spaced, indented paragraphs for the body. Single-spaced block paragraphs are not unheard of. The press release should be one to two pages in length.

Have a few trusted friends look over the release to check for errors or confusing wording. Just like your manuscript, your marketing can always benefit from a second, or third, set of eyes.

For more on writing press releases, check out Jennifer Hagan's chapter The Mighty Pen: Press Releases and Communicating with Print Media!

Pre-Publication Reviewers to Solicit

"Alright, already," I hear you screaming in your head. "I've got galleys. The ink on my press releases dries as we speak! Where the heck do I send these things?"

Settle down.

There are a number of places you want to send the book, but these are crucial: *Publishers Weekly, Kirkus Reviews, Library Journal* and Booklist. If you're writing a children's book, then *School Library Journal* as well.

Publishers Weekly

Basically, anything and everything to do with publishing gets covered in this magazine. Published 50 times a year, *Publishers Weekly* reviews approximately 7,000 books a year, and has a distributorship of around 25,000 publishers, libraries, book sellers, authors, and agents. Everybody involved in the publishing industry reads *Publishers Weekly*.

WWW.PUBLISHERSWEEKLY.COM

Kirkus Reviews

From the Website: "Kirkus Reviews, founded in 1933, is published 24 times annually and reviews, three to four months pre-publication, approximately 5,000 titles per year: fiction, mysteries, sci-fi, translations, nonfiction, and children's books. The reviews are reliable and authoritative, written by specialists selected for their knowledge and expertise in a particular field."

WWW.KIRKUSREVIEWS.COM

Library Journal

Mission Statement, from the website: "*Library Journal* is edited to provide a one-stop source for all the information that library directors, managers, and others in public, academic, and corporate/institutional libraries, need to run their libraries and make all their purchasing decisions... It combines analytical news reports, features, and columns on the cutting edge of library technology, policy, management, and other issues and includes some 7500 evaluative reviews annually of books, audiobooks, videos/DVDs, databases, systems, and more, written by librarians for librarians."

WWW.LIBRARYJOURNAL.COM

WWW.SCHOOLLIBRARYJOURNAL.COM

Booklist

Booklist is the journal of the American Library Association. They review approximately 7,000 titles a year. If you want your book in the library, you want a review here.

WWW.ALA.ORG/ALA/BOOKLIST/BOOKLIST.HTM

Post-Publication Reviewers

After all the aspirin you went through getting your manuscript into the hands of the pre-publication review sources, you'll find that sending your work to post-publication reviewers is a piece of cake. All you need are copies of your book, press releases, and money for postage.

The first source you should try is the local newspaper. A newly-published local author may be newsworthy to many small and mid-sized towns and cities. Getting a review, and working it in with a local signing at a local library or bookstore can get the media ball rolling.

The Internet also makes it easy to find reviewers for your work. You can find several general review sites and science fiction and fantasy review sites that have an appreciable following. Here are several:

Midwest Book Review
  WWW.MIDWESTBOOKREVIEW.COM
ForeWord Magazine
  WWW.FOREWORDMAGAZINE.COM
The Dragon Page   WWW.DRAGONPAGE.COM
SFReader.com   WWW.SFREADER.COM
Science Fiction Book Club   WWW.SFBC.COM
Science Fiction Crowsnest
  WWW.SFCROWSNEST.COM
SF Reviews.net   WWW.SFREVIEWS.NET

The essential post-publication magazine you want to submit your book to is <u>Locus</u> magazine. Serious readers of science fiction and fantasy, as well as those in the sci-fi/fantasy business, read *Locus*. You can find their website at: WWW.LOCUSMAG.COM.

THE PROCESS OF A BOOK REVIEWER

I have to tell you, it's easy to hang your shingle as a book reviewer, or any kind of reviewer for that matter. Got an opinion? Got a web page? Voila, you're a reviewer. And even though I don't review for a major newspaper or magazine, I can email most any large publisher and have an Advance Reader's Copy sent to me free of charge. Kind of sweet for a nobody audiologist from Tucson, Arizona. The point is, even for the small-timers, reviewers can have more material they can review than time to get to them all, so your presentation better be catchy.

Step One—The Selection Process

Of course, my first nods will go to authors I already know and like. As of this writing, I just found out that George R. R. Martin's fourth book in the *A Song of Ice and Fire* series will be published soon. I'm reviewing it, even if I have to go out and buy it off the rack.

If I decide I want to try something new, I do what everybody else does. I simply look some books over and choose the one that interests me most. I read the summary on the back of the book. I look at the cover art. I read the blurbs. I read the first page and see if it grabs my attention.

I also read the press releases we generally get with new submissions. If you send the reviewer a galley or a manuscript instead of a finished novel, the press release is essential, as it's really the only thing the reviewer has to look at. So, unless your name is J. K. Rowling or Stephen King, make that press release engaging.

If the book is by a major press, and it interests me, that's generally enough for me to give the book a try. I know this may sound unfair. I can hear the moans and feel the disturbance in the Force of hundreds of writers and small press publishers rolling their eyes as they read this, but I have to tell the truth. In the realm of non-fiction, I firmly believe that small presses, university presses and even vanity presses can produce products of equal quality to large presses. In the realm of fiction, however, I have found that I must sift through a lot more small press chaff to find the wheat. If what has caught my eye is a small press publication or a self-published book, I give it one more test before I decide to give it chance: The Flip Test.

I find The Flip Test so useful, I should patent it and sell it in bottles. The Flip Test goes like this. I take a book, and flip the pages from back to front. I flip them fast enough that the pages seem a bit animated, not so fast that they become a blur. As the pages flash by, I look to see whether the pages contain mixtures of black and white space in various ratios, or if I see page after page of solid black. Then I look up at a little framed plaque above my desk that says:

Mixture of black and white space in various ratios = Good
Solid black pages = Bad

If the book is one hundred and sixty-seven pages of solid black, I don't waste my time anymore. Solid black pages means there is not enough dialog, there are not enough scenes. Solid black pages mean tons and tons of descriptive narrative. Static storytelling. No sense of forward motion.

In this type of book, you will find paragraphs that run over a page and a half long with frightening regularity. Sentences four to five lines long follow sentences five to six lines long. Books like these haven't been through the hands of an editor, and first time authors who don't need editors can be found in the wild as often as hippogriffs. If the book fails The Flip Test, it has now become a paperweight.

Step Two—Reading the Book
So I start reading the book. If the book was sent in unsolicited, and after twenty to forty pages I know I'm not going to like it, I stop reading it, and I don't review it. I find life depressing enough without having to suffer through bad books. If I told the author I would read and review his book, and I know I'm not going to like it twenty pages in, I will usually just struggle on though. Attempting to spare myself further pain, I have been known to email authors and tell them, as nicely as I can, that their book is the equivalent of a root canal and that I can either stop reading, or carry on to the end. If I carry on to the end, I'm reviewing the book and there is no turning back. Surprisingly, I usually get told to carry on, and be honest in the review, as I've developed something of a reputation for being brutal but sincere in my reviews. I think that the authors believe that reading on will make me change my opinion, or they want some honest contrary reviews. Who am I to deny them?

Of course, if I like the book I just read on to the end. I don't know about other reviewers, but I've never written a review of a title that I didn't read from beginning to end.

Step Three—The Rating Process
At The Dragon Page, we generally rate books on a scale of five, occasionally throwing in the half rating as well (i.e., 3.5 out of 5). So

as I finish the last page, I close the book, close my eyes, and think to myself, "2 out of 5? 3 out of 5? No, 2 out of 5." And then that's the rating the book gets.

I wish I could tell you there's a more elaborate system, something with checks and balances and equations with weights and measures, but I can't. I do have some guidelines I go by, but they are very general: 5 out of 5 are given to books I consider excellent. Not "perfect," but excellent. Books that score 4 out of 5 are "good." Books that score 3 out of 5 are "okay." Books that score 2 out of 5 are "bad." Books that score 1 out of 5 are "awful."

Once you begin collecting reviews, you have to avoid falling into the trap of putting too much store in ratings. First of all, ratings are a shorthand, nothing more. And, more importantly, ratings are not absolute, they're relative. I've read several essays from movie interviewers who get letters demanding how he or she could give three stars to *Return of the King* and three stars to *Waterboy*. Could the reviewer possibly be saying that *Waterboy* is the cinematic equivalent to Sam carrying Frodo on his back up the side of the volcano with the music and the love and the wicked nasty Gollum and how can you say they are the same, they are so not!

Of course they're not. Usually the reviewer thinks to himself, "In the realm of epic fantasy summer blockbusters, *Return of the King* was pretty good. Not enough to get my top rating, but I liked it. I'll give it a three."

Then after watching *Waterboy*, the reviewer thinks to himself, "In the realm of stupid, low-brow comedies, I actually liked this one. Not enough to get my top rating..." etc. etc.

Remember, reviews are simply opinions, and ratings are a shorthand of that opinion. Don't worry too much about them.

Step Four—Writing the Review

I feel a little foolish saying I find writing reviews difficult, since a typical review clocks in at five to seven hundred words and takes around two hours of my life writing, revising, and posting it, while the book I just read came in at just under one hundred forty thousand words and took the author eleven months of his life, but there you go.

The difficulty lies in making each review interesting, unique. As for me, I try to find a hook to hang the review on. For positive reviews, it may story-related (say, for instance, a profound insight stated in the book), or perhaps something technical (like a clever writing device I had never seen before). For negative reviews, the hook almost always tends to be much easier to find: the faulty foundation the plot rests on, the obvious lack of professional editing, the amount of research that should have been done, but wasn't, etc.

Once the review is written and posted, I email the author or publisher with a link to the review webpage. Often, reviewers will send the publisher a "tear sheet," a hardcopy of the review. When the author has the review, he can then use the review for promotional purposes if he wishes.

What do you do when you receive a bad review?

Not a stinkin' thing.

Well, at least don't do all the things you're dying to do. Don't swear; don't get drunk; don't swear, then get drunk, then write a scathing email to the reviewer, telling him or her what you think of his or her opinions, his or her intelligence, his or her clothing choices or his or her parentage. Don't scream about it on your blog.

You have to learn to leave it alone. Why? Because no matter how good it may feel to rant and rave, it won't make the bad review go away, and only makes you look like an unprofessional child.

An example of this occurred on Amazon.com. Author Anne Rice, tired of criticism of her latest book, posted a long, angry retort on the website, belittling the critics and defending her work. Many believed she came off looking foolish.

Let's face it. No matter what we say to people who read our work about how we want honesty and helpful criticism, what we want to hear is praise. You will read over and over again, in every book on writing, that authors shouldn't take bad reviews personally. After all, reviewers aren't rejecting you, they are criticizing the work. But c'mon. Of course we'll take it personally, especially when we're new to the game.

Every new author I've met honestly believes his work is the next *Lord of the Rings* meets *Neuromancer*. Every single one. They believe their work is not just good, it's exceptional. I had a newly-published author tell me that he had been told by others that his book would save science fiction. (Wha—!?!) The book, of course, was dreadful.

To everyone in the profession of the book biz, including reviewers, books are not only possibly fantastic reads, but products as well. So, why did Mr. Bigshot Reviewer give your book the thumbs down? Any number of reasons.

You may have actually written a bad book. It amazes me how many first-time authors can't believe this is possible, but believe me, it is. When you start getting your reviews in, start comparing and contrasting them. Where do you receive consistent praise? Consistent criticism? If seven out of ten reviewers say your dialog sounds soap opera-ish, then maybe you need some work in that area. If two people mention the same glaring plot hole, don't yell that nobody cares about those kinds of things, because obviously some people do.

David Brin, Hugo and Nebula award-winning author, has said that criticism is the only known antidote to error[3]. If you look at the acknowledgments of any of his books, you will see a long list of names of people who have read his book and criticized the snot out of it.

I highly doubt he enjoys having his manuscripts returned in the mail from one of his readers scribbled in red pen, with notes like, "What were you smoking when you wrote this?" etched in capital letters in the margin. But he does it, even though at this point in his career he doesn't have to. So can you, both before the book gets published, and afterward, in the form of reviews.

The reviewer may not like the kind of story you wrote. Everybody has certain kinds of books or stories they simply couldn't like if their lives depended on it. Part of this can be solved by doing your homework ahead of time. Don't send your fantasy book to someone who only likes hard science fiction. No matter how brilliantly your epic medieval lesbian fantasy is written, you won't persuade him that he has been wrong about his reading preferences all this time.

However, sometimes you can't help but unknowingly make a bad match, and you're just going to get a negative review. For example, if you were to send me a time travel story, you've got about a fifty-fifty shot of me liking it. If the protagonist can go back a day or two in time, to change his immediate past, you've got a shot. If, on the other hand, you try to convince me that a secret experiment can send a twenty-first century American back to sixteenth-century England, and that by stealing some local clothes, he can then walk around in any village or town and blend in with the population while searching for someone else who accidentally got lost in the past... you'll lose. The book (or, in this case, movie) will probably get a bad review. I can buy the first story, but not the second, even though I know that both are equally impossible.

Unfair? Maybe. But you have to understand something about reviews. They're opinions. Some are educated and some pedestrian, some insightful and some blunt as hammers, but all reviews are opinions, nothing more or less, and carry with them all the prejudices of any other kinds of opinions. If a reviewer hates superhero stories, your superhero story will flop with him, no matter how well it's written.

The reviewer may honestly make a mistake. This kind of review may hurt the most of all, because it seems the most irresponsible on the part of the reviewer. The reviewer may simply misread something in the book that sours him, and gives a bad review based on that. Or, out of ignorance, he believes you to be wrong about your facts when you are not, and hates the book due to that. When I read Tee Morris's first book *Morevi*, I believed he used the words "pistols" and "bullets" anachronistically. I later discovered I was wrong. Someday, I'll go back and correct that review.

In the end we all know that not everyone is going to like our book. Unfortunately, bad reviews reveal that truth with all the understanding and sympathy of the flu. If you absolutely cannot let it roll off your shoulders, there is one last piece of advice from James Fallows of *The Atlantic Monthly*: "Always write angry letters to your enemies. Never mail them."

CONCLUSION

And so I come to the end of my stretch of the relay with you. I now pass the baton to the next writer, the next chapter, the next topic. I'll leave you with this. As you have undoubtedly realized reading this book, your work does not end once you've finished the novel, or even once it's been published. Like everything else in the writing and post-writing process, getting reviews is work, but work that will reap benefits.

If your book is good it will get reviewed, and it will get good reviews. Just keep at it.

BIBLIOGRAPHY:

[1] I compiled the information to include on galley covers from several sources. The two main sources were The Galley FAQ by Wendy J. Woudstra, found at HTTP://WWW.PUBLISHINGCENTRAL.COM/ARTICLES/20030409-1-0A1C.HTML and Crane's Sample Cover Letters at HTTP://WWW.CRANEDUPLICATING.COM/V1/BOUND_GALLEYS/INDEX.CFM?FUSEACTION=COVER_SAMPLES

[2] A good percentage of the information on galleys and where to send them came from an episode of Writer's Roundtable, an online book-centered interview show. The show took place on July 21, 2004. The guests included Colleen B. Lindsay of Ballantine Books, and Jim Cox of Midwest Book Review. Go to HTTP://WWW.WORLDTALKRADIO.COM/ARCHIVE.ASP?AID=2049 to find a recording of the interview.

[3] The David Brin quote came from a March 3, 2002 interview on Hour25online.com. Go to HTTP://WWW.HOUR25ONLINE.COM/HOUR25_PREVIOUS_SHOWS_2002-03.HTML#DAVID-BRIN_2002-03-03 to find a recording of the interview.

Rejections
BY MARGARET MCGAFFEY FISK

INTRODUCTION

In 1987, I made my first professional submission, a children's picture book, and have managed to accrue upwards of two hundred and thirty rejection letters since. This collection of letters covers a significant timeframe and multiple submission types, including short stories, novels and agent queries. In the time I've been submitting, I've seen more markets move to form rejection letters and away from offering the feedback that writers used to depend on. That being said, there are now many avenues to receive feedback prior to submission, leaving the acceptance and rejection letters to focus on their true intent.

That is where the problem lies. The true intent of rejection letters is to tell an author that a specific piece is not what the editor is looking for. Put that way, it seems simple and straightforward. Why then, is there a whole culture of *rejectomancy*, divination targeted specifically at understanding the hidden messages in those sometimes tiny pieces of paper?

This chapter explores some of the mythology and fact behind rejection letters and their purpose. In my varied collection of rejection letters, I have the ups, the downs and the fun ones. Marion Zimmer Bradley (MZB) liked one story so much she had it typeset before she gave in to the realization that it was not right for the market. Also from MZB, I have a note on another story accusing me of using her magazine as a soapbox because of a flawed humor piece. I have ones telling me the story was trite, unbelievable, unique, almost perfect and close. I even have the much reviled poor photocopy of a photocopy, sent to me by Asimov's in 1988 from the days before word processors became common. My oddest is a note from Weird Tales dating from 1990 which includes a P.S. that asks if I had moved. This shows not only do I have an unusual name, but also that editors do notice frequent submitters (something that can work for or against you).

The majority of the personal notes from pro markets came prior to 2000. Though some pro markets continue to take the time to make specific comments, most have been forced into forms rejections by the sheer volume of submissions. The time of recognizing someone despite an address change is probably past, unless the author consistently rises to the top level of submissions. Still, there is still much to glean from rejections.

GETTING THE MOST OUT OF YOUR REJECTIONS

When a rejection arrives in my inbox or on my doorstep, the first reaction is grief. No submission ever went out without the slightest bit of hope, and no rejection comes back without that hope dying a miserable death. So is there anything else a rejection can offer to make up for killing your dreams? Sure. Some rejections mean nothing more than a line drawn through the possibility of that market for that story. However, others can offer assistance in improving the story, alternative market suggestions or even just a morale boost.

Determining the value of a rejection in that first moment is difficult, if not impossible. The first thing to do when a rejection arrives is set it aside for a day or two. This rest period may be less necessary once rejections become a common part of your submission process, but though softened, the blow still exists. It's a good idea to distance what the rejection offers regarding your story from that moment of grief.

Once the paper has cooled off, the next thing is to think of what you know about the market.

- Does it have different rejection letters for the various levels? Does the wording have specific meaning? Or perhaps the color of the paper?
- Did your rejection come quickly or after a long time in comparison to the market's normal turnaround?
- Who signed the rejection letter? Does the market have a slush reader between your story and the editor?

These questions allow you to identify as best as possible which level of rejection you have received. Here is where the morale boost comes in. For example, when I received my first second-level rejection from a leading market (*Asimov's* in this case), the zing of energy almost entirely eradicated the moment of grief. Additionally, knowing the level a story achieved provides you some information to work with. If this story made it past the slush when other stories you have submitted did not, what is unique or different about this one? What topic, style, environment or other factor makes this tale stand out? And in the best case scenario, which of your other available stories has some if not all of those same criteria?

When a rejection letter includes an alternate market suggestion, the instinct is just to flip that story around and shoot it off to the other market. After all, an editor told you it matched. While that is a good recommendation at times, remember the suggestion may come not from a long-term study of the market, but a gut level "hey, that editor over there is looking for stuff in this category." Always research the market yourself before submitting. You can put a note indicating which editor recommended the story, if you think it will help, but be cautious. Doing so may only tell the new market that this story has been rejected before. If the first editor gave the sense that there is a friendship between them, then it might be worth it, but in general, it's best just to submit as normal.

The trickiest thing to glean from a rejection is something that will help improve a story. Whether or not the editor took the time to offer some suggestions, a full critique of the story is beyond the scope of a rejection letter. Therefore, the writer is left to pick apart a couple of sentences if lucky. Here are a few things to focus on:

- Does the feedback target a specific part of the story, such as the end, the beginning or the resolution?
- Does the feedback target a specific technique, such as dialog, plot or transitions?
- Does the feedback offer any specific comments, such as targeting a character or a moment in the story for improvement?

While it may seem silly, even something as simple as knowing where the editor stopped reading can reveal a flaw that previously went unnoticed. If the story is rich in world building, it's easy for exposition of an irrelevant cultural element to sneak in. This happened to me when Carina (former slush reader for *Realms of Fantasy*) marked her stop point on one of my submissions. Though I had edited the story many times, it took her note to realize there were two paragraphs of irrelevant back story that stopped the plot movement entirely. She was unable to articulate why she stopped there, but I could see it with the pointer she provided. Something as simple as back story, a character's accent, or even the use of a modern word in a medieval story may, when seen through the editor's eye, disrupt the reading.

Feedback in rejection letters should never take the place of critiques, nor should it necessarily bear more weight than a valued critiquer. However, if an editor takes the time to provide some glimpse into why the returning letter held a "no" instead of a "yes," it does the writer good to pay attention and consider that information carefully. Another editor might have a completely different opinion, but at the same time, what the rejection letter mentions could resonate and allow the writer to see something previously invisible.

However, while there are things to learn from rejections, it is important to remember "the right editor, the right story, at the right time." There are too many unique factors for any one rejection to condemn the story it declines.

A publisher told William Golding in 1954 that Lord of the Flies was a promising idea he had not yet successfully worked out. If you had the same reading list as I did in high school, you know this subjective opinion was not shared by all publishers.

TRUTH AND CONSEQUENCES: WHAT NOT TO DO AND WHY

Just as a rejection letter is not about you, your reaction needs to focus on the story and what you plan to do with it next. How many times after a job interview have you badmouthed the hiring managers to their face and to anyone who would listen? I can't imagine that there've been that many. Then why is it some people feel obligated to return a simple form letter, or even one where the editor took some time to offer feedback, with a nasty slap? A writer clutching a manuscript has much in common with a job applicant. Both want something important from the person they're applying to and are one among many seeking that same goal. In both cases, only limited slots are available and the recipients of this attention are usually swamped as they try to process all the requests.

If a hiring manager takes the time to say, "Though we have already filled the position, your resume looked good and we will keep it on file," the almost automatic reaction is "thank you." If an applicant does not get the job, then rarely does the correspondence continue. While editors do not necessarily want their letter boxes or inboxes cluttered with automatic "thank yous," the occasional one is usually gladly received. I recently replied to an unprompted status update from *Book of Dark Wisdom* with a thank you despite my concerns about wasting the editor's time. Not only was my response welcomed, but also I was encouraged to submit another piece even though my first story was still under consideration. The editor commented that he rarely received pleasant responses. If writers would follow the old adage of "if you can't say something nice, don't say anything," editors would be much happier.

If you do not receive a response within a reasonable amount of time (usually what is listed on their guidelines or a minimum of 90 days), you are welcome to request a status update. If you receive no response to the status request, you can always withdraw your manuscript. If you receive a rejection letter, you are welcome to throw it in the trash or otherwise shred to your heart's content, though considering what you could learn from even a form letter, the last wouldn't be very wise.

What you are not welcome to do is reply to the editor with any content that indicates you are unhappy with the rejection, that you found the wording objectionable, or that you have any violent intentions toward them or their families. Some of you may be laughing at this point, but the sad thing is that editors get these kinds of responses frequently enough that the topic comes up at conventions, in blogs, and I'm sure, in discussions between editors. These responses are in no way uncommon. If you do a search of editor blogs, you're sure to find at least one or two stories and sometimes even the letters themselves with identifying features removed.

For example, a new magazine had a tight deadline for the first issue and so expected short turnarounds. It also had a cutoff date. As commonly occurs, the editor experienced some technical problems and had to move Heaven and Earth to get everything in order. In this process, she implemented an auto responder that triggered based on the word "submission" in the subject line. An author requested a status update on his submission using a subject line that triggered the auto responder. Instead of politely inquiring if there was a mistake, he lambasted her for being disorganized, etc. She kept it anonymous when she reported the situation on her blog, but he responded with his true name. How many of her friends in the editorial world took note, do you wonder?

And in case you think this is an isolated incident, pay attention to the later section on magazines that offer feedback. I'll mention at least two that include in their guidelines a statement warning writers who are the type that find feedback offensive to save everyone the trouble and go elsewhere.

Remember the traditional phrase about burning bridges? The editorial community, at least within the speculative fiction book and professional magazine business, is not so large that editors don't see each other at conventions, for lunch, because they share an interest in an author or for any number of reasons. Now imagine this group of people with common interests gets together. What is the likelihood that they share horror stories? What takes an author one or two misguided moments to produce and send, especially for email, could haunt that person for a good long time.

Someone who's difficult to work with will develop a reputation, but someone who slams editors, especially those taking an extra moment to give more than a generic response, will likely never get the chance to prove how they work. If a writer becomes known in editorial circles as a troublemaker, what editor, when faced with ten times or more the number of manuscripts than available spaces, will spare a moment for that author? Would you waste time on someone known to attack if not handled with kid gloves?

Writing is a profession. Submitting is a professional act...or should be. The easiest way to impress an editor is by being so professional that only the story distinguishes your work from any other submission. There are a lot of suggestions about making your manuscript stand out, such as pink paper, perfume and chocolate. I can't say whether such tactics worked in the beginning, but they are generally considered signs of poor judgment. The situation only becomes worse when the editor in question is allergic to perfume or even chocolate.

When writers make names for themselves, as opposed to for their stories, it more often than not leads to a negative reaction when editors see that familiar name come across their desks. Do yourself and all writers a favor: keep your correspondence professional, calm, clear and concise. That is the best reputation of all.

Stephen King was rejected over thirty times before Carrie, his first novel, was accepted.

TYPES OF REJECTIONS

Rejections come in many types, shapes, sizes and even colors. The chart below categorizes the main groups though special, distinct ones will always exist. Also, some crossover between the main groups is to be expected because of their natures.

Type	Description
Holy Grails	These rejection letters are whispered about in the writing halls, rarely seen by new writers and dreamed of by all. While it's true that no one prefers a rejection letter as opposed to an acceptance, some are better than others. This category means the author made it past the gatekeepers and managed to reach the main editor. Though the story is still rejected, this is a sign that the author's work has attained a higher level. One example is a rejection from Gordon Van Gelder of *The Magazine of Fantasy & Science Fiction* as opposed to John Joseph Adams, his slush reader. Another example is a handwritten note from Sheila Williams of *Asimov's Science Fiction* instead of their form letter. Sometimes these rejections come with a rewrite request that, if completed competently, can transform a rejection into an acceptance. If nothing else, this level of rejection carries the understanding that the writer has caught the editor's attention and may be recognized when the next story comes through.
Does Not Play Well With Others	The name is my own, but this type of rejection letter usually comes from anthologies where the editor attempts to choose stories not just around a theme, but also which combine nicely with the other choices to create a mood. This is a second-level rejection and means the story made it into late-stage considerations. No matter how much an editor might like a story, if it conflicts with or has a significantly different tone than the stories already in the acceptance pile, the manuscript will be rejected. These rejections are often accompanied with a note stating that, while the story was enjoyed, it did not fit with the others.
Personalized	These rejections occur at all levels of slush depending on the market or the editor's personal preference. Some markets promise feedback, while others are 90% or more form letters. Pro markets that use email communication rather than print appear more likely to jot a note, but even there, not all stories get feedback. Often, a story has to be disliked or a close cut to get a personal note. While this may seem ungrateful, the time it takes to jot one note multiplied over 300 or more submissions a month becomes significant.

Type	Description
Basic Form Letters	These are perhaps the most frustrating rejections. They offer little to the practitioners of rejectomancy and can appear insulting as they attempt to touch on the most common reasons for rejecting a story. However, the true meaning of these forms is only that the story failed to warrant more than a moment in the editor's already busy day.
Advanced Form Letters	These form letters come in many different styles. Some have a series of checkboxes to give authors a hint as to why their story failed to attract the elusive personal contact. Others are identified by color, such as the yellow form of promise offered by *Realms of Fantasy*, or simply different wording, perhaps with the author's name and story title filled in. Though providing more information than the basic form, the specifics are unique to each market and so any broad analysis falls flat.
Non-Response	Sadly, slush piles brimming with manuscripts that don't even meet the basic guidelines have made this more common. Most markets that use this process do include the fact in their guidelines through a statement such as "after 60 days, assume the material does not fit our needs." Contests also sometimes adopt this policy after they see the response rate. They'll post a notice that winners have been informed and all other stories are rejected. With the albeit small chance of lost email or postal submissions, this could mean a story is assumed rejected when in fact it never arrived. However, in most cases, it did not hold the editor's attention.
On First Page or Query Letter	Writers have mixed reactions to this type among rejectomancy practitioners. Some feel that editors or agents should take the time to use their own paper, while others see this as a benefit because the rejection also identifies which version of the story or query went out to that market.
Please Follow Guidelines	This is, in my opinion, the absolute worst rejection an aspiring author could ever get. It takes very little time to research the specific needs and format for each market, so why take that chance? Despite common advice to use a default format, if a market takes the time to put up guidelines, writers should follow them. Many editors use the ability to comply as a first cut of the slush pile. Why waste their time and yours?

Email Versus Paper Rejections

How a rejection arrives can also influence the content, as described in the table above. Email rejections are more likely to include feedback. There will still be markets that use generic forms for most of their responses, but the odds are in the writer's favor. Also, email rejects can offer a quicker turnaround and reduce or eliminate postal costs. However, the speed of the turnaround does not reflect on the time the editor spent. Whether backlogged for 60 days or able to reject in a few hours (as happened to me once), it's in the editor's best interest to give your story a reasonable chance.

The biggest issue in these days of spam and email filtering is that an email rejection letter (or even an acceptance) will be filtered out. It's important to check all filtered spam and verify that some of it is not precious letters from editors that may contain the gem necessary to take a story from flawed to published.

Email rejections also pose a tracking problem in terms of how they are stored and how easy they are to access. In some ways, they are easier to organize, but can be lost in a computer failure or when an email program is changed.

Paper rejections are rarely lost in the mail, but are also more likely to be the barest of forms, often without the author's name, story title or even the date. A helpful tracking tip is to put the story name and date on the SASE under your address so you'll know what story was rejected regardless of whether the form includes the title. This is where people will complain about the 3X5 cards or 1/4th-of-a-page rejections. Additionally, to receive a paper rejection, the author must always include a self-addressed, stamped envelope (SASE), which increases the postal costs.

The majority of short story markets, as well as most novel publishers and agencies, work on the paper system. It is a long-standing tradition and falls under the "if it ain't broke, don't fix it" approach. Expect to receive your share of paper rejections if you seek publication on a pro level regardless of the perceived advantages of email.

r. Seuss, when shopping around And to Think That I Saw It on Mulberry Street in 1937, heard his manuscript was just too unique for the juveniles market.

MARKETS THAT GIVE FEEDBACK

Let me state clearly that any and all markets can give feedback. Even the leading pro markets can offer a line or two to someone they have met at a conference or for a story that came close. Sometimes the feedback is a single sentence containing a positive comment or a critical clue as to why a particular story failed to catch the editor's interest.

No market has the obligation to provide feedback, though some take it on as a cause. For example, *AlienSkin Magazine* and *Tales of the Unanticipated* warn submitters that feedback will be returned. They then state that the feedback is meant in the spirit of seeking improvement, not to provoke an argument. *Strange Horizons* is a well-known, pro-level market that often provides comments, though not with every story. This once again indicates that some aspect of the story itself must have touched something in the editor, whether positively or negatively.

Though markets that provide comments can help a writer bring a story up to professional standards, the best place to seek feedback is from a critique group. Whether online or in person, this is an opportunity to perfect the story and possibly reduce the number of rejections it may receive. That said, sometimes only an editor can pinpoint the true beauty or flaw in a story, giving a writer the chance to fix the problem before submitting to other potential markets. While I don't suggest submitting to a market solely to receive feedback, which markets offer comments can become one of the factors in deciding where to submit first.

The higher likelihood of feedback in email responses comes because the time necessary to open the document, address and send it is already a given part of the rejection process. All that remains is to add a sentence or more about the story itself. Here is where the "touched the editor in some fashion" comes into play. If, in reading the story, the editor had no particular reaction, then there is nothing to prod the extra effort. If, however, the story prompted either a positive or negative response, then the screen is there and ready for a line or two to pass on that reaction.

A publisher told George Orwell in 1945 that animal stories were impossible to sell in the United States. The manuscript? Animal Farm.

MULTIPLE EDITORS

The traditional path of slush reader to magazine editor is difficult enough, but to make the submission process more complex, many semi-pro and pro magazines work with editorial teams. What does this have to do with rejections? Editorial teams can result in some of the most endearing and heartbreaking rejections of all.

When there are multiple editors, one assumes some commonality in the editorial vision because they collectively affect the look and feel of the publication. However, editors are human beings who have their own quirks that no other can match. This is both the struggle and hope in the "the right editor, the right story, the right time" triumvirate. Multiple editors can skew that balance. A story that's perfect for one might hit on a pet peeve for another or might strike a personal note that the others don't share.

This results in rejections where one editor states that he or she really enjoyed the story but could not get the others to agree. The heartbreak is in the realization that if that one editor had full decision-making power, your story would have made it onto the table of contents. This does not in any way reduce the endearing and uplifting qualities of the rejection. When one of an editorial team stands up for your story, it's a sign that your manuscript, and by inference, your stories in general, have reached the level of quality published by that magazine. When this happened to me with a story sent to Strange Horizons, I didn't know whether to grin or cry. Mixed-response rejections also offer you some insight into both the likes of one and the dislikes of the other editors should you wish to try that market again.

Another side benefit of the multiple editor system is that, if your story makes it past the first cut and is considered by the editors as a group, you'll often get a comment from one or more of the editors that could contain hints on how to improve the story. Some of the multiple-editor markets also provide a line or two for all rejections describing each editor's reaction.

In 1851, a British publisher told Herman Melville that Moby Dick was inappropriate for the juvenile market because of its old-fashioned style.

REJECTOMANCY 101: WHAT RECEIVING A REJECTION REALLY MEANS

Rejection letters, whatever their form, are created for the sole purpose of crushing the hearts and hopes of writers everywhere, aren't they? Well, not really. They are no more intended to inflict emotional harm than notes from a grant committee informing applicants that the recipient was chosen or a company announcing a position has been filled. Writers have imbued rejections with almost mystical properties engineered to destroy and devastate. In reality, they are small slips of paper that serve one purpose and one purpose alone. Receiving a rejection means, simply, that a specific story will not appear in the table of contents of a specific market.

That said, how the information is conveyed can offer some hints. Writers can learn how the story was received, whether the market was a good match, whether the writer did a good job in preparing the submission, and sometimes even how the story can be improved. This is where rejectomancy comes into play. This information isn't always obvious and isn't the same for every market.

Rejectomancy is the art of prying every bit of information from something that, at first glance, seems barren of value. Though some people take this to great extremes, leaving little space for reality, there is factual basis for the careful evaluation of rejection letters.

For example, a writer should be able to take a simple "please submit more" comment at face value. However, that phrase has two very different possible meanings: "we don't want to discourage submissions because we know writers improve," or "this story was a close one and we think the next we see might actually make it into the table of contents." There are many other shades of meaning in between these two extremes, but it's a sign of how little, or how much, a single phrase can mean in a rejection letter.

Thanks to the World Wide Web, writers have access to a huge communal mind that is full of information and willing to compare notes. Sometimes, the only way to tell one market's form letter from another's encouraging one is to ask other authors. This is especially important with emailed rejection letters. I was thrilled at my first *Glimmer Train Stories* rejection. I've since learned that it is nice and comforting, but really does not say anything about my specific submission. Until you've received your third letter with identical wording, there's no way to tell what the message really means. It could be personal and trying to make it clear that your stories are right on the cusp, or a generic "hope you get better" message sent to all those who don't make it to the final consideration pile. If it's the former, the author should follow up with another story of a similar style to take advantage of the possible name recognition. If the later, the submission will have no affect on future ones.

With paper rejections, the difference can be obvious if the editor took the time to hand-write a note. However, in the world of word processors, authors are still stuck with doing rejection comparison to determine if something is a generic form letter or a personal note. The best examples of disguised forms are *The Magazine of Fantasy and Science Fiction*'s basic three rejections. They're all templates (as you learn after the first few) and yet allow the slush reader, John Joseph Adams (JJA), to add small encouragements. These he slips in between the "didn't grab" (he stopped around five pages), "didn't hold" (he didn't finish the story) and "didn't quite work for me" (he finished but didn't pass it up to Gordon Van Gelder). JJA himself has confirmed the intent behind the various wordings. When he adds a comment like "There's some nice writing here," it's a personal note in addition to the form. The first time I got an added note, I dragged out all my others to compare, then searched the Web to confirm that something I'd written caught his attention, if only for a moment. Because notes like those from JJA do not provide specific information and appear in the same typeface, if you don't know the templates, you may not realize what you've actually received.

If "please submit more" can have neutral or positive values, what about form rejections that include negative (and what some consider insulting) elements? The classic example is the <u>Asimov's Science Fiction</u> form letter. It states that an obvious lack of basic English compositional skills is a common reason for rejection. However, general comments on form letters are just that. Of the 300 or more manuscripts some markets receive per month, they observe some patterns.

If you are one of the people these patterns apply to, for example if you don't know standard manuscript format, the provided hints could help you. For the rest, remember the form provides possible reasons and usually ends with a note about how many submissions are received. Most likely this particular story just did not rise above the other manuscripts. These forms are not intended as insults. Think of them more as a desperate cry of the overwhelmed editor who's seeking the proverbial needle in a haystack: the perfect story for the magazine.

What about format? What about when the rejection comes on less than a full page, as three short sentences, as "Dear contributor?" Think back on the overwhelmed editors. The time necessary to customize each rejection is time taken away from considering stories. You might wonder why you should care about a market that has rejected your story. Well, let me ask a question: do you ever plan to submit to them again? If the answer is yes, then you want them to do whatever necessary to maximize focus on the actual stories whether it means no personalization, hiring an editorial team or using short sentences that are less likely to provoke acrimonious letters from rejected authors. All of these efforts produce a tangible benefit for those who submit. Turnaround times on many of the more popular markets have grown to punishing lengths, and for every moment editors spend away from reading slush, those times just get longer.

The only format issue that has nothing, or little, to do with saving time is the size of the rejection note. Often, smaller pages are used as an effort to protect the environment because a single sheet can fit four or more rejections. Other editors might use the small cards so they don't have to fold rejections and can fit the cards in non-standard envelopes when necessary. Neither is any reflection on their opinion of your work.

Rudyard Kipling was told he had an imperfect grasp of the English language in 1889 regarding an untitled submission.

IT IS PERSONAL

Writers are often told not to take rejections personally, but the problem here is direction. Rejections are personal, just not in the sense of an attack on the writer. Rather, they come from one editor, or possibly a team of editors. Negative, positive or neutral, that slip of paper indicates no more or less than one market's opinion about a specific story.

Just as you can't determine the editor's hopes and dreams from the rejection letter, the editor can't tell anything about you beyond what you put into that specific story. As long as you took the time to use proper formatting, followed any market-specific guidelines and edited your story so it wasn't full of sloppy errors, your story tells nothing but what your characters experience. This is true whether or not the editors like the story.

Just as no character in your story embodies you, none of your stories represent you either. Therefore, the best that can be said about a rejection, even one in which an editor states the plot was hackneyed, the characters dull or the ending too predictable, is that an editor has rejected a story. Nothing more, nothing less.

This understanding has two sides to it:

1) Just because the story did not work for this specific editor, doesn't mean another editor will feel the same. Many stories have been rejected by one market only to go on to be published in a bigger market with a stronger reputation.

2) Just because the editor didn't like this specific story doesn't mean the market won't appreciate another submission. Most editors have been around long enough to understand that authors continue to improve or may tackle different

topics that have more appeal. Editors come to recognize authors who submit frequently and some enjoy seeing an author grow. This can be a benefit if your stories are good and getting better. Especially for markets that provide no feedback, it may seem as if the stories are treated the same every time. However, regardless of what form is sent, many editors do notice improvement.

Finally, and most importantly, editors are people too. You can't control when your story crosses the desk, what other stories came just before it, or what's going on in the editors' lives. If yours is the fourth "lead weight saves the world" story in that day's pile, if your story involves the gruesome death of a character the day after a drunk driver drove over the editor's cat, if the coffee bean supplier got confused and delivered only decaf, if the subway air conditioning broke down, etc. All these things are out of your control, and out of the editor's as well. The slush pile has to be read. It can't be put on hold for every minor or major event that might create bias against some stories. The saving grace is that these circumstances are unique to a specific day or a specific editor. The next market might find the manuscript wonderful.

Patrick Dennis searched for a publisher for five years and fifteen different houses before Vanguard Press accepted Auntie Mame.

HOW MANY REJECTIONS SHOULD ANY ONE PIECE HAVE BEFORE YOU TRUNK IT?

It's hard to be professional and calm as your favorite story receives rejection after rejection. The question then becomes when should a writer give up on the story and move on?

The basic answer to this question is very simple. A story should accumulate rejections equal to the total responses minus one, with the final being an acceptance. Publishing is difficult; it requires persistence and dedication. Even if the story is strong, there are many factors influencing its acceptance, and with all the variables, good stories can easily accumulate tons of rejections.

Both J.K. Rowling and Stephen King can tell stories of their attempts to find publishers for their first books that would make any marketing major cringe at the thought of all the lost profit. And yet, there is no way to predict the next bestselling author. Therefore, no particular number of rejections indicates the success or failure of a manuscript. Some are purchased at the first submission and drown in obscurity while others languish in slush piles for years before finding their audience. If a writer truly believes in a story, there's no need to give up just because the stack of rejections has grown tall.

However, with the strict number out of the way, there are some indications of when an author should shelve a particular story. While this does not mean that the story will never have a chance at publication, it does mean the author will stop polishing and submitting actively until the right market or right moment comes.

- One reason to put a story aside is if you no longer believe in it. This happens to writers as they mature. The mechanics of the story can always be improved, but if the story itself is shallow, clichéd or limited in some way, while elements can sometimes be extracted for other works, the particular manuscript is no longer worth the trouble.

- Another reason is the writer's skill might have grown so far beyond that of the story and so the amount of polishing required is prohibitive. If the story requires a complete rewrite to make it into something the writer would be happy to see published, then it might be better to focus on newer works that already incorporate the style and skill improvements. These stories generally make good fodder when a writer experiences a dry period in the production of ideas. They are also useful for anthologies or other themed markets. Rewriting can be faster than coming up with a new idea, executing and editing it, often on a short deadline. I have at least ten short stories falling into this category and have rewritten one for an anthology submission. In general, though, newer works get my attention first.

The time to give up on a story is unique for every author and every story. If you are not prolific, then focusing on rewriting older stories that are no longer at your skill level might be worthwhile. If you are prolific, then maybe shelving some of the ones that require more work than a new manuscript would can allow you to focus on your goal of publication. Every choice is individual, but awareness of the reasons and circumstances should help you make the right decision for each story.

Fourteen publishers passed on the first Harry Potter book before Scholastic took a chance.

SOME WAYS TO STORE YOUR REJECTIONS FOR EASY REFERENCE

So, while your stories are accumulating rejections and your desk starts to look like a poorly managed landfill, what should you do with all these slips of paper and cardstock? The standard joke about rejections is that when you have enough to wallpaper your study, then you have it made, or you should give up. As you can tell from my personal stack, I don't follow either of those patterns. I have easily enough to wallpaper my study, but I'm neither a household name nor ready to give up. The ratio of rejections to acceptances does not necessarily tie into a writer's skill. Too many factors can affect that number including market choice and how prolific the writer is. However, whether you accumulate five or five hundred rejection letters, they provide tangible evidence that you are serious not only about writing, but also about writing professionally.

A quick list of reasons to keep your rejection letters:

- You can identify trends and "hidden" form letters best by comparing the latest ones to past notes.
- You can tell when you might have broken out of the first slush level.
- You can look for something to remind editors who have moved to a new magazine, but who appreciated your writing style at their previous job.

- You can identify stories that were loved by one of multiple editors for submission to new magazines or anthologies edited by the person who loved it.
- You can reminisce on the good old days and see how the world has changed.
- And of course, the most important reason is because rejection letters provide evidence for the taxman that this is not just a hobby.

These are only some of the reasons for keeping your rejection letters. Having made the decision to keep them, the next question is how? While propping an encouraging note on your desk can be a good idea, wallpapering your study is a little much. So, what other options are there?

The two main choices are to store your letters all together or with the related stories. If all you have is a paper system, storing the letters with the stories is a good way to know which markets have already seen this story. However, a quick note on the story folder can provide the same information much more efficiently.

The greatest value in rejection letters is a comparison over time within a single market. For that reason, I recommend storing rejection letters (both paper ones and printed-out emails) alphabetically and chronologically in a three-ring binder. This allows you to browse your history with a specific market easily or to note when a market expresses interest in your writing. Conversely, consistently receiving "not right for this market" rejections can alert you to a difference in interpretation regarding what the market wants. Putting your rejections in a binder also provides an easy way to display your badges of honor to friends, family and the aforementioned taxman. Imagine it as the equivalent of an autograph book. It can be hard to interest people in the nuts and bolts of writing, but they just might tune in when peering at the signature of a well-known editor like Gordon Van Gelder.

Lee Pennington, published in more than 300 magazines, actually did wallpaper all four walls of a room with rejection letters collected in one six-month period.

AFTER THE FIRST ACCEPTANCE

After compiling a folder of rejections; after sticking with it and writing, editing and submitting despite very little positive reinforcement, what about when your first acceptance comes? On that glorious day, whether arriving in the form of a mailed contract or a phone call, you have crossed the line between trying and success. When my SASE first came back with a contract rather than a rejection, I read every word out loud, unable to believe I'd actually succeeded. And that's it, right? All the waiting, angst and horror of rejections is now over. The glory days are here.

Well, not exactly. Remember the adage of "the right editor, the right story, the right time?" That still applies. Yes, having an acceptance, especially from a leading market, is a wonderful thing. However, what exactly does it buy you? Depending on the editor, it may mean you can submit electronically rather than through postal mail; it may mean you bypass the slush reader and go directly to the editor; it may mean your story gets a closer look. However, until you have a big enough name to sell copies just by appearing on the cover, each story must stand on its own merits. That one story has been accepted does not mean any others will be, nor does it mean they will not.

Acceptances are good affirmations for writers, but do not have much meaning beyond that. An acceptance in a small market may even weigh less than a close rejection in a top market as far as identifying where writers are in their careers. Though the tough road doesn't end after the first acceptance, remember that writing is a business and it requires no more, or less, work than many other businesses. Once you have racked up a dozen or more acceptances, then you start to get the notice of editors, but the individual story must always win the sale. If you think about it for a moment, that's actually a wonderful thing. That very focus on the story is what gives newcomers a chance. It gives readers the ability to trust authors not to stagnate after they have a few good contracts. Even bestsellers who are rolling in money have to remember that principle. Fans may forgive one or two poor manuscripts, but show a trend of not improving and many fans will drift to newer authors willing to work for their craft.

*A*gatha Christie was told that The Mysterious Affair *at Styles was not quite suitable for the publisher's list in 1920.*

SUMMARY AND REFOCUS

Pretty much everyone agrees that rejections are hard to take, whether your first or five hundredth. Even authors who receive enough for the rejection letters to become just pieces of paper may feel some letdown or depression when an apparently perfect market rejects a story. However, that low point should not have power over the rest of your life. There are things to learn from some rejections while others are simply data points on the road to publication. I hope this chapter gives you some ideas on how to make the most of your rejections.

Rejections are part of almost all writers' lives, regardless of their professional standing. There are only two ways for a writer with aspirations toward publication to avoid rejections. First, writers could let the fear of small slips of paper keep them from submitting at all. The disadvantage there is that without submitting, there is no chance of acceptance. Secondly, writers can limit their submissions to small markets that only pay in copies or minimal fees, and which provide little benefit as publishing credits. If the writing is good enough, those markets would be happy to print it. However, if the writing is good enough for small markets, then there is a chance a bigger market would also be interested. Writers who only receive acceptances might not be submitting high enough up the food chain.

Yes, rejection's hard, but how can you succeed without taking the chance? Even if several markets offer up rejections, all you need is one acceptance for each manuscript. The trick is to submit professional quality manuscripts to the professional markets. If they reject, often because they have so many strong stories, you can always submit to a smaller market. If a manuscript is accepted by a smaller market before the big markets get a chance, that first print opportunity is lost forever. Does a simple piece of paper seem an adequate threat to hold you back?

The bottom line with any submission still comes down to "the right editor, the right story, the right time." The only way to succeed with that formula is to submit and submit often. Do not let rejections stand in your way.

BIBLIOGRAPHY

Adams, John Joseph. *Reply to What DON'T Editors Want to See, Ever Again?* Night Shade Books. August 14, 2005
HTTP://WWW.NIGHTSHADEBOOKS.COM/
DISCUS/MESSAGES/378/1713.HTML#POST31602

Barker, Laraine Anne. *How to Deal with Rejection.* L.A. Barker Enterprises. August 14, 2005,
HTTP://LBARKER.ORCON.NET.NZ/REJECTION.HTML

Bernard, Andre and Henderson, Bill. *Rotten Rejections: A Literary Companion.* New York: Pushcart Press, 1990.

Where Two or Three or Twenty Are Gathered

THE GROWING PHENOMENON OF THE WRITER'S GROUP
BY DANIELLE ACKLEY-MCPHAIL

Writing, they say, is a solitary endeavor.

I say it is a journey you make with your friends: those you write for, those you write about and those who make it all come together by helping you figure out where you went wrong.

True, for the most part you sit before your computer…or typewriter… or clay tablet…and pretend the world outside your head is not there. But for those writing with the hope of publication, this is only one third of the process (refining the resulting manuscript and promoting the finished product being the other two legs of this triumvirate). With that in mind, it is my task to tell you about one of the writer's most valuable tools: the Writer's Group.

WHAT EXACTLY ARE WE TALKING ABOUT?

On the off chance that it might actually be there, I looked up *writer's group* in The Oxford English Dictionary and alas, though countless trivialities have made it into those exalted pages, *writer's group* has not. The same went for Miriam-Webster's, and the Cambridge Dictionary. Surprising, considering you can't turn around without encountering someone that wants to be a writer. Well, that just leaves me to define the term for myself.

I say writer's groups are meetings of passions, minds and on occasion, bodies. The one unifying factor of such groups is that they be attended by, of course, writers: aspiring, established and every stage in between. While such meetings can have varying objectives, the key element is a desire to write (that is the passion I reference above, so you can stop looking for the X-rating at the top of this chapter).

*W*riter's groups should be supportive and constructive, if you find yourself in one that is not, get out.

TO PUT A FINE EDGE ON IT

While I am sure there are countless variations on writer's groups in the world, I am going to focus on three basic types (and please keep in mind, these labels are my own): The Social Club, the Crucible and the Community. Every group I have ever been a part of or encountered has been some combination of these three elements.

THE SOCIAL CLUB

When you are shopping around for a group of your own, it is important to be sure of both what you are looking for, and what you are getting into. Not every writer's group focuses on polishing the craft.

I know: what's the sense in that? Well, some people like to socialize. This process—especially for someone who sits alone in front of a monitor, pretending the outside world doesn't exist—is made easier when there is common ground. What that means for you is that, though the majority of people in the group are writers, the craft of writing may not be the primary topic of discussion. Participation and structure in the Social Club are characteristically relaxed.

That is not to say that such groups serve no purpose. Not only are they a place to commiserate and unwind among those who can relate, but they are also a means of networking with those in different tiers of the industry, or a pool to be tapped into if you are looking for someone with certain writing-related skills. Think of it as the grapevine for writers, or a community bulletin board.

THE CRUCIBLE

Do you have a general idea what this one is going to be like?

Yeah, you're right, as painful as it sounds—well, for your ego, anyway. This is the intense, no-nonsense writer's group. Think of it as diametrically opposed to the Social Club. There is often a great deal of regulation, a firm obligation to give as much if not more feedback than you receive, and the bitter blow to your ego is not softened when they tear down your work and help you build back up again better than it was before.

The main factor of the Crucible is structure. The process is very formal and regimented, with certain plateaus to be reached and maintained before you can fully benefit from all the group has to offer. One such point could be that those participating must meet an obligation to review and critique a set number of submissions before they are entitled to submit their own work into the process. Once they have reached this point, they must maintain a quota of so many reviews in a given period if they wish to retain their submission privileges. Many times, though not always, emphasis is given to highlighting the flaws of a work that they may be eradicated and repaired, rather than on giving note to the positive attributes of a piece.

This might seem cruel and counterproductive to some, but it is not. The point is not to be brutal and unfair, but to be frank and exacting. For some writers, constructive criticism is the best way to refine their work. They do not want to be told what works, because it does not need their attention. The purpose of the process is not to form a cheering section, but to gain productive feedback that will ultimately lead them as close to perfection as any of us is capable of. They already possess the confidence needed to succeed; what they need is an outside and objective perspective to hone their work to publishable quality.

THE COMMUNITY

This writer's group is about more than just honing skills: it is also about support and encouragement, celebrating successes and commiserating about rejections. This is a writing community that shares its knowledge of both publishing opportunities and the wisdom gained by experience. The topics generally gravitate around writing, though socializing and tangential conversations are not unheard of. A well-rounded environment that is writing-oriented but not narrowly focused. The work is looked at as a whole: what works is praised and what doesn't is addressed. This is the middle ground between the two previous groups. It is for people becoming more serious about their writing, but lacking the knowledge, experience, or perhaps the confidence in their own work to take it to the next level. The community is about nurturing.

Keep in mind that the people you encounter in writer's groups are going to come from varying levels of experience; benefit from what you can and remember to be supportive of those whose experience level may fall below your own.

HOW SHALL WE MEET AGAIN?

There are three methods by which writer's groups are conducted: in-person, on-line and by correspondence. These three methods are also known to cascade into numerous variations on the theme when put into practice, tailored to fit a group's particular needs. The structure of the group decides when and how often "meetings" take place.

In-Person

In-person groups take place just about anywhere: members' homes, libraries, bookstores, diners...the possibilities are, as they say, endless. Depending on the venue and the availability of the members, these groups generally meet weekly or monthly. To connect with one, visit the local community bulletin board or website, check the classifieds of the local weekly paper, or ask at the college campus, bookstore or library nearest you.

One of the drawbacks of these groups is the experience level. It is most often either uniform across the board, with everyone having very little knowledge about the technique of writing or experience with actually being published, or grossly unbalanced, with the majority of members having little or no experience and one or two people being more advanced. In the first case, the majority of the feedback received is going to be subjective (based on the readers' tastes) rather than on any firm understanding of why something works or what the industry is looking for. In most instances, critiques are vague and unproductive. In the second case, those who have little experience will benefit more from the feedback of those who have achieved some level of proficiency, while those with more experience will not get as much out of the group.

On-Line

On-line groups are the most fluid. Conducted by means of message boards, live journals, blogs, newsgroups, list-serves, email or any combination therein, their activity—while dependent on the participation of the members—is for the most part continuous. Its flexibility is in being able to participate when it suits your schedule. Also, because the Web is far-reaching, the experience levels are more varied so everyone is more likely to find something relevant to their writing style.

Because of the diversity of the medium, the resources available to such groups can be more valuable than the member interaction itself. With endless links for writer's resources and submission sites and research pages easily passed from member to member for immediate access, this avenue of meeting has revolutionized writer's groups.

Also, the method in which you access the group can be chosen for the way that most suits you. Message boards, live journals and blogs have features that can send an email alert to let you know when there has been activity on a particular topic. Whereas newsgroups allow you to tailor your user preferences so that you receive posts by email as they are made, once a day by digest, or none at all (in which case you access them at your leisure via the newsgroup home page).

Newsgroups are also the easiest writer's group option to find, though you will have to try out a few before you find one that is a good fit. Check out the classified section of your favorite writer's magazine or run a web search on writer's groups. You will find a plethora of hits. All you have to do is decide if you want one for writers in general, or one tailored to a specific genre or style that you write in. There are benefits to both.

The flaw of this method is volume. There are so many groups to choose from that it might be difficult at first to pin down one that suits both your needs and your personality. With some Internet groups and boards, activity is sporadic and not always helpful, while on others, the members participate with such enthusiasm your mailbox will virtually overflow each day. Such activity can be overwhelming, even if the dialog is stimulating and resourceful. For the most part, it is just a matter of moving on to another group until you find something you are comfortable with. However, after a time the registering processes some groups require can be tedious and off-putting.

Once you have found your group, the next great hurdle is conflict among the members. Sometimes that can be more brutal in the faceless realm of the Internet, where typed words can be misinterpreted or filled with venom to a degree that would not necessarily happen in a face to face encounter. Such occurrences are inevitable.

The mark of a good group is when such occurrences are the exception rather than the rule, and are promptly defused by those running the show.

Correspondence

Correspondence groups are, in a way, a more personal interaction. Conducted by conventional mail, they can be an exchange between you and one other person, or a handful of people. For the most part, groups such as this are small and selective. This method most benefits those who are, for one reason or another, unable to travel to an in-person group and do not have readily available or dependable Internet access.

Interaction is restricted by delivery time in this case. The frequency of exchange is determined by how quickly you receive and review the work, and how dependable the postal service is in returning it. (In theory, it would also be possible to use a fax to go back and forth in this method of "meeting," but given the variable quality of fax print-outs, this may or may not be a good idea.) This method can be supplemented by phone conversations, though depending on the distance, this can grow costly.

To find others who are interested in such an exchange, look to friends, family, or the classified portion of writer's magazines.

Whichever of these methods you choose to employ, take care to protect your work. Any time you exchange ideas or material with an acquaintance you are taking a risk. Whether you know the individual or not, there are those who have no qualms against claiming work or ideas that are not their own. It is horrible, but true.

Protect yourself and discuss your work and ideas wisely, particularly in remote participation groups. Unless the person on the other end is someone you already know, and know well, you are taking a risk.

THE CREATIVE APPROACH:

ALTERNATIVES TO STRUCTURED WRITING GROUPS

As I touched upon earlier, where you live, the type of equipment you have and other physical or time constraints may prevent you from taking advantage of the more standard writer's group options. One alternative I've already mentioned is critiquing by correspondence. Now I will review a few more supplementary options.

Writer's Seminars or Workshops

Run a search on the Internet, or pick up a writer's magazine, and you will find pages and pages of sites or ads for Writer's Seminars and Workshops, ranging from anywhere from a weekend to several weeks in length. Some are extremely discriminating; others are open to all. Almost all of them have a hefty participation fee.

Programs such as Clarion (which holds workshops around the nation and even in Europe) and Odyssey (the annual Fantasy Writing Workshop run by Jeanne Calevos—former senior editor with Bantam Doubleday Dell—in Manchester, New Hampshire) are by acceptance only. Think of them as literary boot camp. These are intensive programs organized and run by industry professionals to prepare those whose work is almost but not quite publishing quality. There are only a limited number of openings and they are allotted for those whose sights are set on a literary career. Your work is evaluated and if it meets their criteria, you are allowed into the program. These workshops can be brutal and costly in both time and money, but they also provide an intense writing evaluation and seminar geared toward honing your talent. They will take your work and tear it down to the ground, and then show you how to rebuild it using the techniques of the master craftsman. Courses are taught by established authors and experienced editors, those who already have an intimate knowledge of the field you are attempting to break into. Courses such as this will not coddle you, but if you let them, they will improve your abilities and understanding of what it is to be a published author.

For those who view their writing as a more casual passion, there are numerous other workshops where the process of admittance is less stringent, where those with the money and a desire to improve their writing are welcome. The structure of such workshops is more discussion panels and mini-seminars that, for the most part, do not need to be signed up for—though there are exceptions to this. Such workshops are generally a weekend, or perhaps a week in length, and attendees set their own schedule based on the topics offered and which they think they will most benefit from. Again, presenters and lecturers are professionals in the field: established authors, editors, publicists and such.

Another draw of these writer's workshops is the networking opportunities. The organizers not only set up programming to help writers polish their work, but they also arrange formal pitch sessions and meet-and-greet receptions.

Literary Conventions

I'm going to include something under this venue that might have some of you looking at me cockeyed, but among the ranks of writer's groups I include the literary convention. On most any given weekend of the year, there is a literary convention taking place somewhere in the world. Though not every panel discussion at such conventions is about the craft of writing, enough of them are that attending would be a benefit to someone wanting to improve their abilities. A lot can be gained from listening to your favorite author explain how they approach their craft.

In addition to such panels, some conventions have actual writer's workshops, which can take two different tacks: a panel of established authors and editors evaluating pre-submitted works, pointing out the strengths and weaknesses and offering constructive criticism on how to improve the story; or an informal panel where the moderator has prepared a series of mini-exercises to show ways to advance your writing. While the duration of such workshops is usually two to three hours, the benefits can be innumerable. Most weekly and monthly writer's groups do not offer the feedback of professionals in the field, especially editors, the very people you need to reach and please.

While time will decide how often you are able to participate, you may want to consider belonging to more than one type, thus benefiting from what each one has to offer.

Who Am I To Talk?

You may ask why I was invited to write this chapter, to share my knowledge on this phenomenon. Well, at the time I am writing this, I am part of no less than five on-line writer's groups, as well as a number of in-person groups, all of them some variation of what I've outlined above. Most notably, though is the fact that I founded, and have been running for the past four years, Yesterday's Dreamers, a writer's group on Yahoo! Groups.

For those of you who have tried what I have mentioned and met with little success, or those whose situations make it difficult to take advantage of my advice, I would make one more suggestion: start your own writer's group. Decide what you are looking for and find others with a similar interest. This isn't easy, but it can be done. For myself, I was already a published author before I even knew what a newsgroup was. I discovered them as a useful tool during a literary convention when I was promoting my work. That made getting started easy for me; all I had to do was set out a sign-up sheet. People interested in me and what I had to say put down their email address and they received an invitation to the newsgroup. Using this method I have gathered people around me not only interested in writing, but also interested in fantasy and science fiction, which is what I primarily write. On top of that, I also had the benefit of starting the initial relationship with about ninety percent of my members in person. Because we met through conventions, we even occasionally reunite real time.

Not everyone is going to have such an opportunity for start-up. What you can do is begin with people you already know that share your interest and desire to improve, then move from there to place an ad in either the local paper or writer's magazines.

When starting your own group—on-line or in person—keep in mind that structure, organization and discipline will be the key to smooth operation. Not only does my group's home page clearly state my intentions for the group, but each time we have a new member join I formally greet them and outline how the group works. We are currently up over sixty-eight members, many of whom are only lurkers (silent and don't contribute, but as they haven't quit, they must get something out of the group). There is a core of about twenty to twenty-five members who regularly contribute to discussions and a handful more who occasionally comment on a topic. Because the majority signed up at literary conventions we have a nice mix of experience levels and everyone benefits.

Decide what you want for you and what kind of group you would like to have. For an in-person group, approach a local library, bookstore, school or diner. Actually, any quiet place where there is space, chairs and someone in charge willing to work out the details with you. Then you are ready to gather your group.

If you are going for an on-line group, there are plenty of list-serves, newsgroup servers and message boards to choose from. All require some form of registration, and naturally some are better organized than others. Look for one that does not clutter your posts with ads and has a dependable reputation.

Once you pick your method of meeting, decide on a schedule (if applicable) and what your objectives are. For me, I intended that my newsgroup would be mainly a support structure; a place where writers could share opportunities and successes, and ask specific questions regarding the mechanics of writing related to snags they have hit in their own work. This has served us well and has kept most people interested, without bogging everyone down with stories to read.

Because some people needed a fresh perspective on their work and feedback based on experience, we also run a critique group by email, separate from but still linked to the newsgroup. The precept for that is simple: everyone submits a story, the names are stripped off, the anonymous selections are sent to everyone participating that round and everyone is free to comment without being self-conscious about commenting on a friend's story or worrying about everyone else knowing which one is theirs. The only guidelines they are given is to be positive and constructive in their comments, pointing out strengths and weaknesses in a piece. The group takes a month and half to read through all of the submissions before sending in their feedback, and then the cycle starts again.

In this way, my writer's group has the flexibility that those who want or need feedback receive it, and those who just require a sounding board can sit back and enjoy the discussions.

Everything in Moderation

Whether you are joining someone else's group or starting your own, policing the members is very important. Knowing when to speak up and when to sit back and let a conflict fade on its own isn't easy, but the situation is going to come up. Any time you bring two or more people together there is potential for disagreement, especially in a group as opinionated as writers. Add ego to that and eventually worlds will collide. If you are moderating or just caught in the crossfire, tact is your most powerful weapon. Redirect the conversation, or intercede in a way that reminds the combatants that everything is a matter of opinion and the important thing is not to confuse different with wrong. If diplomacy doesn't work, take the offenders off to the side (physically or metaphorically) and explain that if they cannot come to an agreement they need to restrict themselves to commenting peaceably on topics unrelated to the disagreement and take the argument outside the group. Anyone who continues to be a disruptive force must be asked to leave. It is harsh, but necessary at times.

Remember, regardless of the type of group you are in: writer's groups are about connecting, support, sharing and improving your ability. Politics are best left by the wayside.

The key word in writer's groups is community, with all the ups and downs that entails. Remember there will be differences of opinion and conflicts of personality. If these are allowed to become too disruptive the group will not be productive.

FURTHER RESOURCES

There are far and away too many writer's groups on-line for me to name them all, or even more than a few, but if you run a search you will find plenty of sources. I have pulled out a few that I have encountered personally to list here.

Forward Motion Writers—open group, must register to use, WWW.FMWRITERS.COM

Science Fiction and Fantasy Writers of America, Inc.—must meet membership requirements, with fee, www.SFWA.ORG

Horror Writers Association—open group, with membership fee, www.HORROR.ORG

Garden State Horror Writer's Association—open group, with membership fee, www.GSHW.NET

Malibu Writer's Group—invitation only

Yesterday's Dreamers—open group, must register to use (those interested can email me at DANIELLE@SIDHENADAIRE. COM for an invitation), HTTP://GROUPS.YAHOO.COM/GROUP/ YESTERDAYSDREAMERS

How Can I Have a Life and Still Write?
AN HONEST LOOK AT THE REAL WORLD
OF A WRITER
BY L. JAGI LAMPLIGHTER

HOW CAN I HAVE A LIFE AND STILL WRITE?

Short answer: Commitment.

Long answer: If you are committed to becoming an author, you can find the time to write, even if you work full-time, have six kids and also run the local soup kitchen. Making a commitment, however, is not the same as knowing how implement it. So the next logical question becomes: now that I have made this commitment, how do I carry it out?

In answering this question, the first point that must be stressed is that no two individuals write alike. This may sound like common sense, yet you would be surprised how frequently people assume otherwise. Articles on this subject are often restatements of what works for a particular author, offering advice such as: "Only those who sit down at midnight, by candlelight, with a full quart of ice cream balanced on their head can produce a worthwhile story. All other methods are for posers."

It would be nice if there were a magic formula that would make words flow from our fingers like honey. Alas, this is not the case. What works for one often merely exasperates another. Keeping this in mind, this chapter will examine numerous strategies for balancing our daily lives with our desire to write. Hopefully, each reader will find a helpful hint or two among the many bits of hard-earned wisdom offered.

Commitment. That Sounds Good...
How Do I Do It?

Short answer: Put aside time to write.

Long answer: Here's where the "each person is different" issue comes into play. There are as many strategies for how to plan your time as there are people who write. Most of these strategies, however, fall into two general categories: quotas and time.

The quota strategy is results-oriented. You commit yourself to writing a certain number of words or pages per day/week/month. It does not matter whether what is written is worthy of Shakespeare or merely fated for the next bonfire. The important thing is that you produce the requisite amount of product.

The time strategy, on the other hand, involves putting aside a certain number of hours each day/week/month to devote to writing. During these allotted hours, you sit at your desk and show bravery in the face of the blank screen. It does not matter whether you produce ten pages or one line. The point is to devote the same number of hours to writing on a regular basis. Eventually, you will produce something worth keeping.

To Quota or Not to Quota?

Short answer: Honestly, it depends on your mental constitution.

Long answer: Quotas are wonderful, if you have the sort of psychology that can manage one. The quota itself can be by word or by page. A page a day, five days a week, for a year will yield two hundred and sixty-one pages, approximately three-fourths of the average 80,000 word manuscript. 1,000 words once a week for a year will yield 52,000 words, about two thirds of the average 80,000 word novel. 1,000 to 1500 words per session seems to be a favorite with many writers, though some do significantly less or more.

A number of authors in the science fiction field are known for keeping strict quotas. One of the strictest is Harry Turtledove, who reports that he produces 2,300 to 2,400 words a day, seven days a week! (It is rumored that he excuses himself from writing on Christmas Day.) At that rate, an 80,000 word novel would take him a little over a month. One of his novels, which are often a bit longer, would take about two months (give or take rewriting time).

Most writers are not that severe, yet many find the quota to be an invaluable tool. As part of a series of articles entitled "So You Want To Be A Writer," author Lawrence Watt-Evans wrote: "Frederik Pohl has a daily quota of three pages. Every day, day in, day out, he writes three pages of something a day. Stephen King, I've heard, has a daily quota of several thousand words, but we won't talk about people like that. That's not normal."

"My quota," Watt-Evans continued, "back when I didn't have kids and could therefore manage one, was a thousand words a day. That's three or four pages, depending. I had to write a thousand words a day, five days a week (I got to pick which five, and could arbitrarily declare any given day to be a "weekend," so long as I hadn't already used up my two weekend days that week). If I hadn't written it, I couldn't go to bed. I wouldn't allow myself to do so any more than I would go to bed without brushing my teeth.

"If I absolutely couldn't write on a given day, then I could put it off—but the amount I owed automatically doubled the moment I fell asleep. That was my inflexible rule. And I didn't allow any carryover, either—if I wrote 8,000 words on Tuesday, I still had to write a thousand more on Wednesday. If I didn't write anything on Wednesday, my quota for Thursday would be 3,000 (Wednesday's doubled, plus Thursday's). No fractions smaller than 500 words were allowed, either. If I wrote 950 words one day, I owed 2,000 the next."

QUOTAS-SMOTAS! SO I SET ONE. SO WHAT?

Short answer: Hey, you're the one who wants to be a writer!

Long answer: Watt-Evans brought up an important issue in his last paragraph. It is often pointless to set a quota unless one can also set some penalty for breaking it. In Watt-Evan's case, if he missed a day, he forced himself to write twice as much the next day. Another writer I know would cancel weekend plans, if he did not meet his quota during the week. That way he could devote Saturday and Sunday to writing. This practice inconvenienced anyone with whom he had made weekend plans. So, he soon altered it to make the next available weekend a writing weekend, rather than the current weekend. He kept this up until he was writing so steadily, he no longer felt he needed a quota.

Exchanging writing with a friend is another way to keep motivated. Every Monday, two writers I know send each other what they wrote during the previous week. They claim the desire to have something to show the other person is a strong motivator. It encourages them to write even when they might otherwise wish to worm out of it. It also offers them the added gratification of near-immediate feedback.

Each person must develop his own enticements, whether it is increased quotas, lonely weekends, or forgoing Starbucks every time the requisite number of pages is missed. Alternately, some writers find it is not penalties that inspire them so much as rewards: a month of met quotas results in a trip to Ben and Jerry's, a new DVD or the pleasure of exchanging what they wrote with a friend. The important point is to find an incentive that motivates you.

QUOTAS DON'T WORK FOR ME. WHEN EXACTLY DO I FIT IN THIS "WRITING TIME?"

Short answer: Any time you can.

Long answer: No schedule works for everyone. That does not mean we writers cannot benefit from the wisdom of those who have successfully managed to produce a book despite their work schedule. Basically, finding the time to write breaks down into: morning, evenings, weekends, other.

Early risers often find the wee hours of the morning to be a productive time. Sounds ideal, doesn't it? You rise refreshed while the morning dew still rests on the grass. With nothing to distract you except a few birdsongs, you bang out your pages before the rest of the world so much as stirs. Kate DiCamillo, author of the Newberry Award-winning *Because of Winn Dixie*, used this method. She got up every day at 4 am and wrote two pages before she went to work. She did this five days a week. At the end of a year, she had finished a novel.

This, of course, assumes you are an early riser. If you wake up blearily, your eyes not focusing properly until after lunch, the chances of your creative juices flowing during the wee hours is probably as likely as roses springing up spontaneously in the Sahara. For the late risers, up early—however ideal—is not an option.

Writing at night is another popular solution. One mother of three reports the only time she ever has a moment to write is three in the morning. Writing at night can be dangerous, however, unless one is quite disciplined about stopping in time to get enough sleep. Late nights work best for stay-at-home parents or workers with a late shift. For those who need to be alert during the morning rat race, late night options are of limited use.

That leaves evenings and weekends. The most successful strategy here seems to be to pick a particular time and stick with it, week in and week out, as much time as makes sense for your situation. If you can swing three nights a week, go for it! If you can only spare every other Saturday, do that. If you can write one Sunday a month, then write one Sunday a month.

Is it worth it to write if you can only put aside a small amount of time? Sure it is! One budding author writes for a couple of hours on Tuesday night. He produces one to three pages on per session, averaging about 50 pages a year. In approximately seven years, he will have completed a novel. Sure, that sounds like a long time to wait. On the other hand, many of us have seen seven years come and go without a novel to show for it.

The commute is another good opportunity for some. Long commute on public transportation? Take your notebook or your PDA. Commuting by car? Buy yourself a small recording device and dictate your ideas. If you can afford modern voice to document software, you might not even have to type it again later.

At-home parents may have the advantage of writing during the day. I emphasize may because watching young children, especially more than one of them, can be a full-time job. To have writing time, parents of young children need a babysitter. Otherwise, they are limited to the same catch-as-catch-can times covered above.

School-age children are completely different animals. While there are always chores to absorb time, some of the hours the children spend at school can often be turned to writing.

Author and at-home-dad Will McDermott said, "My general schedule is to get housework out of the way in the morning and relax a little after the kids leave, and then write for a few hours in the middle of the day. Then once the kids get home, I put it away because the house tends to get too loud. This has changed recently as the kids got a little older. They are more autonomous, which allows me to work later into the afternoon.

> *The hardest part is realizing that you can't work 8 or 9 hours per day like someone who goes to a job. A good day is getting 4-5 hours of productive work done. When you're spouse asks you why you didn't get more writing done that day, you just have to smile and say 'It was slow going today.'*
> — Will McDermott

But Can Anyone Actually Write a Novel This Way? Tell Truth Now!

Short answer: Obviously.

Long answer: Every author who was not in college, retired or independently wealthy wrote his or her first novel while working at something else. Even the really famous guys had to start somewhere. When John Grisham wrote *A Time To Kill* and *The Firm*, he was working as a lawyer. This always astonishes me. My husband worked as a lawyer for a brief time, during which I hardly laid eyes upon him. Lawyers work sixty and seventy-hour weeks on a regular basis. That someone working such a demanding job could produce a novel is simply amazing! If Grisham found the time to write, the rest of us can too.

Other examples? Danielle Steele has been the reigning queen of best-sellers for over thirty years. She wrote her early books at her kitchen table in between caring for her nine children. Jacqueline Carey wrote her acclaimed work of fantasy *Kushiel's Dart* in the evenings and on weekends, while spending her days working in the visual arts field.

Science fiction and fantasy author John C. Wright writes Tuesday and Thursday nights, as well as alternate Saturdays. He fits in extra time as he approaches the completion of a project and reports that it takes him six to nine months to finish a thousand-page manuscript.

Bookstores and libraries are popular day jobs for writers, for obvious reasons. Fantasy writer Michelle M. Welch still works as a reference librarian, despite having published three books. Teaching is another career that can mesh well with writing. *Da Vinci Code* author Dan Brown was originally an English teacher. Eoin Colfer, author of the popular children's book *Artemis Fowl,* taught elementary school while he wrote his first few novels. Paul Levinson was named Teacher of the Year by Fordham University in 2004, yet he finds time to write works of both science and science fiction.

WHAT IF ALL THIS PLANNING DOESN'T TAKE?

Short answer: Keep trying.

Long answer: Some writers claim not to take well to schedules or quotas. Instead, they like to take their notebook or PDA everywhere with them and write as the mood strikes. Reporter Robin Buehler, who must write all day at her job, produces her poetry and fiction in this fashion. Anytime she plans a structured writing day, she finds that events immediately converge to interfere, leaving her frustrated and angry. Rather than get her hopes up and have them dashed again, she prefers to catch each moment as she can. Working in this fashion she has produced quite a few poems that have gone on to publication.

If a catch-as-catch-can system works for you, wonderful. The proof is in the finished manuscript. If at the end of the year, you have something to show for your efforts, you are on the right track. If not having a schedule or quota is translating into not getting any writing done, it might be time to try something more structured.

Which brings me to an important point:

Don't I Have to Be "in the Mood" to Write?

Short answer: No.

Long answer: Many years ago, I believed in the "had to be in the mood" theory. I used to write when I felt creative and avoid writing if I did not. One day, when I was very tired and had just been in a bad argument, I sat down to write anyway. To my utter astonishment, I discovered that what I produced was as good as my normal fare. Since then, I have heard from other writers who have had similar experiences.

Humans are creatures of habit. If you sit down at the same time every week, sooner or later, you may find yourself "in the mood" when that time rolls around. And if not, don't panic. Merely the act of sitting before the blank screen and trying to write often gets those creative juices flowing.

Are There Jobs That Will Hinder My Writing Career?

Short answer: Sure, any job that sucks up your creative energy.

Long answer: Some people have a career and write on the side. Obviously, they are not interested in changing their occupation. Others, however, just want to write. What these folks do for a living is just a place holder; something to keep them afloat until they reach the longed-for day when they can chuck their day job and write full-time. For them, it can be useful to know which kinds of jobs encourages writing and which hinder it.

Humans are versatile, and an exception can be found to every rule. Nonetheless, some professions are more conducive to writing than others. The best job for a would-be author is one where you can write at work. The next-best is one where you can walk away at finishing-time and still have enough creative energy to do your evening writing. The kind of jobs you want to avoid are jobs that require massive overtime, that leave you totally exhausted at the end of the workday or that suck up your creative thought even when you are not in the office.

Are there jobs where you can write your own stuff at work? Sure. Night watchmen, a help desk with a light call load, jobs with long travel times, or long meetings during which you can be writing away and no one will ask questions. Many such jobs have heavy periods, when the calls get busy, and you earn your keep. In between, however, they have long lulls, during which you are being paid merely to be present, and no one cares if you read a book—or write one.

If you cannot find this kind of job, the next best thing is one that leaves you able to write in your off-work hours. The key here is to find work that you personally do not find too taxing. When my husband and I were first married, we decided that we wanted to write in the evenings. To facilitate this goal, we took retail jobs, thinking that we would then be certain that our responsibilities would end the instant we walked out of the store. This proved a mistake. Working at the bookstore in the mall, for instance, proved more exhausting and paid less than the office temp jobs we ended up working half a decade later. Had we but tried our hand at office work earlier, we might both be five years ahead in our writing careers.

If you have a taxing job to which you are not devoted, you may need to bite the bullet and change occupations. If you have a taxing job you love, however, you are going to have to consider which matters to you more, your job or your writing career. If you can force yourself to write in spite of a demanding job, wonderful. If not, one of the two is going to have to go.

What about a Job That Requires Writing, Such as Reporting or Tech Writing?

Short answer: It depends.

Long answer: Writers are divided on this point. Some find the discipline they develop in reporting or tech writing carries over to their fiction. Others claim that writing all day exhausts them, and they are unable to make themselves write more when they come home. Either way, however, a job that requires writing may be a good step in developing your skill, even if you must later change jobs in order to have the energy to produce your own work.

Are There Activities I Can Participate in That May Improve My Writing?

Short answer: Anything that encourages you to write.

Long answer: The kind of activity that requires use of your imagination or your writing skill can be a big help in developing your abilities. In particular, reading, emailing, newsgroups, blogging, writing fan fiction, role-playing games, etc.. Also, any activity that gives you access to a subject about which you wish to write. Reading familiarizes one with writing and what has been written. Emailing, newsgroups, blogging and fan fiction contributions hone writing skills. Role-playing develops characterization and, for moderators, plotting.

ARE THERE ACTIVITIES THAT ARE DETRIMENTAL TO WRITING?

Short answer: Anything that keeps you from writing.

Long answer: Putting aside activities that are detrimental no matter who you are, writers should, in particular, beware of: reading, emailing, newsgroups, blogging, role-playing, and writing fan fiction.

Now, the astute reader might notice some similarities between this list and the one in the question above. This is because the same activities that can help you develop your creative ability can become a hindrance if you indulge in them rather than actually write. These activities are of more use as a learning tool for beginners than they are to the more advanced writer. Advanced writers may enjoy these things, but they sometimes reach a point when they feel the need to put such activities aside, at least until they establish themselves as an author.

A particular note about fan fiction: while any activity that encourages you to write may be good for beginners, there is a danger to becoming too comfortable writing in someone else's background. As Watt-Evans points out in the same series of articles quoted above, very few of those who have won the Hugo for "Best Fan Writer" have ever gone on to make a name for themselves as an author. In the long run, you may find it worthwhile to take the time and energy to invent your own background right from the beginning.

CAN I BE EXCUSED FROM EXERCISING BECAUSE I NEED THE TIME TO WRITE?

SHORT ANSWER: Well, obviously, you could... but it's not such a good idea.

Long answer: One of the nice things about writing is that you never get too old to do it. You'll never be forced to stop and retire unless you wish to—or you become too ill to continue. To a degree, our health is out of our hands. Yet, there are things we can do to increase our chances of a long productive life. One of those things is to stay in some semblance of shape (preferably a shape other than 'sphere'). Therefore, it is best not to remove exercise from your schedule entirely.

Some writers are naturally athletic and already have physical activities they enjoy. If so, wonderful! All you need do now is weigh your commitment to your writing against your commitment to sports, and work out a schedule that balances these two activities.

If you are like the average writer, however, you would like nothing more than to find a way to squirm out of the self-imposed gym class we call exercise. If writing would work an excuse, that would be yet another wonderful reason to recommit yourself to your chosen career! Alas, as explained above, this is not such a keen idea. There are, however, ways to use even the horrific drudgery of exercise to enhance your writing.

For some, it will be the repetitiveness of an exercise machine, a tread mill or rowing machine that will get those creative ideas flowing. For others, taking a walk or even biking may be the answer. The key is to find an activity that gives you uninterrupted time to ponder. Look for an activity that encourages you to spend the exercising time contemplating your latest work, mulling over characters or puzzling out the knotty plot problems. You may even want to find a way to carry a small notebook and pen for jotting down ideas that come to you during exercise.

What you want to avoid is physical activities that require a great deal of thought and therefore takes away from the time you could spend devoted to the mental aspect of your work. A walk that requires you to stop and greet all your neighbors or a bike ride where you must pause for a red light every seven feet may be too distracting to be beneficial. You also might wish to avoid more social sports, such as an adult soccer team or doubles tennis—with all the strategy and talking these activities entail.

Obviously, if you can't get yourself out of the house unless you go with a friend, you might want to jettison the pondering time and take up a team sport or tennis. Any exercise is better than none.

The truly fortunate among us are those writers who have an exercising environment that allows them to work on wording or try bits of dialog aloud without receiving unpleasant stares from the guy on the next stair-stepper. The rest of us must grit our teeth and remind ourselves that we are enduring this for our art.

Added bonus to exercise: some writers find that exercise—especially if performed in silence without TV, music or other distractions—is an excellent cure for writer's block. Just get out there, do some constant, uninterrupted physical activity, and soon the ideas begin to flow!

Can I Give up Eating to Have More Time for Writing?

Short answer: No.

Long answer: Still no. See the part above about needing your health to continue as a writer.

Can I just Eat Junk Food and Take-Out so I Have More Time to Write?

Short answer: Yes, but...

Long answer: Obviously, a diet of junk food brings us back to the health issue. As for take-out: if you can afford to eat high-quality take-out all the time, more power to you! Most of us cannot, so we are left with the small practical steps that can be taken to simplify food preparation and thus maximize writing time.

The ideal situation, of course, is to have someone else prepare your meals: your wife, your mother, etc. That way, you only need to leave your writing long enough to grab your plate (assuming the person preparing the food will not bring it to you) and bring it back to your desk, where you can munch between keystrokes.

Sadly, not all writers are so lucky. For those who are also stay-at-home parents, they often must feed not only themselves but also their hungry brood and tired spouse. Thirty-minute meals and other short recipes are a help. Many grocery stores offer such recipes for free. Food can also be prepared in larger amounts and frozen to save preparation time on another day. The true friend of the stay-at-home writer, however, is the crock pot. You prepare the dish in the morning, when you have not yet gotten into the swing of writing. It cooks all day, and voila! When evening and the ravenous hordes arrive, the meal is already cooked. You have only to ladle it into bowls.

Can I Sedate My Children with the TV so I Can Write?

Short answer: You can...but doing so on a regular basis is really not a good idea.

Long answer: Plopping your kids down in front of a cartoon while you nip upstairs and write can be tempting. However, it is not wise or practical as a regular method of achieving writing time, unless you are disciplined enough to get up early on the weekend and write during Saturday Morning cartoons.

Otherwise, such despicable practices should be saved for last-minute deadlines and other occasions that are few and far between.

Hypnotizing your children with television for the entire month of July while you finish your novel is really not recommended, unless you want to witness first hand the transformation of your sweet little angels into a bunch of cranky whiners. Take it from one who, alas, knows!

CAN I HAVE A FAMILY AND STILL WRITE?

Short answer: Definitely, but it is easier if your family is supportive.

Long answer: Anything is harder if you have to comfort three screaming children who have just brained each other with daddy's golf clubs while you are doing it. No question! Yet many family men and women do become authors. The key is to remember you have a lot on your plate and try not to take on more than you can handle.

Getting the support of your family, particularly your spouse, is very important if you want to be in any mood to write when you finally sit down (much less have your food delivered to your desk). Thus it is important to try to be attentive to that other half when you are not writing. This can be difficult. When not at their desks, writers are often mulling over their stories in their heads. Dragging your thoughts away to notice someone else's needs can be quite a struggle. In the long run, however, it is well worth the effort.

The issue is a bit different when both partners are writers. Some writers swear by this. They claim only another writer really understands when you shut the door of your office, leaving them to be mugged by three rabid children under the age of six. More importantly, only another writer is going to understand why you need to sit for half an hour staring vacantly into space, or playing a level of Doom, or surfing the Web, or pacing and muttering to yourself, or juggling bananas.

(Hey, if that is what helps your ideas flow, juggle, man, juggle!) J. K. Rowling reported she plays Minesweeper in between cranking out pages of Harry Potter. Another author I know plays Solitaire. All these activities (which seem like distractions to the non-writer) are understood by one's fellow aspirant.

On the other hand, unless you are so lucky to live in a house with two offices and, if applicable, a built-in babysitter, two writers means a struggle over the family resources. Who uses the computer and when? Who uses the good computer at the desk and who is consigned to the old clunker in the basement? Worse, who does the housework while the other one writes?

Some writer-couples also complain of jealousy upon the part of whichever spouse's career is not doing as well.

All of this is rather a moot point, however, because very few people deliberately pick their spouses based on whether or not they write. Still, it is wise to make sure your intended supports your desire to become a writer before you tie the knot.

Is There Anything Else?

Short answer: Nope, that about sums it up.

Long answer: Organizing your job, recreation, exercise, eating habits and marriage around your writing career seem a bit too extreme? Maybe you do not need any of this. Maybe quotas or a dedicated writing time will be enough for you. At the end of the month, however, if you are not holding finished pages in your hand, you might want to take a look at the other areas of your life and decide just how important becoming an author is to you. After all, if you hesitate to take steps that are necessary for you to do your best, you may continue to find yourself empty-handed. Meanwhile the fellow who did not hesitate is publishing his fifth bestseller.

Which is just another way of saying that it all comes down to: commitment.

Take Control!
MULTIPLE PROJECTS
BY LAZETTE GIFFORD

Authors who plan to make a career in the publishing business should be on the look out for writing opportunities which will help them get their name in front of the reading public. Sometimes a short article in a writing magazine, for instance, can reach new readers by a venue outside the usual marketing lines. Short stories can do the same, and even writing something like a blog on a regular basis can draw potential fans.

Assessing your time, tracking your work and especially taking control of the larger projects will allow you to know what is safe for you to take on, and make certain that you get your projects done and submitted on time.

PART ONE: OVERALL MANAGEMENT

Time

If you actively pursue new writing opportunities, you might sometimes find yourself deluged with different writing projects and each on its own deadline. These can be everything from a novel under contract to a short story for an anthology or a nonfiction article to a writing magazine. Making certain you get all of your work done on time—and written well—is important to maintaining good relationships with editors and publishers.

The first and most important aspect of project control is to logically evaluate your time constraints. Saying, for instance, you work from nine-to-five and have the rest of the day and weekends free to write is not realistic. You must travel to and from work, have dinner, maybe spend time with your family and friends, do housework and perhaps even have some community obligations.

It may turn out that at best you have only an hour of truly free time to write during each work week day. Counting on anything more would be counter-productive to the process of arranging your work load to best handle the writing.

This hour also involves more than just sitting down at the keyboard and clicking out words. There is research to consider and editing as well. Every project, from a new fiction novel to a short nonfiction article, will require some of both.

Keeping track of the timeframe for a large task (like a novel under contract) is an important aspect of project control. Once you have control of your schedule, you'll know if adding another project is a reasonable decision.

Even if you are working only with short stories, the overall process is the same, and you'll need to evaluate how long each story will take you to write. Try to overestimate the amount of time it will take you, because some padding will help with the projects which inexplicably stall.

The Big S

Stress can have a negative effect on your writing so you will need to avoid it as much as you can. Never underestimate what taking on more work than you can comfortably handle will do to your ability to write. Deadlines are stress-inducing, no matter how well planned the work may be, and any little bit of real life—good or bad—might upset your writing schedule. If you're not used to having a steady writing workload without time to recover and replenish between projects, you may find that having too many of them can create a problem.

One of the hardest lessons (especially for someone just starting out on a career) is learning when and how to say no to a prospective writing assignment, but keep in mind that if you can't make the deadlines it's also not going to help your fledgling career. You must quickly learn to judge how much writing work you can handle. If you have a fulltime day job as well, taking on too many writing assignments can be more work than the return warrants.

Being asked for material is thrilling the first few times and the excitement alone can get you through the work, even if you are already busy. If you already have contracts for manuscripts, like a novel due to a publisher, it must take priority over any new projects, no matter how much fun they look. The wonderful idea for a new short story/book/ series must be put on hold. If you have work under contract, you dare not let your imagination wander too far off the path to explore new territory, and lose the feel for the material which must get done.

Occasionally a writer may be able to postpone a proposed project until later. If a magazine asks for a nonfiction article or short story for their next issue, but you are already strapped for time, ask to have a spot in a future issue instead. Then put the item into your schedule and make certain you get it done early, if possible. If you are working on several small projects, line them up according to due date, make certain that you have time to do the research you need, and work your way through them.

Once again, be sure to give yourself plenty of leeway so that if something does not fall together the way you imagined, you have time to step back and rethink the material.

Once you have a larger project, like a novel under contract, you need to start thinking in terms of more complex schedules. Even if you only have a single novel to get through, and no side projects, giving yourself a timetable is a good way to make certain that you get the work done on time.

In fact, you would be wise to set your timetable so the novel will be done ahead of the date the book is due to the publisher. Giving yourself as much leeway as possible will allow for moderate vacations and "real life" disasters—or even an occasional smaller project along the way.

If you have more than one project that needs to be done, you'll need to sit down and figure out which one is going to take more time. A nonfiction article of a thousand words may look like something you can write in a weekend, but—once again—don't forget to factor in research and edits. Don't underestimate the time it will take to complete. Better to have extra time than not enough.

Many new writers with novel contracts, seeing that they have months to do the work, put it off in favor of doing other things. Here's something to consider though: Are you one of those people who end up making your holiday gifts the week after they should have been in the mail? Do you find yourself rushing to get the last minute work done before you go off on vacation, even though you had weeks to prepare before hand?

Then make a schedule, start early and work on your material without fail. Writing a novel is not something you want to leave to the last minute.

Give yourself ample time not only to write, but also to take breaks, to rethink material and to rewrite— and still get the manuscript turned in on time.

Organization

Ideas, character creation, worldbuilding, outlines for novels, research notes, interviews and outlines for nonfiction articles—there are numerous pieces that go into projects, and that's even before you get to the manuscript writing. You will want to have some way so that you can keep all of this information in a readily-accessible format. A plain paper notebook can be good for many of the pieces, especially if you can carry it with you and are able to add notes at any time. A three-ring binder is better because you can put both handwritten and computer-generated notes in one, rearrange them to suit you and easily add in extra pieces of information as you find them.

For those who keep everything on the computer, it doesn't hurt to make periodic printouts and to occasionally replace the older copies of information with updated ones. It's also wise, of course, to make back up files and keep them somewhere safe and away from the computer. In fact, even if you handwrite most of your material, you may want to set up a schedule where you either type or scan the material into the computer, thereby making a back up of your handwritten material as well.

Note cards can be kept in notebooks by either taping them to pages or buying plastic pages into which they can be slid. This last will allow you to rearrange them as you need to, and to easily group them for reading.

A PDA (Palm, Visor, Clié or even the more expensive pocket computer) is also a very handy way to do notes at any time and place and have them in an easily accessible format since the PDA will download the information to your computer.

Keeping track of your information is one of the most important parts of project control. It helps you make the best use of your time.

How you organize the material is up to you. However, remember that it doesn't help you to do the hard work of research, worldbuilding and character creation if you can't find or access the information when you later need it.

Charting Your Progress
Many writers find it useful to chart their progress and word count totals, especially if they have a deadline to make. Such a chart, done on Microsoft Excel™ or any other like program, can allow you to track

the number of words you've written along with how many more you need to do per day to meet your deadline. You can, of course, do the same on paper or on a calendar where you can write the information. Making certain that you stay on track during the actual story writing is very important. All the preparation in the world won't help if you don't apply yourself to the writing and stick to it. This is one of the main places where the ability to self-motivate is essential. Having something that tracks the work and makes you look at your results can help.

This will also give you a way of watching which projects need your immediate attention before they fall too far behind. You may not have the choice of setting aside all other writing work in favor of a big project like a novel. If not, keeping a calendar and checking it regularly is going to be very important. You may also need to build in alerts that give you plenty of time before a deadline to get work done. Having an alert that says "send article today" will not be nearly as helpful as "article due in three days" with follow ups on the next two days. Computer programs like Microsoft Outlook™ are an excellent way to organize such warnings, but only if you keep them updated and pay attention to them when they arrive.

Writing to any regular schedule will work—every day, three days a week, only on weekends—whatever works best for you. However, if you have fewer writing days, you will need to write more material at each sitting. If you fall behind, don't worry—as long as you continue to write, you will get the novel done.

A writer who has trouble sitting down and working might join in dares, challenges, marathons, and other anti-procrastination games that can be found at various places on the Internet. Forward Motion (HTTP://FMWRITERS.COM) runs something every month, besides having regular two month long challenges of various types. It might be just what you need to focus on the work and learn how to pace yourself for longer writing projects.

PART TWO: ORGANIZING PROJECTS

There is no sure way to schedule in something like the writing of articles or short stories when you are working on a bigger project like a novel. You have to decide when you're comfortable with writing them. If you find that writing something else breaks your feel for a novel, then don't do smaller projects during the writing phase. You might even find that you do an entire novel project from idea to submission, and then take some time to write smaller projects before you start a new novel. If you have projects that are time-sensitive, make certain you get them done as quickly as possible. There is nothing that will induce writer's block faster than an article you haven't started that needs to be completed in the next day.

There's something else worth mentioning: Avoid projects you don't want to write. Just because you are offered a possibility doesn't mean you have to take it. It's better to turn down an article, book or short story possibility than to find yourself stuck working on something you dislike. That dislike can translate into two problems. First, your prose isn't likely to shine in something you don't like. Second, a disagreeable project can slow you down and take time from other

Handling Small Projects

Once you start thinking of your writing career as a series of individual projects, some of which overlap, you will see the need to keep track of the pieces and arrange your writing schedule to accommodate them. Those projects may come in various sizes, from novels to short articles. It is, unfortunately, easy to lose track of material as it begins to pile up, or to leave it until the last minute and rush through something that should have had better research and editing. Not keeping track of projects can put you in a contract bind and even take the joy out of writing.

Project control for writers is almost entirely about time management and self-motivation. Without a boss standing directly over you, it can be easy to put off work until later. If you aren't careful, it's also easy to lose track of smaller obligations. When you decide to take on a new project, make certain you know what it requires before you agree, including the expected word count, deadlines and how much research you will need to do. Also make certain that whatever else you have already committed to is not going to suffer for taking on a new job. A weekly blog entry is relatively easy to track and remember, even when you are working on a big project like a novel. However, add a couple nonfiction articles, a story for an upcoming anthology and a query to a publisher and you might find yourself floundering.

Short Stories

Writing short stories, even while working on a larger project, can be a nicely fulfilling way to use your creativity. They can also give the writer a sense of actually accomplishing something since it's far easier to get to "The End" than it is with a novel. Not all people are short story writers, and it's not a requirement for novelists to write and sell short stories as well. Many published authors have written only novels, and some have written only short stories. Authors have to find what they're comfortable with.

Unlike a novel, a short story often does not need a huge amount of pre-work. The lesser amount of worldbuilding needed, and the fact that the plot can usually be held in the head for the entire short time it takes you to write, make these nice additions to slip in now and then. If you find your story is taking longer to write than you expected, one thing you can do which will help you stay focused is to end each day's work with a list of steps for the rest of the story.

Be sure to take the time to properly edit the story. Afterwards, look for a publisher to submit to—unless you have written a story for a specific market. If you have, get it off to them early. If it's rejected, find another market. Keeping stories in circulation is relatively easy compared to writing and editing them, and much easier than novel submission since you don't need anything but a cover letter and the story. Don't let short stories sit around gathering dust.

Nonfiction articles

Writing nonfiction articles can be a great boost to your income. Nonfiction articles almost always pay better than fiction. However, they take a lot more care than writing a quick short story.

The first step is to decide if there is a market for your material. There are markets for just about everything out there, so the chances are good that whatever you've come up with will find a home. However, check first. Some topics may only be open to professionals in the field. Some may require you to write in a way which would make the article more work than you care to do.

Many markets require that you query with an article idea. You may be able to put out several queries without having to write the material first.

The second step is to research your article. It doesn't matter if you think you know exactly what you're talking about—double check those facts. You will also likely be asked to give references for the article, so it doesn't hurt to find some material that supports what you want to write about.

The third step is to write and edit. With a short article these two actions can often be handled at the same time. Get the manuscript done as quickly as you can, and send it off to the market. Don't try to second-guess yourself on whether it will work or not. Trust your research and your writing. If you have done both to the best of your ability, then reworking the article again and again will not make it better. Also, remember that anything seasonal has to be to the publisher months in advance. Get that holiday article out in July!

Handling a Novel Project

Keeping track of a number of smaller projects is difficult enough, but once you have a manuscript which is going to take months to develop and write, it becomes more complicated.

Many writers make their first novel sale based on a book they spent years writing, editing and nurturing. They make the heady first sale and suddenly they have a contract saying the publisher wants a second book...in one year! Sometimes they have even less time. Knowing how long it took them to complete the first novel, some writers have even turned down contracts because they didn't believe they could fulfill the 'second novel' clause. Publishers are often unwilling to give the writer more time in the contract, and for a good reason. Once your book is on the stand, you will want to have a second one there as soon as possible to reinforce name recognition for those who enjoyed the first book.

Nevertheless, having taken several years to get your first novel done, how can you hope to get a second one written, edited and ready in so short a time?

You need to evaluate the steps needed to move from the formation of the original idea all the way to submission. There are pitfalls along the way, and places where you can get stuck and that have nothing to do with the actual writing process. This can be one of the most fearful challenges for new authors. One way to overcome this obstacle is to start preparing yourself before you have a publishing contract in hand.

Treat each of your novels as though you have already sold it, both in the quality and in the timeframe during which you work. Preparing now for a time when you have to meet time constraint obligations will make the first contract—and the ones after it—far less frightening.

Planning to write in a timely manner doesn't make the writing any less fun. In fact, by focusing on the work, you may find you are more attuned to the story and the characters than if you spread the writing over a longer period of time. By preplanning and sticking to the schedule the story will have a better chance of remaining coherent, whereas a novel abandoned for months can lose focus and require extensive reworking.

Whether you also take on other new projects, and how many you're comfortable with, is going to depend on you. No one else can tell you how much work you can handle and at which point the workload will start affecting the quality of the individual pieces. You have to learn to be honest with yourself.

The Steps in a Novel Project

An idea! It comes racing through your head, and your heart beats a little faster. You suddenly smile for no reason anyone around you can see. If the people present know you, they'll just nod and say it's a "writer's moment." If they don't know you, they'll just consider you strange. It's all the same. You're a writer.

However, if every writer immediately leapt up and started writing novels based only on those first impressions and ideas which come flooding into their heads, the chances are they wouldn't finish anything. An idea is not enough.

The first step in a novel project is to look at your wonderful idea and see if you can expand it enough to create a viable story. Starting something which dies in the second or third chapter is a waste of your time and counterproductive to producing publishable work. It becomes easy to abandon projects if you are not prepared to take them from the first idea all the way to the end.

You also need to think about the story and the characters who are going to people it. Are these people and events you want to live with for the next year or more?

The second step is to do research. If you're writing a contemporary fantasy based in the real world, you really don't need any research, right? Wrong. Never skip on the research. Get as much background material sorted out for your story as you can, though beware of overindulging in your fact-finding mission. Some people love research so much that they sometimes never get around to writing the book. If you are writing a fantasy set in an imaginary world, you will need to create an entire world and everything in it. The good side is that you can make something fit, rather than worrying if you missed something in your research of the world as we know it.

What does this have to do with project management? Doing the prework to a novel can save the writer considerable time later. There's no reason to rush. Let your mind work on the story and the characters, and do whatever research you think you need. Chances are you'll end up doing more as you get into the novel, but getting the obvious stuff out of the way will allow you to move forward on the novel with few delays.

Character creation may come before the research, during it, or afterwards, depending on the type of writer you tend to be. Many plotdriven writers imagine a situation and then create characters to fit into the scenario. Others are character-driven and imagine their characters followed by what sort of world they would live in. It doesn't matter which way you work; when the book reaches the shelves readers can rarely tell the difference. The best stories weave character, plot and world together no matter which came first in the author's mind.

The third step is the outline. Yes, outline. I know some of you are shaking your heads in dismay and vowing you will never write an outline; it will stifle your creativity, you'll lose interest in the story, your characters will no longer have the freedom to explore that they need.

Outlines are not set in stone directions you have to follow from start to finish without any deviations. They are nothing more than roadmaps which will keep you on a general course from the first line of your story to The End. The outline isn't going to dictate every move your character makes, who he sees and what he does. Even with your roadmap/outline, you are likely going to end up taking detours to see odd and exotic things along the way. Your imagination is in no way constrained by the words on the paper. Then why bother with an outline at all?

An outline makes certain your important scenes fall where they need to for story pacing, and that you remember to cover all aspects of the complicated story line. If you do follow something unexpected that turns up as you write, the outline will help direct you back to where you need to be in order to reach the next important step in your novel. An outline can note not only events, but thematic revelations, mystery clues or any other aspect of the story the writer wants to track. An outline is a writing tool. There is one important reason to get used to writing an outline of some sort; many publishers and agents require the submission of one before you write your novel. This form is usually called a synopsis, and is essentially little more than an outline in paragraph format. This is an important tool for professional authors who cannot afford to take a year to write a novel that doesn't sell. Learn to write one now and you'll have yet another hurdle crossed before you have to face it under more demanding circumstances.

The fourth step is to start writing. If you have done the research, character creation and outlining, you're probably going to find it remarkably easy.

If you already have a contract in hand and the promise of an advance when the book is delivered, you'll probably have enough reason to keep going. For other writers, self-motivation, the need to tell the story and even promising yourself a reward for staying on track may work. With or without a contract, give yourself a deadline. Use a chart like I mentioned before and keep close track of how many words you need to do to get the novel done on time. If you do have a contract, don't forget to allow time to edit once you have completed the novel. Even if you are an "edit while you write" novelist, you will still have to go over the work again.

If you have a year to write the novel, you might take the first two months to do all the pre-work of research, character creation, and outlining. You will want to give yourself at least two months to edit, as well. So you now have eight months to write the novel. That's about 244 days.

But not everyone wants to work every single day. So let's round this off too 200 days in which to write a novel that needs to be about 120,000 words. Sounds horrible, doesn't it? This works out to a mere 600 words a day.

If you apply yourself to keeping a schedule, this will give you plenty of time to not only write the novel, but also take on other projects if you find that you have the time and that they won't interfere with what you are already doing. The trick is to make sure you stay focused and get each project done.

The fifth step is editing. Once you have finished the novel, let it sit for a few days. Relax. Enjoy life in the real world again! If you find you want to write, now is again a good time to take on another small project. It can even help you get a little distance on your novel which will make it easier to edit.

When you're ready to get back to work, you'll have to start new goals based on editing. They will be similar to the writing phase, only now you'll have goals for "pages edited" rather than "words written." Using the simplified system of saying a book has an average of 300 words per page (when properly formatted), this would mean a book of 120,000 words would be 400 pages long. Following the suggestions I've made for a year long schedule, you will not have two months left before your deadline. Like the eight months to write, you will not likely want to edit every single day, so set your goal at 50 days, which will give you 8 pages a day to edit.

Depending on how you go about your editing, you may have to up the number, or work out a multiple pass system. Study books specifically on editing, read on-line tips and take your time at this phase. And remember that the sooner you get the novel written, the more time you will have to edit it.

After you've gone over the work, you might even want to find a beta reader or two to make some final suggestions. The author is sometimes blind to some problems, and getting them corrected before you send the work for submission can sometimes make the difference between a rejection and an acceptance. You need not ask your beta reader for a line edit (you should have already fixed any of those problems), but do have him point out any obvious problems, both in plot and grammar.

Do not send the novel to a beta reader before you do your first edit. A beta reader is best used to gauge a virtually finished product and point out any last changes which need to be made. Having a person read a book too early in the process wastes his time, and ruins him as a beta reader for a later version. You want the impression that the book would make on a person who bought it off a shelf. Work your way through the edits with care. This may take extra time if you engage a beta reader. Do the best you can, but—like overindulging in research—don't keep editing when it's really time to let go.

The sixth step is the last one! As soon as you finish the editing, start preparing your submission package. For those who are working on the second book for a contract, this is pretty easy. Get the work done and deliver it to the publisher. Sending early is good, as long as you've really done all the work. Never send an unedited draft, or one you haven't gone over even after the final edit. Make certain the impression you present is one of professionalism.

For those who are using this timetable but still have to submit the material to a publisher, this means a bit more work. Query letters, cover letters, synopsis and first three chapters are all pieces you might have to put together for a submission.

Read the guidelines to whatever place you want to submit and write up a small template which includes everything they want. Afterwards, start filling in the spots. You need not do this in order. Writing the synopsis might be your first step since it is often the most difficult. If the process calls for a query letter before you send a submission package, do it and get it off—but then go on with rest of the work without waiting for an answer.

Writing a synopsis is often considered one of the most difficult parts of working toward publication. Find books and web sites to give you hints, and don't fret too much over it. Do the best you can, but realize this is another piece that takes practice and will get easier the more of them you do.

After you have sent off this submission package is another good time to find some smaller projects to do. This is also a great time to start working up ideas for the next novel. Don't sit back and wait—and waste time. A short break can be rejuvenating, but as soon as possible start the process again. The more work you have completed, the better your chances for sales.

If you do make a novel sale, be aware that you will have at least one more round of editing to do, and you'll have to fit this into your schedule as well. It will be easier to do if you already have a grasp of how much time the work takes you.

More than one novel at a time

Some people work on a number of novels at once. There can be problems with this method, and one of them is that the novels sometimes tend to a "sameness" in the story and characters. Be wary of writing the same book in several versions.

If you are working on more than one novel at a time, I suggest you vary the steps. Don't start research on a second novel until you have at least started the writing phase of the first one. In this way you will have a good round of work going:

Novel One		
Pre-writing work (idea though outline)	Novel Two	
Writing	Pre-writing work (idea though outline)	
Editing and Submission	Writing	Novel Three
	Editing and Submission	Pre-writing work (idea though outline)

Working on projects other than just novels might go something like this:

	Novel	Other Projects
Month One	Story idea and Expansion	This is a good time to write shorter material.
Month Two	Research, character creation, outline	Research can be a wonderful time to get ideas for short stories and articles. Take advantage of the time while you're not doing other writing. Also jot down any notes for future novel ideas as well.
Month Three through Ten	Writing	Try to stay focused on the novel during this time. Trying to do too many projects can distract you from the main one and make it harder to write.
Month Eleven through Twelve	Editing and Submission	Taking a break between writing and editing is another great time for a shorter project—or to start looking at ideas and pre-work for a new novel!

While you are researching your novel project you may find this is a good time to work on short stories and articles. Doing research can lead to a number of side ideas, and working those into short stories, or writing articles about something fascinating that you're researching, can add both income and a nice release for all that writing energy you're building up.

During these pre-novel-writing months be on the lookout for other writing opportunities that you can handle relatively quickly before you get into the part of writing where you should be concentrating on the novel. Give yourself definite word count limits, and don't let this material interfere with your research, worldbuilding and character creation for the novel.

Part Three: A Look at Managing Multiple Projects in Real Life

Besides what I've already written in this chapter, I have two additional rules that I apply to all my own writing:

1. Finish everything I start.
2. Complete projects within one year.

Some people will find those two rules excessive, but they keep me from wasting time on piles of unfinished material or setting aside projects when I hit a bad spot with the intention of getting back to them "someday." I don't have time to waste, so I don't start any project until I have thought it out and made certain that I want to write it, and can do it in a reasonable time frame. A project which stretches out too long loses coherency, and I lose interest as other projects start slipping in ahead of it.

Not every story works as well as I hoped when I start—but I still finish them. I've learned more about writing from the ones which gave me trouble than from the easy ones. Forcing myself to rework a plot that didn't fall together right, or to recreate a character who couldn't hold up her part of the story, is a good exercise. It has shown me where some of my weaknesses are and how to avoid them in the future. I always start a new novel every January 1st. These are always books I want to write, and I've done the planning as the previous year winds down. It's good to start the year out with this kind of enthusiasm and it helps to set the mood for the year. I consider myself primarily a novelist, although I usually write at least a dozen short stories and at least as many articles during the year. I also take part in NaNoWriMo (National Novel Writing Month, every November), and write a couple novels in thirty days. Those are the only things which I have planned to write from year-to-year. Whatever else I write comes from inspiration, requests, and contracts. You cannot plan for any of those; you can only be ready to take them on when they arrive.

Within a couple weeks of the start of the year I'll already have multiple projects lined up, and some of them started. I keep track of them all on a webpage in my journal which also includes my word count per month and my submissions. On a table in this page I note the title, day began/finished, type (novel, short story, article, etc.), genre and number of words. I note all unfinished projects with a different color so that they're easy to find as I look through the list. (HTTP://ZETTESWORLD.COM/JOURNAL/PROGRESS/PROGRESS04.HTM)

I do not list every project, but that's just because I often get things written without remembering to enter them. Articles are rarely listed. Neither are things like the weekly class I write at Forward Motion. You will, however, find outlines listed. For my records, I consider an outline (and the research that goes with it) as a separate project from actually writing the book. In fact, outlines might be written a year or more before I start the novel.

Many of my first draft novels tend to be short. That's just the way I write. It's not unusual for a novel to gain 30,000 to 50,000 words in the edit. I write a linear and sparse first draft and fill in details on the second round, sometimes adding in subplots and additional characters.

This means my writing time and editing time usually balance out more than they will for people who write a good, solid full first draft and only have to edit it afterwards, without massive amounts of additional material.

Maintaining daily word counts is another very important aspect of how I work. My goal is to average at least 1,000 words per day at the end of the month. I rarely write that "little," however. Writing every day trains the mind to slip easily into the work, and having the research done makes it easier to move forward on a story, novel, or article. I keep track of my daily word count in an Excel spread sheet and I've written over one million words for several consecutive years.

Writing every day will give the author a lot of finished first drafts, which are just as useless as unfinished stories and articles. So I also edit at least five pages every day, and this is entered on the Excel sheet as well. Editing, done in five to ten page chunks, is a lot easier than editing an entire novel all at once. It's an easily achieved goal, and I learned early that setting goals too high only result in frustration rather than progress.

The trick to doing this much work is in exactly what I explained in the first part of this article: keep track of the work, don't over step what you can do and follow through on all the projects. Half-finished projects are no help to you. They're a waste of time and they won't further your career. On the other hand, I obviously write far more than I sell. Those projects are potential future sales, of course. I send out a couple of them every month.

A schedule will not automatically make you a better writer. You have to work at the craft and be willing to learn how to improve your prose, and that's something far more than just writing a lot of words. However, if you are interested in a career as a writer, being able to make the best use of your writing time is essential. Learning to work to deadlines and handle multiple projects will help you enjoy the work by lessening the stress involved, and allow you to concentrate on the story, rather than the time you need to write it.

About the Authors

LAZETTE GIFFORD

Lazette Gifford owns and runs Forward Motion for Writers, a website with several thousand members (www.fmwriters.com). She is the editor and publisher of *Vision: A Resource for Writers* (www.lazette.net/vision), and is the head of the fantasy imprint for Double Dragon Publishing (www.double-dragon-ebooks.com). She has had several nonfiction writing-related books published. Her fiction has been published in both short story and novel formats, and in electronic and print venues.

In her free time (yes you can laugh now) she works with digital photography and art, and has had pictures appear in several magazines.

Her website is www.lazette.net.

MICHAEL D. PEDERSON

Mike Pederson is the creative mind behind for the popular semiprozine, *Nth Degree*. He began life as a semi-pro in 1988 when his SF short story, "Dust Storm," won first place in a local writing contest. In the nineties he wrote and published the *Raven* comic book series, and edited and published *Scene*, a Virginia-based entertainment magazine. He is an active member of the Washington Science Fiction Association and known on the con circuit as "that Nth Degree guy." Most recently, his time, talents, and energetic enthusiasm have been invested into RavenCon, a Science Fiction-Fantasy-Mystery Convention in Richmond, Virginia. RavenCon 2006 went better than anyone dreamed possible with Terry Brooks as the Guest of Honor, and 2007 went even bigger and better with Hugo and Nebula winner Rob Sawyer as Guest of Honor. Find out more about this realized vision of Mike's at http://ravencon.com.

HELEN FRENCH

Helen French has worked in book-selling, book publishing and currently magazine publishing. Book-selling came first—she managed a SF/F section in a bookstore just after university. Then came a two-year stint at Harlequin Mills and Boon, where she was an editorial assistant, working on historical, women's fiction and fantasy imprints. Freelance editing followed, but she found true love in magazines, where she now works full-time as a production manager, focusing on writing her own fantasy fiction during her free time.

JENNIFER HAGAN

Jennifer Hagan wants it all: a home, travel, family, a good career, and to write the Great American Novel. Fortunately at 28-years-old, she still has time to achieve it. An avid reader, photographer, and Discovery Channel addict, Jennifer has a number of interests that she tries to work into her fiction.

After graduating from college with a degree in English, Jennifer worked as a reporter for a daily newspaper and a weekly newspaper for several years. Choosing to leave the tempo of a newspaper, Jennifer then started working with individuals who have developmental disabilities at a non-profit organization. She has continued to write although put it on hold while pursuing other opportunities.

Jennifer recently bought a house in the White Mountains of New Hampshire and lives there with her cat, Artemis, and do, Pepin the Short. She now works at a private non-profit with troubled teens. She is doing freelance writing work and still working on her first novel.

TEE MORRIS

Tee Morris began his writing career with his 2002 historical epic fantasy, *MOREVI: The Chronicles of Rafe & Askana*. Tee then appeared in Dragon Moon Press' 2003 release, *The Complete Guide to Writing Fantasy* and the served alongside Valerie Griswold-Ford as co-editor of *The Fantasy Writer's Companion*. Both books were finalists for *ForeWord Magazine*'s Book of the Year Award. 2004 also saw the release of Billibub Baddings and The Case of The Singing Sword which received an Honorable Mention for *ForeWord Magazine*'s Best Fiction of 2004.

Tee entered 2005 with an idea, and that idea — podcasting *MOREVI* —went on to become the first book podcast in its entirety. That experience led to the founding of Podiobooks.com, collaborating with Evo Terra on *Podcasting for Dummies* and earning him a nomination for the 2006 Parsec Award for excellence in podcasting. Along with that title and *Legacy of MOREVI: Book One of the Arathellean Wars*, Tee's article "Dear John" appeared in BenBella Books' *Farscape Forever:*

Sex, Drugs, and Killer Muppets. In 2006, Tee appears in the podcast anthology *VOICES: New Media Fiction* (edited by Mur Lafferty), and in BenBella Books' *So Say We All: Collected Thoughts and Opinions of BATTLESTAR GALACTICA.* He is also a columnist for *Blogger and Podcaster Magazine,* and is currently gearing up for the 2008 premieres of *Billibub Baddings and the Case of The Pitcher's Pendant* and *Exodus from Morevi: Book Two of The Arathellean Wars.*

Find out more about Tee Morris online at www.teemorris.com.

JANA G. OLIVER

Jana Oliver admits a fascination with mystery, usually laced with a touch of the supernatural. An eclectic person who has traveled the world, she loves to pour over old maps and dusty tomes while rummaging through history for plot lines. In 2006, *Sojourn,* the first book in the *Time Rovers*™ Series debuted from Dragon Moon Press, a riveting story of time travelers and shape-shifters in Late Victorian London.

When not herding verbs and annoying nouns, Jana teaches writing classes and serves as host of The Fancy Dress Albert Public House podcast. She lives in Atlanta with one husband, two cats and her overactive imagination.

SUMMER BROOKS

Summer Brooks is an avid reader and writer of fantasy and science fiction, with a deep passion for good SF television and movies in general. In 2004, that passion led her into the den of The Dragon Page Radio, a haven where she could likely live happily ever after. She started out as a book reviewer for the talk shows, but soon after experiencing the fun of live radio, she became an additional on-air voice for many of the Dragon Page talk shows and podcasts.

A year and a half later, Farpoint Media was created as a parent umbrella for the growing number of the shows Michael and Jeffrey manage, and Summer is now producer or co-host for 5 of those shows, with more new projects constantly being developed. She currently handles guest interview bookings for "Slice of SciFi", "Cover to Cover," and "With Class," and she's featured on the shows "Slice of SciFi", "The Babylon Podcast", and "The Kick-Ass Mystic Ninjas" and "Michael and Evo's Wingin' It."

In addition to reveling in numerous SF/F media fandoms, Summer is hard at work writing articles and novels, and her passion is to write and produce a TV series or miniseries that leaves a mark on people. Summer is also a licensed massage therapist with a small but very happy client base.

More info on the shows and other projects can be found at http://farpointmedia.net/

JOE MURPHY

Sweet little Joe from Illinois awoke to the horrid sound of a twister one morning. After the storm passed, he was deposited in the alien landscape of Arizona and a vague feeling of homesickness. That quickly vanished when Michael R. Mennenga and Evo Terra offered him piles and piles of free books, and killer desserts when in the studio.

Appreciating science fiction and fantasy in all forms, Joe went in to the profession of…Audiology? His Bachelor's came from Illinois State University and his Master's from Western Illinois University, and with these degrees Joe help people hear the world around them. Joe reviews books for The Dragon Page, remains the sober voice of Wingin' It, goes old school on The Kick Ass Mystic Ninjas and voices his opinions on Slice of SciFi.

Joe Murphy passed away April 1, 2007, after a battle with leiomyosarcoma, an aggressive form of cancer. Onthe week of his passing, many podcasts went silent while others simultaneously podcast a tribute show. In his memory, the Joe Murphy Memorial Fund was established in order to increase awareness of this devastating disease and to raise money for hospice. His voice continues to be heard in *Give Us a Minute*, hosted by Tee Morris. Find out more about Joe's legacy at http://joemurphymemorialfund.org.

MARGARET MCGAFFEY FISK

Margaret McGaffey Fisk has been writing since grade school, back in the days when everyone still wrote with pens on paper. She started submitting manuscripts in her second year of college and hasn't kicked the habit since. To support herself until that million dollar contract, she has held a variety of positions from pizza parlor cleanup crew and breakfast cook to technical writer/editor and computer systems analyst. A moderator and active member of Forward Motion (www.

fmwriters.com), she enjoys helping other writers pass the hurdles between the first word and publication. Her short stories have appeared in *Cloaked in Shadow: Dark Tales of Elves* from Fantasist Enterprises and *Triangulation 2004: A Confluence of Speculative Fiction from PARSEC*. She has had several non-fiction articles on writing published in *Vision: A Resource for Writers* and is now the Features Editor for the e-zine.

DANIELLE ACKLEY-MCPHAIL

Danielle Ackley-McPhail has worked both sides of the publishing industry for over a decade. She has used her talent and her passion for writing to expand her knowledge of the rich mythology of her Celtic heritage and to make her mark in the world of fantasy.

Her works include the urban fantasy, *Yesterday's Dreams* (Mundania Press, www.mundania.com, 2006), its pending sequel, *Tomorrow's Memories*, the chapbook, *Children of Morpheus* (Lite Circle Books, www.litecircle.org, 2004), an edited anthology, *No Longer Dreams*, (Lite Circle Books, 2005), and contributions to numerous anthologies and collections worldwide, including *Post-Modern Tempraments: Fifteen Poets* (Cyberwit Press, www.cyberwit.net, 2003), *For Better or Worse* (Poets Work Press, 2005) and *Dark Furies* (Die Monster Die! Books, www.diemonsterdie.com, 2005). Her work has also appeared in *Nth Degree* (on line and in print), *Sabledrake Magazine*, and on Darkwalls.com.

Currently, in conjunction with Laughing Pan Productions, she is working on the upcoming anthology *Bad-Ass Fairies*. If you would like to learn more about her work, please visit www.sidhenadaire.com. Danielle lives in New Jersey with husband and fellow writer, Mike McPhail, mother-in-law Teresa, and three extremely spoiled cats.

L. JAGI LAMPLIGHTER

L. Jagi Lamplighter is a fantasy author. She has published several short stories and numerous articles on Japanese animation. She recently sold her first trilogy, *Prospero's Daughter*, to Tor. The first volume, *Prospero Lost*, scheduled for the Spring of 2008. When not writing, she switches to her secret identity as wife and stay-home mom in Centreville, VA, where she lives with her dashing husband, author John C. Wright, and their three darling boys, Orville, Roland Wilbur, and Justinian Oberon.

About the Editors

VALERIE GRISWOLD-FORD

Born in South Carolina, and raised in New England, Val Griswold-Ford inherited several things from her bibliophile parents: a love of books, and a talent for telling stories. Both contributed to an early start to her writing career.

After writing short fiction and her first novel in high school, Val switched to journalism in college. She covered several political beats, wrote a weekly column and rose to associate managing editor of *The Daily Campus*, the fifth largest daily newspaper in Connecticut.

Post-college is when she began writing in earnest. After her first chapter in *The Complete Guide to Writing Fantasy*, Val co-edited *The Fantasy Writer's Companion* with Tee Morris. She released her first solo novel, *Not Your Father's Horseman*, at Westercon 58 in Calgary in July 2005, and is working on the sequel, *Dark Moon Seasons*.

Val writes dark fantasy, horror, paranormal romance and urban fantasy, in addition to her nonfiction works. Val lives with her husband and three kittens in Merrimack, New Hampshire.

LAI ZHAO

Fantasy, with generous servings of other genres, is Lai Zhao's favourite feast, with plenty of maniacal laughter and insane plots added for taste. Known to talk to stuffed bunnies and converse intelligently with cats, Lai has been accused of being "crazy" and "weird." Fortunately, no one has ever labelled her "certifiable." *(Yet.)* When she surfaces from her fiction-writing, Lai lives and works in Hong Kong. She is immersed in all things Chinese punctuated with healthy doses of Japanese. To date, she has been involved in various commercial non-fiction projects and has had her fiction published online. Currently, Lai is working on two fantasy novels. *The Fantasy Writer's Companion* marks her first non-fiction foray into the world of Fantasy Writing.

About the Artist

ANNE MOYA

Anne Moya began her career at the age of seventeen with her being commisioned to design a granite sculpture in her home town of Snohomish, Washington. At eighteen, she began Angel Press Studios as a small press comic publisher in 1993. The same year she was awarded the Washington State Artist of the Year as well as her first solo art exhibition. In 1996 she received her AA in Print. After winning various state recognition for her fine art and illustrations, Anne expanded into Graphic Design. Working for 6 years in corporate in-house design, Anne received her BA in Graphic Design in 2002 and entered the freelance field. With her expansive knowledge of print, design and multimedia, Anne continues to return to her roots and persue her passion of fine art and book illustration in her new home of Chicago.

Find out more about Anne Moya and Angel Press Studios online at www.angelpressstudios.com.

Index

DON'T MISS THESE EXCITING TITLES BROUGHT TO YOU BY DRAGON MOON PRESS, EDGE SCIENCE FICTION AND FANTASY AND TESSERACTS!

ALIEN DECEPTION, Tony Ruggiero (tp) ISBN-13: 978-1-896944-34-0
ALIEN REVELATION, Tony Ruggiero (tp) ISBN-13: 978-1-896944-34-8
ALPHANAUTS, J. Brian Clarke (tp) ISBN-13: 978-1-894063-14-2
ANCESTOR, Scott Sigler (tp) ISBN-13: 978-1-896944-73-9
APPARITION TRAIL, THE, Lisa Smedman (tp)
    ISBN-13: 978-1-894063-22-7
AS FATE DECREES, Denysé Bridger (tp) ISBN-13: 978-1-894063-41-8

BILLIBUB BADDINGS AND THE CASE OF THE SINGING SWORD, Tee Morris (tp) ISBN-13: 978-1-896944-18-0
BLACK CHALICE, THE, Marie Jakober (hb)
    ISBN-13: 978-1-894063-00-5
BLUE APES, Phyllis Gotlieb (pb) ISBN-13: 978-1-895836-13-4
BLUE APES, Phyllis Gotlieb (hb) ISBN-13: 978-1-895836-14-1

CHALICE OF LIFE, THE, Anne Webb (tp) ISBN-13: 978-1-896944-33-3
CHASING THE BARD by Philippa Ballantine (tp)
    ISBN-13: 978-1-896944-08-1
CHILDREN OF ATWAR, THE by Heather Spears (pb)
    ISBN-13: 978-0-88878-335-6
CLAUS EFFECT by David Nickle & Karl Schroeder, The (pb)
    ISBN-13: 978-1-895836-34-9
CLAUS EFFECT by David Nickle & Karl Schroeder, The (hb)
    ISBN-13: 978-1-895836-35-6
COMPLETE GUIDE TO WRITING FANTASY, THE VOLUME 1: ALCHEMY WITH WORDS, edited by Darin Park and Tom Dullemond (tp)
    ISBN-13: 978-1-896944-09-8
COMPLETE GUIDE TO WRITING FANTASY, THE VOLUME 2: OPUS MAGUS, edited by Tee Morris and Valerie Griswold-Ford (tp)
    ISBN-13: 978-1-896944-15-9
COMPLETE GUIDE TO WRITING FANTASY VOLUME 3: THE AUTHOR'S GRIMOIRE, edited by Valerie Griswold-Ford & Lai Zhao (tp)
    ISBN-13: 978-1-896944-38-8
COMPLETE GUIDE TO WRITING SCIENCE FICTION VOLUME 1: FIRST CONTACT, edited by Dave A. Law & Darin Park (tp)
    ISBN-13: 978-1-896944-39-5
COURTESAN PRINCE, THE, Lynda Williams (tp)
    ISBN-13: 978-1-894063-28-9

I-ROBOT POETRY, Jason Christie (tp) ISBN-13: 978-1-894063-24-1

JACKAL BIRD, Michael Barley (pb) ISBN-13: 978-1-895836-07-3
JACKAL BIRD, Michael Barley (hb) ISBN-13: 978-1-895836-11-0

KEAEN, Till Noever (tp) ISBN-13: 978-1-894063-08-1
KEEPER'S CHILD, Leslie Davis (tp) ISBN-13: 978-1-894063-01-2

LAND/SPACE, edited Candas Jane Dorsey and Judy McCrosky (tp)
    ISBN-13: 978-1-895836-90-5
LAND/SPACE, edited Candas Jane Dorsey and Judy McCrosky (hb)
    ISBN-13: 978-1-895836-92-9
LEGACY OF MOREVI, Tee Morris (tp) ISBN-13: 978-1-896944-29-6
LEGENDS OF THE SERAI, J.C. Hall (tp) ISBN-13: 978-1-896944-04-3
LONGEVITY THESIS, Jennifer Tahn (tp) ISBN-13: 978-1-896944-37-1
LYSKARION: THE SONG OF THE WIND, J.A. Cullum (tp)
    ISBN-13: 978-1-894063-02-9

MACHINE SEX AND OTHER STORIES, Candas Jane Dorsey (tp)
    ISBN-13: 978-0-88878-278-6
MAËRLANDE CHRONICLES, THE, Élisabeth Vonarburg (pb)
    ISBN-13: 978-0-88878-294-6
MAGISTER'S MASK, THE, Deby Fredericks (tp)
    ISBN-13: 978-1-896944-16-6
MOONFALL, Heather Spears (pb) ISBN-13: 978-0-88878-306-6
MOREVI: THE CHRONICLES OF RAFE AND ASKANA, Lisa Lee
& Tee Morris (tp) ISBN-13: 978-1-896944-07-4

NOT YOUR FATHER'S HORSEMAN, Valorie Griswold-Ford (tp)
    ISBN-13: 978-1-896944-27-2

ON SPEC: THE FIRST FIVE YEARS, edited On Spec (pb)
    ISBN-13: 978-1-895836-08-0
ON SPEC: THE FIRST FIVE YEARS, edited On Spec (hb)
    ISBN-13: 978-1-895836-12-7
OPERATION: IMMORTAL SERVITUDE, Tony Ruggerio (tp)
    ISBN-13: 978-1-896944-56-2

ORBITAL BURN, K. A. Bedford (tp) ISBN-13: 978-1-894063-10-4
ORBITAL BURN, K. A. Bedford (hb) ISBN-13: 978-1-894063-12-8

PALLAHAXI TIDE, Michael Coney (pb) ISBN-13: 978-0-88878-293-9
PASSION PLAY, Sean Stewart (pb) ISBN-13: 978-0-88878-314-1